The people's science

The people's science
The popular political economy of exploitation and crisis 1816–34

NOEL W. THOMPSON

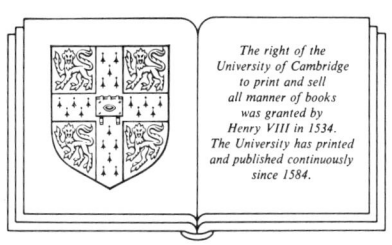

CAMBRIDGE UNIVERSITY PRESS

Cambridge
London   New York   New Rochelle
Melbourne   Sydney

Published by the Press Syndicate of the University of Cambridge
The Pitt Building, Trumpington Street, Cambridge CB2 1RP
32 East 57th Street, New York, NY 1002, USA
10 Stamford Road, Oakleigh, Melbourne 3166, Australia

© Cambridge University Press 1984

First published 1984

Printed in Great Britain at the University Press, Cambridge

Library of Congress catalogue card number: 84–7069
British Library Cataloguing in Publication Data
Thompson, N.W.
The people's science.
1. Great Britain – Economic conditions –
1760–1860 2.Great Britain – Politics
and government – 1800–1837
1. Title
330.941′07′04 HC255
ISBN 0 521 25795 6

M U

To my Mother and Father

The history of economic and social thought travels, for the most part, a highway through the air, moving from peak to peak, from great mind to great mind. It pays little attention to those streams and rivers of communication that carry the lighter matter of the summits and hillsides down into the valleys of common occupation... This is a history that leaves few records, but it is an important history, and if, in its discovery surmise must substitute to a great degree for documents, that is a fact which preaches caution but not neglect.

    S. Gordon, 'The *London Economist* and the high tide of laissez-faire', *Journal of Political Economy*, 1955.

A study of the unstamped press is important not only as showing its tendency to degrade public taste and lower the tone of the legal journals but also as illustrating the increasing prevalence of levelling and communistic ideas among working-men after 1815.

    J. H. Rose, 'The unstamped press', *English Historical Review*, 1897.

Contents

Preface	*page*	viii
Introduction		1
1 Changing attitudes to political economy in the working-class press 1816–34		8
2 The need for a working-class political economy		35
3 Charles Hall and Robert Owen: anti-capitalist and socialist political economy before the Ricardian socialists		65
4 Ricardian socialists/Smithian socialists: what's in a name?		82
5 The theory of labour exploitation and the working-class press 1816–30		111
6 The theory of labour exploitation and the working-class press 1830–34		136
7 Early socialist political economy and the theory of capitalist crisis		158
8 The popular political economy of crisis 1816–34		191
Conclusion		219
Bibliography		229
Index		245

Preface

In the course of writing this book I seem to have contracted debts of Brazilian proportions. The research upon which it is based was begun in Belfast under the tutelage of Professor R. D. C. Black whose patient efforts to steer me to a more profound understanding of the work of past economic writers served both to enlighten and enthuse. A Peterhouse Research Studentship enabled me to continue my labours, supervised by Maurice Dobb, whose death in 1976 removed not only a great academic but also a source of personal inspiration. It was, paradoxically, through this loss that I gained the guidance of two people without whose constant encouragement, interest and support this book would not have been written – John Saville and Phyllis Deane. It is difficult to give suitable expression to the debt which I owe them but it was their faith and confidence in what I was doing which saw me through when others, who deservedly must remain nameless, counselled despair.

I have also benefited from the criticism and comments of Gareth Stedman Jones, Greg Claeys, Michael Ignatieff and Gavin Kitching – the latter's continuing capacity to evince an interest in what I have to say about the Ricardian socialists meriting some kind of award for intellectual tolerance. I would also like to make particular mention of the penetrating dissection of my PhD thesis during a memorable (for me) *viva voce* with Professor A. W. Coats. These have played a part in the shaping of the final product but are in no way culpable for the failings and deficiencies which remain.

Library staff in numerous institutions have suffered in the course of my research but I would like to thank specifically those of the Goldsmiths Library, the Library of the University of Cambridge, the Butler Library, New York, and the Newspaper Lending Division of the British Library, the porters in which have trundled their trolleys many miles on my behalf.

Finally I would like to thank Catriona, Siân and Kirstie for mitigating the loneliness of the long distance academic.

N. W. T

Introduction

Discussing the works of Mrs Marcet and Miss Martineau in an *Edinburgh Review* article of 1833, William Empson lamented that political economy, 'The science, which from its object ought to be pre-eminently the people's science, has yet made but little way to popular power and favour.'[1] Such chagrin was justified. A generation of propagandists and would-be educators[2] had plied their pens, with a vigour matched only by their conviction, to popularise what they saw as the fundamental tenets of classical orthodoxy. Yet, by 1833 at any rate, there was little indication that their proselytising had won the hearts and minds of the labouring classes for whose benefit they wrote. Nevertheless, Empson's outburst of annoyance is, in a sense, misleading. The labouring classes had not rejected political economy *per se* but only that brand of political economy purveyed by the classical popularisers. Indeed, by the date of Empson's review political economy had gone a considerable way towards achieving the status of a people's science. However, the science espoused was not that of the Mills, Ricardo, Torrens, McCulloch, Senior and their admiring acolytes but rather that of Hodgskin, Thompson, Gray, Owen and other, lesser, anti-capitalist and socialist political economists. It is with *this* people's science that this study is concerned or, more specifically, with the theoretical approach of anti-capitalist and socialist political economists to the twin evils of labour exploitation and general economic depression and

---

[1] W. Empson, 'Mrs Marcet – Miss Martineau', *Edinburgh Review*, 57 (April 1833), 8.
[2] Harriet Martineau, Jane Marcet, James Mill, Henry Brougham, Charles Knight, Francis Place *et al.*

the manner in which these were dealt with by writers in the working-class press of the period 1816–34.

The study begins with a survey of changing popular attitudes to the discipline of political economy as manifested in the working-class press and discusses the growing recognition of the need to utilise political economy to defend the material interests of the labouring classes. Why this occurred, why it occurred when it did and why this defence assumed the form which it did, are questions considered in chapter 2.

Chapter 3 examines the explanations for working-class emiseration provided by Charles Hall and Robert Owen, discussing some of the analytical deficiencies of anti-capitalist and socialist political economy in Britain prior to the advent of the Ricardian socialists and, together with chapter 2, seeks to highlight the decisive nature of the Ricardian socialist contribution to the formation of a people's science which could, by the late 1820s and early 1830s, confront popularised classical orthodoxy on its own conceptual terrain.

This contribution is discussed in more detail in chapter 4 where the structure and implications of Ricardian socialist labour exploitation theories are considered. Here histories of anti-capitalist and socialist economic thought such as those of Max Beer, G. D. H. Cole and Alexander Gray proved initially helpful but ultimately unsatisfactory, as it became obvious that an understanding of Ricardian socialist political economy necessitated some careful delving down to its possible classical roots. Chapter 4 undertakes this task with respect to their thinking on the determination of exchange value under capitalism and argues that their tendency to think through this problem along Smithian rather than Ricardian lines had profound repercussions, not only for the thrust of their own critical analysis but also, as is argued in chapter 6, for the form which popular, anti-capitalist and socialist political economy assumed in the working-class press of the late 1820s and early 1830s.

While chapters 4–6 consider theories of labour exploitation and their filtration into the working-class press, chapters 7 and 8 do the same for that other distinctive component of anti-capitalist and socialist political economy, the theory of general economic depression. Again, the purpose of these chapters is to consider critically the contribution of formal theorists, before examining the treatment of this phenomenon by their popularisers.

Given that it is the working class of the period which is taken as the major popularising medium, three questions arise. First, which papers may be legitimately deemed to constitute the working-class press and why? Secondly, how popular was the people's science purveyed by working-class papers? Thirdly, why limit the study to the period 1816–34?

With reference to the first question, Royden Harrison's categorisation of 'labour periodicals' has been taken as a guide. Thus Harrison distinguishes three sub-species. First, those papers which were 'produced by an organised body consisting wholly or mainly of wage-earners or collectively dependent employees... Second... periodicals which were produced in the avowed interest of the working class – where that class was thought to have interests exclusive of the interests of other social classes or actively opposed to them... Third... those which were produced for wage-earners by members of other social classes.'[3] For the purpose of this study, the term 'working-class press' has been applied to those papers which fall into the first two of these three categories[4] while the third category has been ignored because it comprises papers which were produced simply to entertain or as a counterblast to all forms of radicalism by those who sought, primarily, to defend the status quo.

As regards the chronological limits of the work, it is tempting to state that for any study of the history of ideas the choice must inevitably be somewhat arbitrary but such evasion merits the obvious retort that some choices are more arbitrary than others. The short answer to the question, therefore, is that the chronological span of the work has been determined in large measure, though not exclusively, by the availability of primary source material of a 'popular' kind. Thus the study begins in 1816 because this date marks the advent of a cheap, radical press[5] with views to suit the predilections and a price to suit the pockets of a working-class readership. From this date, therefore, there is

[3] R. Harrison, G. Woolven and R. Duncan, *The Warwick Guide to British Labour Periodicals 1790–1970: A Check List* (Hassocks, Harvester Press, 1977), pp. xiii–xiv.
[4] ibid. p. 638, for a full list.
[5] S. Harrison, *Poor Men's Guardians, a record of the struggles for a democratic newspaper press 1763–1973* (London, Lawrence and Wishart, 1974), p. 41.

sufficient literature to make feasible a study of the popularisation of economic ideas, though, in this context, it must be admitted that the early 1820s are particularly lean years.[6]

The closing date of 1834 is more difficult to justify. Thus a case could be made for extending the study to 1839 and the publication in that year of John Francis Bray's *Labour's Wrongs and Labour's Remedy*. This would have allowed a discussion of the economic writings of all the Ricardian socialists and thus obviated the need to confine consideration of Bray's political economy to cursory notice in chapters 4 and 7. Yet extending the study to 1839 would have involved other difficulties, particularly as regards length, for not only would it have necessitated the detailed examination of many more newspapers but it would also have required some discussion of the early Chartist press and thence the role of Chartists and Chartism in disseminating or failing to disseminate anti-capitalist and socialist economic ideas. To do full justice to these questions would require a separate study and one which would need to be carried through to 1848 or even 1850.

The year 1836 represents another possible terminal date as it saw the reduction of the stamp duty on newspapers in the Budget of that year and hence the virtual elimination of the significant price differential which had existed in the early 1830s between unstamped and stamped journals. It was this differential, together with the illicit nature of its radical offerings, which had given

[6] The newspaper stamp duty had been raised by ½d to 4d in 1815 but this had not prevented an efflorescence of radical journalism in the immediate post-Napoleonic War period (1816–19). However, in 1819, as part of a package of repressive legislation rushed through parliament in the aftermath of Peterloo, the Newspaper Stamp Duties Act was passed 'which by broadening the definition of a newspaper brought the cheap, Radical papers within the scope of the 4d stamp duty', A. Aspinall, *Politics and the Press c.1780–1850* (London, Hone and van Thal, 1949), p. 9n. The purpose of this piece of legislation was made explicit in its preamble and was 'to restrain the small publications which issue from the press in great numbers and at a low price' and this to a large extent it succeeded in doing. Radical papers, in order to avoid prosecution, either had to pay the stamp tax and sell at a prohibitively expensive 7d or more or become monthly pamphlets retailing at an equally discouraging 6d. Some papers such as Carlile's *Republican*, Cobbett's *Register*, the *Medusa* and the *Cap of Liberty* made the transition but their popularity necessarily declined and it was only with the emergence of a co-operative press in the late 1820s and the burgeoning of the 'unstamped' in the early 1830s that the 'working-class press' recovered from this legislative blow. On these points see also P. Hollis, *The Pauper Press: a study in working-class radicalism of the 1830s* (Oxford University Press, 1970), p. viii, and S. Harrison, *Poor Men's Guardians*, pp. 53–4.

the unstamped press of the 1830s its great appeal and after 1836, therefore, the character of much of the working-class press changes as radical publishers were forced to compete with stamped journals. In effect, 1836 marks the end of the 'Great Unstamped'.[7]

The year 1834 has been chosen, however, because it marks both a qualitative and a quantitative change in the popularisation of economic ideas by working-class papers. It marks the date when many papers which had provided an important forum for economic debate ceased publication. This year saw the demise of papers like the *Crisis*, the *Pioneer*, the *Voice of the West Riding* and the *Destructive*; and while the *Poor Man's Guardian* continued to be published until the end of 1835, among papers which devoted significant space to the discussion of economic questions, it proved the exception. In addition newly established papers in the period 1834–6 were increasingly oriented to the discussion of political and related issues such as universal suffrage and the campaign for the repeal of the stamp tax on newspapers. This was certainly true of the *Twopenny Dispatch* (1834–6), the *New Political Register* (1835–6), the *People's Weekly Dispatch* (1835–6), the *Political Register* (1834–5), the *Weekly Herald* (1836), the *Reformer* (1836) and the *Radical* (1836). Papers such as these discussing primarily political matters had of course existed, indeed flourished, in the early 1830s but not to the exclusion of those which devoted significant space to a consideration of those economic questions of specific interest to the labouring classes. Even a cursory examination of the working-class press after 1834 reveals a much less extensive dissemination of anti-capitalist and socialist economic thinking than had previously been the case.[8] It is primarily for this reason that the study has been terminated in 1834.

The question of how popular was the political economy purveyed by working-class papers is both interesting and important. However, the available evidence allows only a tentative answer. Some crude indication of popularity is given by circulation figures where these are available but such figures undoubtedly

---

[7] ibid. p. 98; 'working-class publishers' were brought 'face to face with a wide new field of competition'.
[8] There is a comparable and undoubtedly related diminution in the intensity with which classical doctrine was popularised.

underestimate the popular impact of the working-class press in this period. Indeed, one contemporary observer suggested that crude circulation figures should be multiplied by thirty to give an accurate indication of the numbers who read each paper printed.[9] This may be an exaggeration but it was undoubtedly the case that 'Remarkable efforts were made to get at the news. Men clubbed together to buy single copies. Old newspapers circulated through entire streets. Coffee houses and public houses took in newspapers for their customers to read. The 'pothouse oracle' read aloud extracts from newspapers and commented on what he read.'[10] In addition, readers could gain access to newspapers via Political Reading Societies, 'Political Protestant Associations', reading rooms attached to bookshops and by hiring and lending arrangements, while some newspapers were read out at large public meetings.[11]

Yet this still gives no clear indication of the extent to which the ideas, economic or otherwise, purveyed by these papers were understood or assimilated by their working-class readers; still less does it reveal whether the labouring classes accepted or approved the opinions and ideas which these papers contained. It is not possible to assume, for example, that the views on social, political and economic questions of articulate and literate, middle-class editors and writers such as 'Bronterre' O'Brien or J. E. 'Shepherd' Smith were imbibed indiscriminately by those of the working classes sufficiently motivated and literate to read and understand the *Poor Man's Guardian* or the *Pioneer*, for these writers were undoubtedly attempting to educate or mould working-class opinion in addition to reflecting it.[12] Nevertheless, as one writer has put it, 'We might none the less risk the generalisation that from 1816 to the early 1840s the relationship between radical

[9] G. Merle, 'Weekly newspapers', *Westminster Review*, 10 (April 1829), 478.
[10] R. K. Webb, 'The Victorian reading public', *Universities Quarterly*, 12 (1957–8), 37.
[11] A. Aspinall, 'The circulation of newspapers', *Review of English Studies*, 22 (1946), 33, 31, 42, 34.
[12] See, for example, the remarks of R. Johnson: 'we cannot assume that the attitudes of radical leaders and writers were those of 'the workers' ... radical leaders were clearly involved in a process that was part mediation or expression of some popular feelings, and part a forming or an 'education' of them', 'Really useful knowledge, radical education and working-class culture 1790–1848' in J. Clarke, Chas. Critcher and R. Johnson (eds.), *Working-Class Culture, Studies in History and Theory* (London, Hutchinson, 1979), pp. 75–6.

leadership and working-class people was extraordinarily close'[13] and certainly it can be said that in the period after 1816 radical economic and political ideas sold newspapers and in some cases sold them in considerable numbers. 'The People's Science' would therefore appear to be a legitimate epithet to apply to the popular political economy of the working-class press.

[13] ibid. p. 93.

1

Changing attitudes to political economy in the working-class press 1816–34

The attitude to political economy of writers in the radical press of the immediate post-Napoleonic War period embodies a strong anti-intellectualist strain. This anti-intellectualism is most apparent in *Cobbett's Weekly Political Register* but it also finds expression in such papers as Richard Carlile's *Republican* and, to a lesser extent, T. J. Wooler's *Black Dwarf*. Cobbett in particular would seem to have had little time for political economy judging from his acerbic castigation of its leading theorists. His condemnation of them was unhesitating, unqualified and liberally spiced with personal abuse. Thus addressing one issue of his paper to Malthus, 'that impudent and illiterate Parson', he stated with pungent simplicity, 'I have during my life detested many men but never anyone so much as you.'[1] Smith was dismissed with similar contempt as 'verbose and obscure'; a writer who took care to hide the implications of his theories 'from vulgar eyes';[2] while Ricardo was the butt of a continual stream of virulent, anti-semitic rhetoric that does not bear repetition.

Nevertheless, it must be emphasised that readers of Cobbett's *Register* and other radical journals were not dissuaded from all attempt to make order out of the seeming chaos of the economic world. Cobbett might loathe the political economists and their reification of human relationships but he was not entirely averse to explicating those laws and forces which he saw as governing

---

[1] *Cobbett's Twopenny Register*, 34, 33 (1819), col. 1019, 'A Letter to Parson Malthus on the Rights of the Poor'.
[2] ibid. 34, 32 (1819), cols. 992–3.

the economic fate of the working man.³ Thus he complained that while there was much talk about 'plunder and the distribution of plunder', there was no 'manuel' (sic) on such matters to which the labouring classes could refer.⁴

T. J. Wooler in the *Black Dwarf* also exhorted his readers to give serious attention to the principles of political economy. 'As the errors of antiquity fell before the deductions of modern science', he wrote, so would 'fall the evils of which the reformers complain by the development of the real principles of political economy'.⁵ While even Richard Carlile, ever more prone to violent anti-clericalism than speculation on matters economic, printed in his *Republican* an admonishment from one correspondent that 'as a guide of the honest and industrious order of the people' he should be prepared to give greater consideration to 'such causes as impoverish the labourer and enrich the sluggard'.⁶ These early radical papers did not, therefore, purvey a uniformly negative attitude to political economy.

One paper of the immediate post-Napoleonic War period which took a particularly positive approach to the discipline of political economy was John Wade's *Gorgon*. Wade was convinced that political economy could prove an important analytical tool with which to investigate and explain the impoverished condition of the labouring classes and he offered in his paper to 'bring forward [the] best writers not only to prove that the situation of the working classes is much worse than it has been, but also to establish the mischievous tendency of low wages'.⁷

An equally positive attitude finds expression in the two cooperative papers of the late 1810s and early 1820s, the *Mirror of*

---

³ J. W. Derry is quite correct in stating that Cobbett 'loathed the science of economics' because 'it was too dismal [and] too inclined to justify everything that Cobbett hated' but he is wrong in seeing this loathing as a general 'horror' of discerning 'laws governing economic development, trade, supply and demand and the growth of population', *The Radical Tradition, Tom Paine to Lloyd George* (London, Macmillan, 1967), pp. 64–5. Rather, what horrified Cobbett was the specific nature and import of the laws which classical political economy established. He would have been quite content if the laws discerned had been those propounded by Paine in his *Decline of the English System of Finance* or those which he had discerned himself in *Paper against Gold*.
⁴ *Cobbett's Twopenny Register*, 33, 3 (1818), col. 95.
⁵ *Black Dwarf*, 3, 44 (1819), col. 716.
⁶ *Republican*, 6, 9 (1821), 286, a letter from 'Regulator'.
⁷ *Gorgon*, 38 (1819), 299.

Truth and the *Economist*. Significant space was given over to a discussion of economic questions in these papers. Indeed George Mudie, the editor of the *Economist*, was congratulated by one correspondent for 'the plain and intelligible manner in which the working... of some of the most abstruse principles of political economy had been placed before [his] readers'.[8] 'It is by Political Economy alone that our system must triumph,'[9] wrote Mudie to Robert Owen in 1823 and such sentiments do seem to reflect a growing awareness, among Owen's adherents and the proponents of co-operation generally, of the need to advance their opinions and develop their arguments in the language of political economy.

Yet, despite the importance which writers in the early radical and co-operative press attached to a knowledge of political economy, they were severely limited as to the sources upon which they could draw for inspiration or which they could recommend to their readers, given that they wished to assert and defend the material interests of the labouring classes. Thus Cobbett could only recommend as 'sound' Thomas Paine's *Decline of the English System of Finance* (1796) and his own *Paper against Gold* (1815), while Richard Carlile was equally adamant that political economy must be established on the principles enunciated by Paine.[10] John Wade in the *Gorgon* solved the problem by recommending and utilising classical authors. Thus 'the name of Ricardo' was denominated 'a tower of strength' when it came to attacking 'the mischievous tendency of low wages'[11] and Adam Smith 'the enlightened and benevolent author of the *Wealth of Nations*' was quoted as a staunch advocate of

---

[8] *Economist*, 12 (1821), 189, a letter from a 'Co-operative Economist'.

[9] George Mudie to Robert Owen, 3 January 1823, *Owen Correspondence*, No. 25, Co-operative College, Manchester; see, for example, Anon., *Mr Owen's Proposed Arrangements for the Distressed Working Classes shown to be consistent with sound principles of Political Economy: in three letters to David Ricardo Esq., M.P.* (London, Longman, 1819), which was written to convince '*every enlightened economist* and opulent proprietor' of the sound economic principles upon which Owen's plans were based, ibid. p. 109 (my emphasis); also, J. M. Morgan, *Remarks on the Practicability of Mr Owen's Plan to Improve the Condition of the Lower Classes* (London, Samuel Leigh, 1819), pp. 5, 7, 10, who as well as defending the soundness of Owen's economic opinions was at pains to point out that they were consonant with the political economy of Adam Smith.

[10] *Republican*, 3, 12 (1820), 411; also ibid. 4, 14 (1820), 504.

[11] *Gorgon*, 20 (1818), 154.

raising wages to a level which would allow those 'who feed, clothe and lodge the whole body of the people ... to be themselves tolerably well fed and clothed'.[12] This is not to suggest that all contributors to the *Gorgon* accepted consistently and uncritically the dicta of the major classical economists. Indeed, the attitude of classical writers to the poor laws led to their condemnation in the *Gorgon*'s pages as 'frozen-hearted philosophers' whose opinions it was necessary to 'translate ... out of their own heathenish dialect'.[13] Nonetheless, the important point remains that the *Gorgon* often considered their opinions worthy of such translation.

Writers in the early co-operative press had, of course, works such as Robert Owen's *A New View of Society* (1813), *Two Memorials on Behalf of the Working Classes* (1818) and the *Report to the County of Lanark* (1821) upon which to draw for theoretical inspiration and ideas. However, while the significance of these works should not be underestimated, they only began the work of establishing the theoretical foundations of a working-class political economy[14] and did little to define the scope and methodology which was to distinguish it from classical economics.

In contrast, the years 1824–7 were to see not only the articulation of the theoretical fundamentals of a distinctively anticapitalist and socialist political economy but also discussion of its scope, method, content and aims. For these years ended the dearth of acceptable economic works upon which writers in the working-class press could draw. Three writers were primarily responsible for this – William Thompson, Thomas Hodgskin and John Gray.[15] This short period saw the publication of Thompson's *Inquiry into the Principles of the Distribution of Wealth* (1824) and

[12] ibid. 11 (1818), 86; see also ibid. 14 (1818), 110, where Smith is mentioned in a similarly approving fashion.
[13] ibid. 48 (1819), 377–8, 'these philosophers laugh at all attempts to better the condition of the poor, by alms-giving or otherwise; they say that such attempts do not in the least tend to eradicate the evil, but only to defer it to a more distant period'.
[14] See below, pp. 74–81.
[15] For biographical information on these writers see E. Halévy, *Thomas Hodgskin*, translated with an introduction by A. J. Taylor (London, Benn, 1956); J. Kimball, *The Economic Doctrines of John Gray, 1799–1883* (Washington, Catholic University of America Press, 1946), and R. K. P. Pankhurst, *William Thompson, Britain's Pioneer Socialist, Feminist and Co-operator* (London, Watts, 1954).

Labor Rewarded (1827), Hodgskin's *Labour Defended against the Claims of Capital* (1825) and *Popular Political Economy* (1827) and John Gray's *Lecture on Human Happiness* (1825) which, taken together, provided a significant micro- and macroeconomic appreciation of the reasons for working-class emiseration.

These writers all placed great emphasis on the need for the working classes to confront and defeat the political economists with the constructs, concepts and analytical tools of political economy. For them, the mere vilification of classical writers was not sufficient if classical economic doctrines were to be effectively countered and existing economic arrangements assailed. As Hodgskin perceptively pointed out, 'We cannot acknowledge . . . that we are incapable of ascertaining and understanding the natural laws which regulate the progress of society, without giving into the hands of one class of men the power of interpreting them according to their views and interests.'[16] Thus Hodgskin saw political economy as a powerful instrument which, by establishing and interpreting the 'natural laws' of economic life, could, in effect, define the economically possible and the economically efficacious. That the efficacious and the possible should be defined by 'one class of men' according to 'their views and interests' was not acceptable. Such competence should not be the exclusive possession of one class. For Hodgskin, political economy was too important to be left to the classical political economists.

Co-operative papers published in the late 1820s and the *Trades Newspaper* (the only authentically working-class newspaper outside the co-operative press in the late 1820s) both reveal the widening range of palatable sources available to writers in the working-class press. Thus the early issues of the *Trades Newspaper* contained a series of extended excerpts from Hodgskin's *Labour Defended*,[17] which amounted to a limited serialisation of the work with minimal editorial comment. In addition, notice was taken in the lifetime of the paper of William Thompson's *Inquiry* and the same author's *Labor*

---

[16] T. Hodgskin, *Popular Political Economy, Four Lectures delivered at the London Mechanics Institute* (London, 1827), p. 263.

[17] *Trades Newspaper*, 6 (1825); ibid. 7 (1825), 97–8; ibid. 8 (1825), 113–14; ibid. 11 (1825), 161–2; ibid. 14 (1825), 209–10.

Rewarded,[18] while both Thompson and Owen contributed to the paper when, under the editorship of William Carpenter, it became a vehicle for the propagation of co-operative ideas.[19]

Yet the *Trades Newspaper* also showed that in the late 1820s a working-class paper was still susceptible to the influence of classical orthodoxy. Extensive and favourable notice was taken in the very first issue of the paper of J. R. McCulloch's *Lecture on the Wages of Labour*.[20] In addition, after significant space had been devoted to Hodgskin's *Labour Defended* in the early issues of the paper, there was a rehabilitation of classical principles initiated by Francis Place. The subject chosen by Place, free trade, shows typical tactical insight for not only did it allow him to put the work of the classical economists in a favourable light, as something concerned with attacking harmful, government-supported monopolies, it also allowed him to avoid, initially, any overt clash with the economic opinions of Thomas Hodgskin, who, as he desired a general liberation of all economic activity from artificial constraint, was a staunch advocate of free trade principles. Thus any suggestion of a fundamental antagonism between the views of Hodgskin, still apparently in favour with the *Trades Newspaper*, and the popularised classical orthodoxy of Place was obviated.

The *Trades Newspaper* did not, in fact, jettison the political economy of Hodgskin immediately after the proselytising incursions of Place. Indeed, it printed a letter from Hodgskin on 'the real object and aim of the science of political economy'.[21] However, after this epistolary swan-song, the work of Hodgskin was not noticed again and for a considerable time thereafter the *Trades Newspaper* was dominated by Francis Place and the

---

[18] For example, notice was taken of the respective rent theories of Thompson and Ricardo with editorial comment favouring the former, ibid. 88 (1827), 281; given the line of argument pursued in chapter 4 it is interesting to note a writer who, in a review of Thompson's work in the *Trades Newspaper*, saw him as striving 'hard to prove that the inequality of wealth in society arises not from individual differences in the power of production *but chiefly from superiority in effecting the exchange of commodities*', ibid. 104 (1827), 410 (my emphasis).

[19] This occurred in the period 1829–30. As one correspondent wrote to the editor, 'You seem enraptured with the new co-operative system now in vogue', *Weekly Free Press*, 215 (1829), 1.

[20] *Trades Newspaper*, 1 (1825), 1.

[21] ibid. 29 (1826), 452.

principles of popularised classical orthodoxy.[22] Articles on free trade and the Corn Laws proliferated, with great stress being laid on the importance of repeal for the rate of capital accumulation and thence the demand for the services of the labouring classes. More revealingly, Place soon felt able to strike out with confidence upon topics of a more sensitive nature such as the rights of property and the economic consequences of mechanisation and innovation.[23] In addition, Place's crudely mechanistic views on what determined the rate of wages were printed[24] and supplemented by a warm recommendation of McCulloch's *Essay on the Circumstances which determine the Rate of Wages*.[25] 'If workmen are wise', wrote Place, 'they will contrive the means of obtaining this little manual... Masters employing a number of workmen could hardly do anything more useful to themselves... than purchasing a number of these books... selling them to their intelligent workmen.'[26] Not only were the labouring classes to imbibe sound principles of political economy, they were to pay for the privilege.

Place also informed the working classes through the medium of the paper that political economists such as McCulloch were 'the great enlighteners of the people': 'Look at their works from the time of the great man Adam Smith, to the *Essay on Wages* just published by Mr McCulloch and see if they have not all

[22] The replacement of John Robertson as editor after No. 35 (March 1826) was undoubtedly decisive here. Robertson had been a close associate of Hodgskin. Together they had edited the *Mechanics Magazine* (1823–4), a paper which not only carried articles by Hodgskin on the plight of the Spitalfields silk weavers but also served as a medium through which to criticise Francis Place, George Birkbeck and others during the struggle for control of the London Mechanics Institute. I. Prothero lists some of Robertson's economic opinions and suggests they could almost have been those of Place, *Artisans and Politics in early Nineteenth Century London, John Gast and his Times* (Folkestone, William Dawson, 1979), p. 199. However, Robertson's favourable attitude to the anti-capitalism of Hodgskin and the marked change in the economic views purveyed in the *Trades Newspaper* after Robertson ceased to be editor would suggest that the economic opinions of the men were decidedly different.

[23] See, for example, *Trades Newspaper*, 41 (1826), 641.

[24] ibid. 44 (1826), 689–90; Place saw the wage level as being determined by the size of the population or workforce and the availability of funds (the wage fund) to employ them. Curtailment of the former and expansion of the latter would raise the level of wages.

[25] The *Trades Newspaper* actually carried advertisements for McCulloch's *Essay on Wages*. See, for example, ibid. 48 (1826), 788.

[26] ibid. 44 (1826), 689–90.

along deprecated anything which was in any way calculated to do injury to the people.'[27]

That Place could oust the opinions of Hodgskin in favour of his own brand of popularised classical orthodoxy is impressive; that he did so with such openly apologetic intent in a paper avowedly defending working-class rights and interests, was little short of a *tour de force*. Well might one correspondent express discontent with the paper 'in consequence of its dogmas being too frequently at variance with the interest of those it is supposed to advocate'[28] and well might Place congratulate the paper on its first birthday,[29] though the congratulations for making the paper what it was by July 1826 should really have gone to Place himself.

Writers in the co-operative press of the late 1820s also concerned themselves with the discipline of political economy,[30] though they were more selective than the *Trades Newspaper* when it came to works to recommend to their readers.[31] In addition, like the early co-operative press these papers exuded a confidence in the discussion of economic questions which stemmed from the certainty that in all that pertained to political economy they had the truth while classical writers had not. Thus the editor of the *Co-operative Magazine* echoed the opinion of many when he wrote that 'Some of the ablest and most liberal of the political economists of the new, or Malthus, Mill, Ricardo and McCulloch school have before now entered the lists with

---

[27] ibid. 49 (1826), 799–800.
[28] ibid. 46 (1826), 739, a letter from 'Edge-tool Man'. This speedy and effective counter-revolution does call into question the importance which E. P. Thompson attaches to the appearance of excerpts from *Labour Defended* in the early issues of the *Trades Newspaper*, *The Making of the English Working Class* (Harmondsworth, Pelican, 1975), p. 857.
[29] *Trades Newspaper*, 52 (1826), 827.
[30] The co-operative press of the late 1820s included such papers as the *Co-operative Magazine and Monthly Herald*, the *Co-operative Magazine*, the *London Co-operative Magazine*, the *British Co-operator*, the (Brighton) *Co-operator*, the *Birmingham Co-operative Herald*, the *Associate*, the *Associate and Co-operative Mirror* and the *Advocate of the Working Classes*.
[31] See, for example, the *Associate and Co-operative Mirror's* recommendation of Thompson's *Labor Rewarded* and *Distribution of Wealth* (i.e. his *Inquiry*), John Gray's *Lecture (on Human Happiness)*, Hall's *Effects of Civilisation* (listed as scarce), Owen's *Report to the County of Lanark* and J. Minter Morgan's *Revolt of the Bees*, 2 (1829), 11. What this amounted to was a basic reading list for the study of socialist political economy. William Thompson had, of course, direct access to the press writing as he did for the *Co-operative Magazine*.

us and retired.'³² Such confidence may have lacked a firm theoretical base but it was an effective antibody to the virus of popularised classical orthodoxy.

While the *Trades Newspaper* might circulate more widely the anti-capitalism of Hodgskin and the co-operative papers popularise the socialist political economy of Thompson, Owen and Gray, the number of papers involved in the 1820s was small. Popularisation of anti-capitalist and socialist economic principles among the labouring classes was not on a scale sufficient to pose a significant threat to the hegemony of classical thought and, in any case, as the *Trades Newspaper* showed, classical popularisers could still gain access to working-class papers. However, all this was to change in the early 1830s, which saw a proliferation of working-class papers which both zealously and extensively disseminated anti-capitalist and socialist economic doctrines. This was the 'new class of literature... avowedly for the millions' which William Lovett referred to in his autobiographical *Life and Struggles*.³³

G. J. Holyoake wrote of Thompson's *Inquiry* that it required 'a sense of duty to read through his book – curiosity is not sufficient'³⁴ and at ten shillings a copy even a sense of duty may have proved insufficient for a labourer to become acquainted with Thompson's economic ideas. In the years 1830–4, however, the barrier to popularisation represented by the high cost of books was effectively eliminated. Those who wished to imbibe the elements of anti-capitalist and socialist economic thinking no longer required a sense of duty and a tidy sum of money to do so. These years saw a plethora of cheap, unstamped papers in which the works of writers such as Hodgskin, Thompson, Gray,

---

[32] *Co-operative Magazine*, 1 (1826), 10; this lumping together of classical economists did have the advantage of allowing co-operative writers to damn classical political economy as a whole without having to disperse their fire.

[33] W. Lovett, *The Life and Struggles of William Lovett in Pursuit of Bread, Knowledge and Freedom* (London, Bell, 1920), p. 81; see also J. H. Wiener, *A Descriptive Find List of Unstamped British Periodicals, 1830–36* (London, The Bibliographical Society, 1970), p. vii: 'The years 1830–6 were especially fruitful in the history of British periodical literature... The penny newspaper and the cheaply priced periodical received an initial impetus during these years, as scores of journals deluged the growing urban centres. Hundreds of printers, publishers, and aspiring journalists plied their trades successfully. Radical ideas were given increasing journalistic expression.'

[34] G. J. Holyoake, *A History of Co-operation* (London, Unwin, 1906), p. 14.

Owen and others were both recommended and quoted; they saw the growth of a medium which by the constant reiteration of anti-capitalist and socialist economic slogans and doctrines laid the basis of a popular working-class political economy. It was this constant dripping of new ideas upon the already weathered stone of traditional modes of thought which was fundamental in reshaping the way in which many of the working classes perceived, and the language they used to describe, those economic forces which moulded their material existence.

Thompson's *Inquiry* was quoted by papers such as the *Lancashire Co-operator*[35] and later the *Lancashire and Yorkshire Co-operator*,[36] which begged 'to recommend ... Mr Thompson's works as conveying the best information on Co-operative Political Economy'.[37] Excerpts from Hodgskin's *Popular Political Economy* also found their way into the *Lancashire and Yorkshire Co-operator*,[38] while parts of *Labour Defended* appeared in the *Destructive* and the *Natural and Artificial Rights of Property Contrasted* was quoted extensively in the *Poor Man's Guardian*.[39] This latter work was one with which the editor of the *Poor Man's Guardian*, 'Bronterre' O'Brien, expressed himself 'fully in accord' adding that he would 'often have recourse to it on future occasions'.[40] John Gray also seems to have provided a source of theoretical inspiration with his *Lecture on Human Happiness* being quoted both in *Carpenter's Political Letters* and the *Destructive*,[41] while O'Brien in the *Poor Man's Guardian* cited his views on the 'reform of the social state'

---

[35] *Lancashire Co-operator*, 6 (1831), 8.
[36] *Lancashire and Yorkshire Co-operator*, 1 (1831), 6; Thompson was quoted to answer the charge that individual gain was necessary as a stimulus to productive effort.
[37] ibid. 5 (1831), 4; Thompson's works are recommended along with J. M. Morgan's *Revolt of the Bees*.
[38] ibid. August 1832, p. 15.
[39] *Destructive*, 1 (1833), 6–7; *Poor Man's Guardian*, 90 (1833), 59, and 98 (1833), 125.
[40] *Poor Man's Guardian*, 87 (1833), 34, 'The Subject of Property Investigated'; the obviously strong influence of Hodgskin's ideas upon O'Brien is, surprisingly, not emphasised by A. Plummer, *Bronterre, A Political Biography of Bronterre O'Brien* (London, Allen and Unwin, 1971), though he does suggest in general terms, in a much earlier article, that O'Brien did owe a considerable intellectual debt to the early English socialists, 'The place of Bronterre O'Brien in the working class movement', *Economic History Review*, 2 (1929–30), 80. The influence of Hodgskin on O'Brien seems to have been particularly important with respect to the latter's views on property and the exploitation of labour.
[41] *Carpenter's Political Letters*, 12 February 1831, p. 13; *Destructive*, 46 (1834), 202–3, where the work is referred to as the *Essay on Human Happiness*.

as being well in advance of Paine's, praise indeed from a writer and a paper that held the ideas of Paine in such high regard.[42]

Yet more significant than the mention of these writers' works was the fact that, in the years 1830–4, the editors of between fifteen and twenty working-class newspapers[43] were prepared to devote extensive space to discussing the causes of exploitation and poverty, the reasons for impoverishment in the midst of abundance, the repercussions of mechanisation, the consequences of free trade, the causes of glutted markets and redundant labour, the efficacy of trades unions in improving the material lot of the labouring classes, the poor laws and the population question, and were prepared to do so in the idiom of political economy. These papers purveyed a 'new' form of critical discourse which they used to question both the existing social and economic order and the fundamentals of that economic 'orthodoxy' which was viewed as its theoretical mainstay.[44]

The most important papers of this period, though in varying degrees, treated political economy as a discipline of real consequence. The *Crisis* referred to political economy as 'in our day the alpha and omega of the sciences [which] ... dominates over others',[45] and many other papers considered an understanding of it a necessary and sometimes a sufficient condition for the working classes to remove the economic distress by which they were afflicted.[46] 'Perhaps the works most needed and best adapted to the present state and condition of the working people are to be found among those which treat of moral and political economy',[47]

---

[42] See, for example, *Poor Man's Guardian*, 80 (1833), 646, article on the 'Character of Thomas Paine'.

[43] This makes allowance for those such as O'Brien who were editors of more than one paper.

[44] 'Thus, in the social and economic spheres as in the political, the ideas propagated by the unstamped press appeared dangerous to propertied reformers. Hume, Place, James Mill, and others...' J. H. Wiener, *The War of the Unstamped, the Movement to Repeal the British Newspaper Tax 1830–36* (Ithaca, Cornell University Press, 1969), p. 231.

[45] *Crisis*, 2, 21 (1833), 164, editorial signed 'A'.

[46] See, for example, *Voice of the West Riding*, 25 (1833), 199, 'Address to Members of Trade Unions: The Character of the Working Classes'. Discussing the exploitation of labour in general terms, the writer of this article viewed it as something that 'nothing can remove but a general diffusion of useful knowledge throughout the working classes and an unreserved dissemination of truth, *particularly in relation to ... moral and political economy*' (my emphasis).

[47] ibid. 1 (1833), 2, 'Opening Addresses'.

stated one writer in the *Voice of the West Riding* and, indeed, in its opening 'Address' the paper had pledged, among other things, to produce literature of this very type to combat and confound the ideas of the 'Political Economists'.[48] In similar fashion the *Exchange Bazaars Gazette*, in its prospectus, set itself the task of dissipating 'the errors of spurious Political Economy' and in subsequent issues it did devote space to attacking the 'fashionable but ridiculous theories' purveyed by the political economists.[49] Even the *Destructive*, a paper oriented more to a consideration of purely political matters, stated, with respect to William Thomson's *Age of Harmony* (1834),[50] that it noticed 'this and like publications in preference to crowding our pages with comments upon Parliamentary debates',[51] while the collected issues of the co-operative paper the *Birmingham Labour Exchange Gazette* were published under the title, *Essays and Articles on subjects connected with Popular Political Economy illustrative of the Condition and Prospects of the Working Classes* (1833), so dominated was the paper by a discussion of economic issues.[52] Many writers in these papers would have applauded the sentiments of O'Brien when he stated that 'the battle of labour against capital is not to be fought wth guns and swords . . . it will be of enlightened against foolish labourers, who are ignorant dupes of the capitalist',[53] and have argued further that a necessary prerequisite of 'enlightenment' was a sound knowledge of political economy.[54]

If, therefore, as one writer put it, 'Hodgskin's economics [and] the reputation of Malthus and Ricardo . . . were subjects of general discussion in . . . rendezvous of the London artisans';[55] if Owenite and anti-capitalist political economy did reach the

[48] ibid.
[49] *Exchange Bazaars Gazette*, 1 (1832), 7.
[50] N.B. Not William Thompson, though broadly defined this was a work of political economy.
[51] *Destructive*, 28 (1833), 221.
[52] In contrast, therefore, to the Romantic critics of early industrial capitalism, it would seem that writers in the working-class press were not driven to a complete rejection of the science of political economy. In this context see the remarks of C. C. Ryan, 'The fiends of commerce: Romantic and Marxian criticisms of classical political economy', *History of Political Economy*, 13 (1981), 82.
[53] *Poor Man's Guardian*, 169 (1833), 238, editorial.
[54] Thus, for example, one commentator wrote that the 'ignorance of the people' could be attributed 'in a great measure to the ignorance of their instructors the political economists', *Crisis*, 3, 9 (1834), 69, editorial.
[55] M. Hovell, *The Chartist Movement* (Manchester University Press, 1925), p. 49.

'thinking portion of the British working class'[56] precipitating the formation of 'two Radical Publics', the dividing line between which was 'alternative notions of political economy',[57] it was in the years 1830–4 and primarily as a result of the efforts of writers in the working-class press that these things occurred. Thus it is interesting to note Place's assertion that Hodgskin's doctrines 'were carefully and continually propagated among them [the working classes] . . . by small publications. Many of them were sold for two pence a dozen. They were carefully and cleverly written for the purpose intended and were very widely circulated.'[58] For Place, an informed if sometimes paranoid observer of such matters, the anti-capitalist political economy of Hodgskin was certainly reaching a wide and receptive working-class audience in the early 1830s.

However, writers in the working-class press of this period did much more than merely emphasise the importance of political economy and suggest to their readers the sources from which a sound knowledge of the discipline might best be culled. They also mounted a vigorous assault on the scope, methodology, aims and content of what was perceived as classical orthodoxy and, in addition, they suggested some of the essential characteristics which an alternative, working-class political economy might possess. In this task the writings of Hodgskin and Thompson once again seem to have pointed the way. Certainly these two writers developed in their respective works many lines of attack upon the classical approach to political economy, which were subsequently to be elaborated and more widely disseminated in the working-class press. In particular, they were quick to assail the essentially apologetic intent which they saw as pervading much classical writing and which took the complementary forms of obfuscating the economic evils of

---

[56] M. Beer, *A History of British Socialism* (2 vols., London, Allen and Unwin, 1953), Vol. 1, p. 280.
[57] E. P. Thompson, *Making*, p. 799.
[58] *Place Collection*, BM Add. MSS. 27, 791, fol. 270; in addition, Place viewed 'even the best' of the unstamped press of the early 1830s as constantly inculcating 'absurd and mischievous doctrine respecting the right of property'; see also J. H. Rose, 'The unstamped press', *English Historical Review*, 12 (1897), 715–16: 'A study of the unstamped press is important, not only as showing its tendency to degrade public taste and lower the tone of the legal journals, but also as illustrating the increasing prevalence of levelling and communistic ideas among working men after 1815.'

capitalism which bore most heavily on the labouring classes and directly defending the economic interests of capitalists and landowners. The point was made forcefully by Thompson in his *Labor Rewarded*:

Some of the partisans of the diffusion of knowledge, use all their exertions to shut out from the consideration of the Industrious Classes, all views on matters of social science, particularly on detached and still disputed points of political economy, which do not exactly square with their notions. So far they resemble inquisitors, who mean, by diffusing knowledge, training human beings to implicit belief in their dreams, that they and their political associates may the more securely prey and fatten on the fruits of the industry of the industrious. This is remarkably the case with those of the leaders of the school of Competitive Political Economy.[59]

Hodgskin and Thompson saw in the writings of the classical economists the insidious fusion of a mystificatory and apologetic intent. 'Such are the doctrines of political economy', wrote Hodgskin, that 'capitalists may well be pleased with a science which both justifies their claims, and holds them up to our admiration, as the great means of civilizing and improving the world'[60] and Thompson too saw classical political economy as an attempt 'to stifle inquiry respecting those great principles which question their [competitive political economists'] right as well as that of the capitalists, to larger shares of the national produce than those which the physical producers of wealth themselves enjoy'.[61] Political economy in the hands of these writers was an ideological buttress of the inequitable status quo; it was a theoretical rationalisation of the impoverishment of labour,[62] a rationalisation too which was articulated in a language designed to confuse rather than enlighten.[63] As used

[59] W. Thompson, *Labor Rewarded: The Claims of Labor and Capital Conciliated By One of the Idle Classes* (London, Hunt and Clarke, 1827), p. 46.
[60] T. Hodgskin, *Labour Defended against the Claims of Capital*, 2nd edn (London, Steil, 1831), p. 17.
[61] W. Thompson, *Labor Rewarded*, p. 46.
[62] 'It is the overwhelming nature of the demands of capital sanctioned by the laws of society . . . enforced by the legislature, and *warmly defended by political economists*, which keep . . . the labourer in poverty and misery', T. Hodgskin, *Labour Defended*, p. 23 (my emphasis); see also ibid. p. 5, where Hodgskin writes of 'the claims of the capitalists . . . [being] supported by the theories of political economy'.
[63] See, for example, Thompson's remarks on the manner in which 'Political Economists of the school of Competition' abused or failed to define the term 'free competition', *Labor Rewarded*, pp. 52–3.

by classical writers, for example, the term 'capital' had become 'a sort of cabalistic word, like Church and State, or any other of those general terms which are invented by those who fleece the rest of mankind to conceal the hand that shears them'.[64] These 'general terms' and the manner in which they were applied introduced confusion into a science which might otherwise be used to lay bare the underlying nature of the relationship between 'shearer' and 'sheared'.

Such criticisms of classical writers were echoed both in the co-operative press of the late 1820s and more extensively and with greater vigour in the working-class press of the early 1830s. Thus a writer in the *Co-operative Magazine* (1826) accused political economists of purveying as a science what was merely a medium through which to articulate the views of the 'leading interests of society',[65] and to propagate 'doctrines [which] have tended during the whole of the present century to discourage the expectation of any great improvement in the condition of the labouring people'.[66]

It was in the early 1830s, though, that the work of the political economists was most frequently derided as linked to the articulation of class and sectional interests. Political economists were condemned as being 'in the pay of the capitalists',[67] as 'attached to the upper classes to whom they look for advancement',[68] as constructing their 'systems only for the good of particular classes, instead of exploring sources of natural wealth'[69] and as writing 'for narrow minded beings with money in their pockets called capitalists'.[70] Thus they were seen as writing with the intention of justifying or concealing economic inequalities and injustices from which they and the classes whose interests they defended derived benefit. Such an opinion was clearly expressed by 'Senex' in his 'Letters on Associated Labour' in the *Pioneer*, where he

---

[64] T. Hodgskin, *Labour Defended*, p. 17.
[65] *Co-operative Magazine*, 1, 5 (1826), 140.
[66] ibid. 2, 9 (1827), 387.
[67] *Pioneer*, 31 (1834), 283, 'Letters on Associated Labour', by 'Senex'.
[68] *Crisis*, 2, 21 (1833), 164, editorial signed 'A'.
[69] ibid. 1, 40 (1833), 159, report of a speech by W. Hawkes Smith at a meeting in Birmingham.
[70] *Pioneer*, 28 (1834), 244, 'Letters on Associated Labour', by 'Senex'.

condemned classical writers for having 'bewildered themselves and the world in endeavouring to prove that hireling labour at the lowest possible rate, is the proper condition of the vast and overwhelming portion of our race, from whom proceed all the wealth and strength of communities'.[71] More specifically O'Brien attacked the Society for the Diffusion of Useful Knowledge (SDUK) for producing economic tracts and pamphlets which aimed 'to cause the few to take from the millions the whole produce of their labour and to accomplish this object... by all sorts of sophistry, to delude the wealth producers into a belief that the labour of human beings is regulated precisely on the same principles as any other commodity'. For O'Brien this 'juggle of the political economists' meant 'neither more nor less than this... Give up the whole produce of your labour.'[72] In similar vein William King in a pamphlet had condemned 'A work... recently published entitled *The Rights of Industry* but which is more properly a work recommending the plunder of industry'.[73] Thus were the writers of the SDUK popularly pilloried for their defence of capital and profit.

Writers in the working-class press and the authors of cheap pamphlets, like William King, believed not only that 'Political Economists' were treating an economic system abounding in evils and injustice as something rational, fixed and immutable but also that they wrote with the deliberate intention of making it appear so, thus persuading their readers that all was for the best in the best possible of all economic worlds. As one writer put it, 'I leave political economists to their jargon. They wrote under a system of evil and they wrote not for the purpose of getting rid of that evil but to cut down man to the endurance of it.'[74] Classical orthodoxy, or what was perceived as classical orthodoxy, was thus denied the critical function, the radical

---

[71] ibid. Senex was probably J. E. (Shepherd) Smith; see, for example, J. Saville, 'J. E. Smith and the Owenite movement, 1833–4' in S. Pollard and J. Salt (eds.), *Robert Owen, Prophet of the Poor, Essays in Honour of the Hundredth Anniversary of his Birth* (London, Macmillan, 1971), pp. 115–44, and J. Sever, 'James Morrison of the *Pioneer*' (unpublished monograph, 1963).
[72] *Poor Man's Guardian*, 30 (1832), 237.
[73] W. King, *To the Useful Working Population* (London, 1831), p. 1.
[74] *Pioneer*, 28 (1834), 243, 'Letters on Associated Labour' by 'Senex'.

crusading role which Francis Place had attempted to attach to it in the pages of the *Trades Newspaper*.[75] Rather, it was revealed to readers of the working-class press as an essential bulwark of the inequitable and unjust; a weapon designed for the defence rather than the critical analysis of existing economic arrangements. Political economists were accused of assuming as given what should be their primary object of investigation, i.e. they were condemned for building their theories upon the assumption that labourers must necessarily exist at a basic level of material subsistence rather than examining critically the arrangements that made that so.[76] As such 'the imposters of the Malthusian and McCulloch schools' were seen as cheating 'the public into hard heartedness by false dogmas and assumptions',[77] by stressing continually the idea that abject poverty was a necessary, immutable and even beneficial fact of communal life. Thus it was that Harriet Martineau was accused of making 'believe that the worst that could be is the envy and admiration of the world'.[78]

This attack upon their apologetic character ensured that the opinions of classical writers and their populorisers did not make the same inroads into the working-class press of the early 1830s as they had previously done in the case of papers such as the *Black Dwarf*, the *Gorgon* and the *Trades Newspaper*. The opportunity for constructing a radical, critical, political economy based on the more enlightened sentiments of classical writers was effectively, if temporarily, destroyed.

In this respect it is interesting to note that those institutions and individuals who attempted to disseminate classical principles among the labouring classes were subjected to particularly vituperative attack in the early 1830s. Thus the *Voice of the West Riding* warned its readership against writers such as Martineau

---

[75] It was quite easy, for example, to cite writers like McCulloch as being in favour of the legalisation of combinations, the repeal of the Corn Laws and a high wage economy. In this respect it is fundamentally wrong to view the classical economists as suggesting that 'misery was the precondition of economic development; in their eyes poverty was the stimulus to production', G. Hardach, D. Karras and B. Fine, *A Short History of Socialist Economic Thought* (London, Edward Arnold, 1978), p. 1.

[76] See, for example, *Carpenter's Political Letters*, 9 December 1830, p. 9, article by 'Economist'.

[77] *Destructive*, 46 (1833), 361.

[78] *Voice of the West Riding*, 23 (1833), 180.

and McCulloch who were dismissed as 'Pseudo Political Economists'.[79] Other papers attacked Harriet Martineau as a good writer of fiction but a poor writer of political economy[80] and more scurrilously as the 'anti-propagation lady, a single sight of whom would repel all fears of surplus population, her aspect being as repulsive as her doctrines'.[81] In addition the Society for the Diffusion of Useful Knowledge was condemned as an organisation with 'base and insidious intentions'[82] and the *Penny Magazine* through which, amongst other media, it disseminated its ideas was dismissed as displaying the 'anti-social' and 'cannibal pretensions' of the 'properties of the rich' as 'accumulations of industry'.[83]

This criticism of the popularisers, as of the classical economists themselves, tended to be assertive and abusive rather than reasoned and analytical. However, it may be seen as effective in a tactical sense as it discredited classical economics *en bloc*, leaving the way clear for the propagation and reception of an alternative political economy.

Classical writers were also discredited in the late 1820s and early 1830s by associating their work, in the minds of working-class readers, with particularly unpopular policies. Thus the classical economists were accused of believing that there existed a 'redundant population' and of being supporters of emigration as a remedy for this ill. Such beliefs undoubtedly sprang from a popular conception and hatred of the doctrines and implications of Malthusianism, but what popular writers did was to assert that such beliefs were generally adhered to by the 'modern school of Political Economy, who consider over-population as the main cause of the depression of the industrious classes'[84] and who 'with a Christian clergyman at [its] head, wish . . . the surplus population of the country to transport themselves to different shores and climes'.[85] In this way writers in the working-class

---

[79] ibid.
[80] *Crisis*, 2, 21 (1833), 167, editorial signed 'A'.
[81] *Poor Man's Guardian*, 167 (1834), 220, article on the 'Bastardy Clauses of the Poor Law Amendment Bill'.
[82] ibid. 44 (1832), 359, 'A Labourer'.
[83] ibid. 86 (1833), 25, article on 'The Relative Condition of the Rich and Poor Considered'.
[84] *Crisis*, 2, 24 (1833), 108, editorial signed 'A'.
[85] ibid. 1, 4 (1832), 13, report of a speech by W. Carson.

press gave the impression that classical political economy as a whole was attempting to impale the labouring classes upon the horns of an economic dilemma which implied that either 'superfluous' labourers fled the country with the aid of government finance or else they must perish from lack of physical subsistence.[86] It seemed that the working classes were being forced to 'submit to the insults of the Malthusians ... by being told that there are too many of them ... that they breed too fast; while the condoling followers of Wilmot Horton advise them, nay compel them to leave their native land'.[87] Thus in the early 1830s writers in the working-class press managed to associate classical orthodoxy with the 'wrong' side of one of the most emotive issues of the period. Classical political economy was tarnished in consequence.

In addition to this increasingly vigorous attack on the apologetic nature of classical economic thinking, an examination of the working-class press of the period 1816–34 also reveals mounting criticism of classical writers for their obsession with certain economic questions to the neglect of others more intimately concerned with the material condition of labour. In particular, classical economists were seen as being overwhelmingly concerned with the factors affecting the rate of capital accumulation and the expansion of output to the neglect of questions related to the distribution of the national product. Thus they were seen as narrowing the scope of the discipline to exclude analysis of those economic questions in which the working classes were primarily interested.

In the *Economist*, for example, classical writers were accused of being exclusively concerned with maximising the rate of capital accumulation[88] and as viewing 'the wealth of nations as something distinct from the comfort, the abundance, the enjoyments of their members' and so ignoring 'that hitherto most

---

[86] The real state of affairs was more complex. Most classical political economists were critical of emigration on the grounds of cost and efficacy. As R. N. Ghosh has pointed out, Malthus himself had serious misgivings about Wilmot Horton's emigration plans, 'Malthus on emigration and colonization', *Economica*, 30 (1963), 45–61.

[87] *Lancashire Co-operator*, 5 (1831), 6.

[88] See, for example, the *Economist*, 7 (1821), 103–4: 'There are few errors which have been more fatal to humanity ... than that of Political Economists regarding capital.'

Changing attitudes to political economy 1816–34   27

difficult problem of political economy viz. the true distribution of the immense amount of production which manufactures aided by machinery can now create'.[89] This line of attack in an early co-operative paper such as the *Economist* was more fully developed in the economic works of Thompson and Hodgskin. As early as 1818 Hodgskin had declared himself 'an enemy of those doctrines of the political economists that praise the accumulation of capital'[90] while criticism of interference with the 'natural' laws of distribution to promote capital accumulation remained a constant theme in his writings.[91] In similar vein Thompson wrote in his *Inquiry* that 'The ultimate object [of economic activity] is not accumulation, is not capital, but enjoyment immediate or future. Herein differ the mere political and moral economist. The accumulation of wealth or capital, and particularly in large masses is the sole object of the mere political economist.'[92] Such political economists were therefore seen as being concerned with how the product of labour was distributed only in so far 'as it may influence reproduction and accumulation'.[93]

Thompson set his attack upon the *political* economists' obsession with capital accumulation within a more broadly based critique of the scope of classical political economy. What Thompson desired was to synthesise his economic theorising with a particular moral perspective[94] and in the attempt he was led to challenge the very categorisation of the discipline as *political* economy. Thompson preferred to define his role as that of a moral economist[95] and indeed in some respects he may be seen as attempting to re-establish on a more 'scientific' basis the old 'Moral Economy' which was receiving its death blows in the closing years of the Napoleonic Wars and the immediate post-

---

[89] ibid. 36 (1821), 161; ibid. 32 (1821), 102.
[90] T. Hodgskin to F. Place, letter, 12 November 1818.
[91] See, for example, T. Hodgskin, *The Natural and Artificial Rights of Property Contrasted* (London, Steil, 1832), p. 173.
[92] W. Thompson, *An Inquiry into the Principles of the Distribution of Wealth most conducive to Human Happiness* (London, Longman, 1824), p. 413.
[93] ibid. p. ix; Thompson believed that questions of distribution had been wrongly left to 'moralists and politicians'.
[94] Thus R. K. P. Pankhurst rightly remarked that for Thompson there was 'no hope of progress as long as the science of morals remained divorced from that of Political Economy', *William Thompson*, pp. 27–8.
[95] W. Thompson, *Inquiry*, p. 413.

war period.[96] Thus with Thompson, 'just prices' and 'fair wages' are transmuted into 'natural price' and the 'natural value' of labour. Thompson in effect appropriates the language of the political economists while eschewing the ethical neutrality with which they tried to imbue it.[97] In this way Thompson was able not only to retain the moral fervour of an earlier mode of critical discourse but also to attack the assumptions and concerns of classical political economy on a front sufficiently broad to harness and reflect a discontent with early industrial capitalism that was more than purely economic.[98]

Broadening the scope of 'political' economy in this way also allowed for a more direct consideration of those distributional questions which most obviously concerned the working classes. In fact how wealth, once produced, might best be distributed was for Thompson the kind of question to which only a moral economist was competent to give an answer. It was the moral economist who concerned himself with the ultimate destination and utilisation of wealth; it was the political economist who concerned himself with the magnitude of the national product.

---

[96] E. P. Thompson, *Making*, pp. 594–7.

[97] In this context see J. S. Schumpeter's remark that in the hands of the Ricardian socialists the labour theory of value assumed the significance of an ethical law, *Economic Doctrine and Method* (London, Allen and Unwin, 1954), p. 121.

[98] K. Tribe, *Land, Labour and Economic Discourse* (London, Routledge and Kegan Paul, 1978), pp. 153 and 156, has written of Thompson that he used 'economic terminology ... to construct a moral discourse in which this terminology is invoked as a mode of proof of the rectitude of the moral positions put forward'. Similarly, of Hodgskin he has stated that his 'introduction of economic categories is deployed as a form of evidence in a moral argument, establishing the veracity of the moral analysis'. This is altogether too simplistic. Tribe ignores what may be termed the connotative ambiguity of many of the terms and concepts used by Thompson, Hodgskin and the other Ricardian socialists. Thus taking the term 'natural' as applied to value and price, it may be argued that at one level this is used by Thompson and Hodgskin to construct a moral argument to the effect that commodities should exchange at their natural values if labour is to be guaranteed economic justice. However, the use of the term is also meant to imply an underlying material reality which would surface in 'natural' values if it were untrammelled by state interference or the coercive economic power of the capitalist. Thus their theories of value are not only a means of indicating the value at which commodities ought to exchange but also the value at which they will naturally exchange in the absence of man-made market imperfections. In a sense too the strength of Ricardian socialist political economy lies precisely in this connotative ambiguity which can allow a term such as 'natural' to embody an ethical imperative and a sense of scientific objectivity.

It was to be in the working-class press of the early 1830s that this condemnation of the narrow nature of classical political economists' analytical concerns was to receive its most forceful popular expression. Once again it was writers in these papers who gave popular voice to the views of Thompson, Hodgskin and other anti-capitalist and socialist writers of the 1820s. Political economists were attacked for their obsessive concern with those factors facilitating capital accumulation. They were accused of being 'unfeeling worshippers of mammon' and condemned because 'all their views ... and all their ideas of advantage to society have reference and are confined to the accumulation of capital'.[99] They were seen as having stripped economic questions of their ethical dimension by relegating Man to the status of a mere instrument of production.[100] For them Man had become simply a means to attain certain economic ends, 'a mere secondary consideration: in lieu of Trade being a means of HIS welfare, HE is considered as an engine to be worked for the good of trade'.[101] In similar vein O'Brien exclaimed against Henry Brougham that 'His whole structure of argument ... [was] based upon the Ricardo dogma that labour is a marketable commodity ... a most impudently false assumption, disguised under the form of an abstraction.'[102] Political economists had reified Man: they had ceased to know anything 'of Man, his nature, his rights and his powers'[103] and in such circumstances with Mankind stripped of its human attributes and reduced to the status of a commodity or instrument of production, ethical considerations had been effectively eliminated from economic questions.

In addition to concealing the true causes of working-class economic distress, defending the interests of the rich and

---

[99] *Poor Man's Advocate*, 9 (1832), 70, provides one example among many of this type of criticism in the working-class press.

[100] Or as one anonymous pamphleteer put it in *Words of Wisdom Addressed to the Labouring Classes* (Armagh, 1830), p. 13, 'Economists ... consider man as a mere wealth-producing machine, whose remuneration is to be regulated by the value of food and clothes ... Just as any other piece of machinery [he] must be kept in working order.'

[101] *Voice of the West Riding*, 6 (1833), 41, 'The Working Classes and Political Economists' by 'Verax'.

[102] *Poor Man's Guardian*, 135 (1834), 407.

[103] *Pioneer*, 28 (1834), 244, 'Letters on Associated Labour' by 'Senex'.

powerful exploiters of labour, concerning themselves with those economic questions of exclusive interest to capitalists, ignoring those economic developments which affected the material lot of the labouring classes and purging political economy of any ethical dimension, classical political economists and their popularisers were also accused of constructing their theories on shaky methodological foundations. In particular they were accused of having scant regard for the actual facts of economic life. Thus McCulloch was rebuked by the editor of the *Trades Newspaper* for falling, in his consideration of the Irish problem of landlord absenteeism, 'into a common error of the Ricardo School, namely that of urging from half the facts of a case and creating a general principle upon partial analysis... On parochial questions the disciples of Ricardo are frequently... dangerous counsellors, in as much as they disregard facts, argue from half cases and mistake hasty generalisations for a complete analysis.'[104] Classical economists lived in an ideal world of their own theoretical construction and one which failed to 'take into consideration the habits and instincts and all the natural passions and propensities belonging to human nature'.[105] In addition classical writers were accused of abstracting from distinctions of time and place to give a spurious universal validity to the economic laws which they believed they had discovered. As one writer put it when discussing the economic opinions of James Mill, 'In laying down the LAWS which regulate the production, the distribution, the exchange and the consumption of commodities, Mr Mill makes no distinction of time or place. For aught that appears... the same laws are everywhere in force.'[106]

Such methodological criticisms were constantly reiterated in the working-class press of the early 1830s with political economists accused in particular of founding their theories upon inadequate empirical foundations. As one writer stated:

Their [the political economists'] professed object is to exalt the condition of the producers of wealth, yet they countenance and seek

---

[104] *Trades Newspaper*, 12 (1825), 182.
[105] ibid. 18 (1825), 273, a letter from Thomas Single.
[106] *Co-operative Magazine*, 2, 9 (1827), 389, article by 'Philadelphus', i.e. B. S. Jones; see G. Claeys, 'Benjamin Scott Jones alias 'Philadelphus': an early Owenite socialist', *Bulletin of the Society for the Study of Labour History*, 43 (Autumn 1981), 14–15.

to encourage the spirit of competition in our commercial system, either unmindful of or unacquainted with the ravages it is everywhere making. But in this there is nothing which will surprise us when we reflect upon whom they are and how they are situated. Though talented and deeply read, yet they are persons removed by their conditions from that intercourse with their poorer brethren which can really make them acquainted with the condition of society; and all their writings prove them to be not practical men but mere theorists who state only certain facts and draw from them erroneous inferences.[107]

The political economists could not, therefore, posit viable solutions to the fundamental economic and social problems generated by capitalism because they were temperamentally, geographically and socially divorced from those whom the problems most intimately affected. Their economic theories and the practical policies which they based upon them were necessarily derived from perniciously incomplete information. Formulated in ignorance of the facts of economic life, they were the product of 'closet theorists' unacquainted with the economic realities which were the everyday experience of the labouring classes. Thus it was believed that classical writers could legitimately be accused of an 'antipathy... to almost every known fact in the actual world'.[108]

By 1834 the methodology, scope, aims and content of classical political economy, or what was perceived as classical political economy, had been utterly condemned by writers in the working-class press. But what did they wish to put in its place? Given that by the early 1830s so many writers saw political economy as a discipline of real consequence which could not be ignored, what should be its essential characteristics – or, more specifically, what were to be the distinguishing features of an alternative, working-class political economy?

In a sense, its essential characteristics can be dialectically derived from the popular critique of classical orthodoxy. An alternative, working-class political economy should be all that classical political economy was not. Thus it should be based

---

[107] *Lancashire and Yorkshire Co-operator*, July 1832, pp. 2–3, article on 'Co-operative Missions' by 'M'.
[108] *Carpenter's Political Magazine*, February 1832, 'On Political Economists'.

upon a scientific regard for facts and it should be characterised by, as one writer believed, 'a rigid adherence to inductive philosophy'.[109] It was a discipline which should be primarily concerned with the causes and consequences of the maldistribution of wealth as these affected the labouring classes, rather than with the factors making for the rapid accumulation of capital. It should be a discipline which embodied a distinctive moral outlook and which worked from the assumption that Man was not simply a means to a preconceived economic end. It should be a 'moral' or 'social'[110] rather than a 'political' economy. Above all, an alternative, working-class political economy was to be a discipline stripped of apologetic intent and based upon the work of those writers whose analysis transcended the mere defence of vested interests, i.e. it should be based upon the work of those who obviously wrote from the standpoint of the oppressed. A working-class political economy should challenge the quietistic attitudes and implications which could be and were derived from popularised classical orthodoxy; 'Some Political Economists of the present day are patiently waiting till things find their level... till Distress shall have checked and diminished the population.'[111] The work of such writers was dismissed as riddled with an 'immoveable apathy'[112] permeated by an acceptance that the material lot of the labouring classes could not be significantly ameliorated. This despair, which was an inevitable consequence of the 'gloomy and unnatural dogmas'[113] of classical political economy, was to be banished by a working-class political

---

[109] *Co-operative Magazine*, 2, 3 (1827), 144, quoted from J. M. Morgan's *Revolt of the Bees* (1826); see also the remark of 'W. T.', i.e. William Thompson, that 'Till the competitive economist can prove from FACTS and not from ideal tendencies that the industrious classes are not constantly reduced to severe distress by loss of employment from scientific improvement his assertions will be in vain... The general result is not to be ascertained by theories of what writers think ought to be the effects, but by overlooking into the world of industry and seeing what the effect IS', *Co-operative Magazine*, 1, 6 (1826), 185.

[110] William Carpenter, for example, favoured the term 'Social Economy' to designate a 'science which treats of the internal arrangements of a society or a community and of the method by which the greatest quantity of wealth and happiness may be secured to the greatest number of individuals at the least possible expence [sic]', *Carpenter's Political Magazine*, September 1831, p. 79, article entitled 'Social Economy'.

[111] *Economist*, 2 (1821), 28.

[112] ibid. 21 (1821), 325–6, 'Investigator'.

[113] ibid.

economy; a working-class political economy was to pose and answer questions which would shake fundamentally the 'immoveable apathy' of classical economics. 'Pseudo political economy' might 'shy off' questions which concerned the right of labour to its whole product[114] and 'how it is that those who do not work grow rich, while those who do work grow poor'[115] but it was the belief of many writers in the working-class press of the early 1830s that political economy could and should be used to investigate just such matters. O'Brien in the *Poor Man's Guardian* gave some idea of the questions with which a working-class political economy should be concerned:

3. How it comes that the labourer and the capitalist are different persons, or why they are not the same person? ... 5. If labour has been originally able to create capital without the aid of capital ... ought not labour unaided by capital, to be competent to produce the same results now? ... 7. Does the labourer receive as large a portion of the produce of his labour now, as he used to a century ago ... ? Has the condition of the labourer improved or declined with the growth of middlemen or with the improvements of machinery? ... 9. Is the amount of taxation ... sufficient of itself to account for the workman's degradation?[116]

It was to be the answers to these questions which were to provide the substance of an effective popular economic critique of early industrial capitalism.

Whether in the period 1816–34 classical political economy in its pure or its popularised form was characterised by all the deficiencies attributed to it by writers in the working-class press is a debatable point but it is also, in significant respects, an unimportant one. In a situation where 'labourers [were] beginning to think for themselves. And [were] turning their attention to the science which treats of the production and distribution of wealth',[117] the popularisation of these perceived deficiencies by writers in the working-class press undoubtedly inspired an unfavourable reaction to the works of the classical political economists among their readers. Classical popularisers were,

---

[114] *Pioneer*, 6 (1833), 42.
[115] *The Co-operator*, 3 (1828), 2, article entitled 'Value of labour'.
[116] *Poor Man's Guardian*, 90 (1833), 57–8.
[117] *Co-operative Magazine*, 2 (1826), 64, a letter from 'S.F.'

therefore, forced to sow the seeds of orthodoxy upon a peculiarly infertile working-class soil.[118] In addition, through its attack on the essentially apologetic nature of classical writing the working-class press prepared the way for a favourable reception of the economic thought of those like Hodgskin, Gray, Thompson and Owen who wrote with obvious critical intent. In this respect even the vilification of writers such as Martineau, McCulloch, Malthus and Ricardo and the abusive attacks on the proselytising activities of the Society for the Diffusion of Useful Knowledge had their positive consequences. Such abuse of classical political economy and its popularisers ensured that it was to those anti-capitalist and socialist writers positively recommended in the working-class press that readers would have been inclined to turn to furnish themselves with a knowledge of political economy and a theoretical understanding of those economic problems which afflicted them. However, before considering the works of these writers it is necessary first to consider the reasons for this remarkable burgeoning of popular interest in political economy itself.

[118] N. B. de Marchi, 'The success of Mill's *Principles*', *History of Political Economy*, 6 (1974), 119–57, argues that J. S. Mill's *Principles of Political Economy* (1848) was designed in some measure to counter the opprobrium which had been heaped upon political economy in the previous twenty years but he makes no mention of that portion of the opprobrium for which the working-class press of the early 1830s was responsible.

2

The need for a working-class political economy

Scrutiny of the working-class press would suggest, therefore, that by the late 1820s and early 1830s the labouring classes were concerning themselves increasingly with 'the science which treats of the production and distribution of wealth'[1] and also that they were determined to use it for critical rather than apologetic purposes. The question arises, then, as to why at both a formal[2] and a popular level, this period should have seen the emergence of an anti-capitalist and socialist political economy.

One possible answer to this question is that the particularly severe economic distress experienced by the labouring classes in the aftermath of the Napoleonic Wars inevitably turned the attention of radical thinkers to matters economic and thence to the discipline of political economy. Such a suggestion does of course raise the vexed question of whether or not working-class living standards were or were not being significantly eroded in this period. However, at the risk of oversimplifying the outcome of a debate which has exercised the minds and engaged the passions of generations of economic historians, it is probably fair to say that in the immediate post-Napoleonic War period particular economic hardship was indeed experienced by large sections of the working population. In fact most historians would probably accept Professor Deane's view that

for the distressed years of the immediate post-War aftermath when the demobilised soldiers and seamen flooded the labour market and

---

[1] *Co-operative Magazine*, 2 (1826), 64, letter from 'S.F.'
[2] The major economic works of the Ricardian socialists were published in the immediately preceding period, 1824–7.

the industries which had thrived in the war were facing a slump in demand, it is likely that higher real wages earned by those who were lucky enough to be in regular employment were insufficient to compensate for the loss of earnings experienced by the unemployed ... It seems probable that the real earnings of the average, working-class family were lower in these years than they had been in the 1780s.[3]

Yet what this distress seems to have provoked was an upsurge of radical political activity and the unparalleled proliferation of a complementary literature, rather than the emergence of a distinctively radical anti-capitalist or socialist political economy such as that disseminated in the period 1824–34. Also statistical evidence tends to suggest that it was in just this later period, the later 1820s and early 1830s, that per capita consumption and average real wages began to rise. Thus it has been estimated that per capita consumption rose from £11.3 per annum in the decade 1811–20 to £14.6 per annum in the decade 1821–30; while real wages rose from an index figure of 104 for the decade 1811–20 to 128 for the years 1821–30.[4]

Of course such aggregate data conceal the deteriorating living standards and particular hardship suffered by those sections of the workforce who were feeling the cold economic blast of intensified competition and/or technological advance. Thus groups of workers such as the Spitalfields silk weavers and the Midland framework knitters did experience significantly lower earnings and prolonged periods of underemployment or unemployment in the 1820s. However, this impoverishment seems to have provoked the spokesmen for these labourers to furnish an explanation of poverty which was narrowly and specifically related to the particular difficulties of their trade, rather than a more generally applicable economic critique of the functioning of competitive capitalism. Thus the main complaint of the framework knitters and silk weavers was that while other interests, occupations or trades had their economic position protected by legislation, they alone were

---

[3] P. Deane, *The First Industrial Revolution*, 2nd edn (Cambridge University Press, 1979), p. 265.
[4] C. H. Feinstein, 'Capital accumulation in the industrial revolution' in R. Floud and D. N. McCloskey (eds.), *The Economic History of Britain since 1700* (2 vols., Cambridge University Press, 1981), Vol. 1, p. 136; G. N. von Tunzelmann, 'Technical progress during the industrial revolution', in ibid. p. 159.

The need for a working-class political economy 37

being asked to weather the rigours of untrammelled competition. Andrew Larcher, for example, asserted that it was neither legitimate nor just to argue that the wages of silk weavers should be left to find their own level in a free market when 'house rents, food and all other necessaries' did not.[5] Robert Hall, on behalf of the framework knitters, similarly attacked the partial application of laissez-faire principles. 'It is evident', he wrote, 'that the vaunted maxim of leaving every kind of production and labour to find its own level is not adhered to . . . it has always been violated in this country from the remotest times.'[6]

What these writers then proceed to advocate is legislative protection for the workers in their particular trade. Given the ruinous nature of partial competition, it was imperative that Parliament pass or retain on the statute books legislation which would allow the control of product prices and thence the earnings of those who produced them. Thus Hall wrote: 'if every other expedient should fail, we see no reason why its [the legislature's] aid should not be exerted in favour of the Leicestershire framework knitters as well as of the Spitalfields weavers, who were a few years ago effectively relieved by the establishment of a minimum [wage]'.[7] A similar point was made in a petition which declared that 'adequate wages, and their concomitant advantages, cannot be secured without the enactment of some regulatory law'.[8]

Severe economic distress seems, therefore, to have produced sectionalism or particularism rather than an attempt to formulate a general critique of existing economic arrangements applicable to the material plight of the labouring classes as a whole.[9] Certainly some writers did attempt to derive from the particularly

---

[5] A. Larcher, *The Good and Bad Effects of High and Low Wages; or, a Defence of the Spitalfields Acts* (London, 1823), p. 13.
[6] R. Hall, *An Appeal to the Public on the subject of the Framework Knitters Fund*, 2nd edn (Leicester, T. Combe, 1820), p. 7.
[7] ibid. p. 8.
[8] Anon., *A Petition of the Journeymen Broad Silk Weavers of Spitalfields and its vicinity* (n.p. 1828), p. 5.
[9] Thus R. A. Church and S. D. Chapman wrote of Gravener Henson, the framework knitters' leader and spokesman, that he 'and the framework knitters had no notion of promoting equalization either of wages or of opportunity among the working classes', 'Gravener Henson and the making of the English working class' in E. L. Jones and G. E. Mingay (eds.), *Land, Labour and Population in the Industrial Revolution* (London, Edward Arnold, 1967), p. 158.

impoverished condition of the silk weavers and framework knitters a more general appreciation of the economic vulnerability of wage labour. Thus Hall made the point that while political economists regard labour as just another commodity which should be left free to find its own level in the market place, it was in fact a commodity whose conditions of supply rendered it qualitatively different from all others.[10] Similarly William Hale[11] (who quotes Hall) in a pamphlet defending the Spitalfields Acts and William Jackson[12] in *An Address to the Framework Knitters* contrasted the capitalist's power of withholding his goods from the market with the powerlessness of labourers likewise to control the supply of the only commodity which they possessed. However, with the exception of Jackson's *Address*[13] there is a failure to integrate these insights into anything resembling a general critique of capitalism. Indeed, the pamphleteers of the 1820s carefully distinguished between good employers, who maintained a fair level of wages, and bad masters irrevocably intent upon the kind of cut-throat competition which necessitated wage cutting. William Hale, defender of the Spitalfields silk weavers, was in fact an employer[14] who stressed the essential community of interest between employers and employed and the relative industrial peace which had prevailed in the past when prices and wages had been regulated. What Hale and other writers attacked was not the general division of society into capitalist and labourer, employer and employed, but rather the impoverishment, social antagonism and abrogation of responsibilities which resulted from untrammelled competition. These writers were not anti-capitalists, nor can their economic writings be said to represent an embryonic

---

[10] R. Hall, *An Appeal*, p. 6.
[11] W. Hale, *An Appeal to the Public in Defence of the Spitalfields Act* (London, Justins, 1822).
[12] W. Jackson, *An Address to the Framework Knitters* (Leicester, J. Fowler, 1833), p. 29.
[13] It should be remembered that Jackson's *Address* was not written and published until after the major works of Hodgskin, Thompson and Gray had seen the light of day.
[14] 'Hale was in a considerable way of business; he employed from three to four hundred looms; but... there was more capital on the repealers' side than on his', J. H. Clapham, 'The Spitalfields Acts 1773–1824', *Economic Journal*, 20 (1916), 470. In this context it is also interesting to note the increasing stress which, from the mid-1820s onwards, Gravener Henson placed on bringing masters and men together, R. A. Church and S. D. Chapman, 'Gravener Henson' in E. L. Jones and G. E. Mingay, *Land, Labour and Population*, p. 150.

anti-capitalist political economy. What they desired was a regulation of trade which would guarantee 'just and merited wages', 'a just price for ... labour', 'a fair and equitable price for labour', 'an equitable reward'.[15] Thus it has been said of Gravener Henson that he looked 'back to an age early in the eighteenth century when, as it seemed to him, a regulated trade had prevented many of the evils which were evident in the industrial society in which he lived'.[16] What he desired was to re-create, by means of paternalistic legislation, a world where 'the poor would live ... with ease and were not subject to a state of uncertainty for want of employment or apprehension of a reduction of means'.[17] Such aspirations were certainly shared by most of those who wrote in defence of the interests of the framework knitters and silk weavers.

Where poverty and hardship were rife in the post-Napoleonic War period, therefore, they seem to have been productive of a nostalgic yearning for a secure and stable past, rather than any generally applicable explanation of labour's impoverished material condition, such as that furnished by the Ricardian socialists. Thus it would seem unwise to argue that the general economic critique of early industrial capitalism which emerged in the mid-1820s was prompted by the direct experience of increasing emiseration.

It may be argued, though, that too narrow a view has been taken here of what constituted falling living standards; that what the labouring classes experienced in the 1820s and 1830s, regardless of what real wage or consumption data might suggest, was a marked deterioration in the quality of life; that the poverty, uncertainty of employment and the general squalor of urban life were qualitatively different from anything which had previously been experienced by the working population and that it was this qualitative emiseration which provoked radical writers to formulate a 'new', theoretical, economic explanation of labour's impoverished material condition.

---

[15] A. Larcher, *Good and Bad Effects*, p. 6; W. Hale, *An Appeal*, p. 16; ibid. p. 29; Anon., *Petition of the Journeymen*, p. 4.
[16] R. A. Church and S. D. Chapman, 'Gravener Henson' in E. L. Jones and G. E. Mingay, *Land, Labour and Population*, p. 146.
[17] G. Henson, *The Civil, Political and Mechanical History of the Framework Knitters in Europe and America* (Nottingham, 1831), Vol. 1, p. 216.

This is certainly nearer the mark. More important than the degree of poverty and economic distress suffered by the labouring classes were the qualitatively different forms which these perennial problems were assuming in the 1820s and 1830s as the industrial transformation of Britain gathered momentum. They demanded quite simply different explanations from those which had previously been provided and it was to furnish them that working-class writers or those who wrote from a working-class standpoint increasingly had recourse to the tools, concepts and constructs of political economy. To establish and amplify this point it is necessary to consider briefly the economic writings of Thomas Spence, William Ogilvie and Thomas Paine in order to highlight the deficiencies which rendered the existing agrarian radical analysis inapplicable to the forms which poverty, general economic distress and uncertainty of employment were assuming in early-nineteenth-century Britain.

For Thomas Spence, poverty was the necessary consequence of the exploitation and oppression of the labouring classes which followed historically and logically from the forcible abrogation of Man's natural right of access to the land. 'If we look back to the origin of the present nations', wrote Spence, 'we shall see that the land and all its appurtenances was claimed by a few and divided amongst themselves ... so that all things, men as well as other creatures were obliged to owe their lives to some other's property',[18] and it was through the exercise of the economic power thus acquired by 'conquest or encroachment on the common Property of Mankind' that the earth came to be 'cultivated either by slaves, compelled, like beasts, to labour, or by indigent objects whom they [the landowners] first exclude from a share in the soil, that want may compel them to sell their labour for daily bread'. Thus landlords 'by granting the means of life ... granted the life itself; and of course, they thought they had a right to all the services and advantages that the life or death of the creatures they gave life to could yield'.[19]

---

[18] T. Spence, *Lecture on Land Reform to the Newcastle Philosophical Society* (1775) in M. Beer, *Pioneers of Land Reform* (London, Bell, 1920), pp. 7–8; republished as *The Real Rights of Man* (London, 1793) and again republished as *The Meridian Sun of Liberty or The Whole Rights of Man displayed* (London, 1796).

In effect, for Spence, these 'indigent objects' were doubly exploited. First, by being denied their natural right of property in the land they were deprived of 'the natural fruits of the earth being the fruits of our undoubted common',[20] i.e. the produce spontaneously yielded by the earth independently of productive endeavour. Secondly, landless labourers were exploited by being deprived of the greater part of the fruits of their actual labours. Thus 'the privileged orders' were seen as being on a par with 'their humble imitators the highwaymen who have the impudence to deprive men of their labours for nothing'.[21] While it was 'The toil of the labouring classes ... [which] produce[d] provisions', it was the landowners who secured 'a perpetual influx of wealth by their Rents without toil or study'.[22] So for Spence this second mode of exploitation took the form of rents which represented the physical appropriation by 'a few, haughty, unthankful landlords' of the 'Cream of [labour's] Endeavours', 'the fruits of the earth', the 'provisions' created by 'the toil of the labouring classes'.[23]

William Ogilvie too saw Man as having a natural right to property in the land. Thus he wrote, 'The earth having been given to mankind in common occupancy, each individual seems to have by nature a right to possess and cultivate an equal share.'[24] Denial of these rights led to the aggregation of landholdings and hence the concentration of economic power in the hands of a small number of landowners, many of whom 'by exacting exorbitant rents ... exercise a most pernicious usury, and deprive industry that is actually exerted of its due reward'.[25] Thus it was the landless labourer who was peculiarly vulnerable to exploitation and indeed Ogilvie compared his lot

---

[19] T. Spence, *The End of Oppression being a Dialogue between an Old Mechanic and a Young One concerning the Establishment of the Rights of Man*, 2nd edn (London, 1796), p. 4; *The Rights of Infants* (London, 1795?), pp. 15–16; *Lecture*, p. 8.
[20] T. Spence, *The Rights of Infants*, p. 6.
[21] ibid.
[22] ibid.
[23] T. Spence, *Lecture*, p. 15; *The History of Crusonia or, Robinson Crusoe's Island* (1782) in Anselm Schlösser (ed.), *Essays in Honour of Willie Gallacher* (Berlin, Humboldt University, 1966), p. 299; *The Rights of Infants*, p. 16.
[24] W. Ogilvie, *An Essay on the Right of Property in Land* (1781) in M. Beer, *Pioneers of Land Reform*, p. 35.
[25] ibid. p. 60.

unfavourably to that of the mechanic and manufacturer who were seen as being able to 'find the materials whereon to exercise ... [their] talents at a moderate price' and to bring the produce of their labour to a 'freer market'.[26] Such advantages were not enjoyed by the 'cultivator of the ground' despite the fact that he was 'the most essential artisan to the welfare of the community'.[27] Ogilvie accepted that where he had the opportunity the cultivator could 'now bring his produce to a free and open market' but the problem was that unlike the artisan and manufacturer 'he cannot so easily find the rude materials of his industry at a reasonable price' and this was because landownership in any district was monopolised by a few. Thus, for Ogilvie, the situation of the cultivator was 'much inferior to that of the artisan, who can go to a cheap market wherever it is found, and can bring his rude materials from a great distance to his home'. In contrast 'the cultivator must carry his home to his raw materials'.[28] So the cultivator was vulnerable to exploitation and economic oppression in a way that the artisan was not. In fact Ogilvie argued that where artisans or manufacturers did suffer the unjust appropriation of their product it was by landlords who owned the land upon which their workshops were sited.

For Ogilvie, like Spence therefore, exploitation took the form of excessive rent exactions and the impoverishment of labour was a by-product of this. Like Spence too he conceived of exploitation as the direct physical appropriation of labour's product. Thus, for example, when Ogilvie discussed the conditions which had to be met to ensure that rents were fair he stated that 'the rent to be paid ought always to be fixed at a determined portion of the *real or estimated annual produce of the soil*'. It was in physical terms that Ogilvie thought.[29]

Two points can be made at this stage about Ogilvie and Spence's explanation of labour's impoverished material condition.

---

[26] ibid. p. 61n.
[27] ibid.
[28] ibid.
[29] ibid. p. 104 (my emphasis); see also, for example, Ogilvie's remark that 'The labour of men applied to the cultivation of the earth tends more to increase the public wealth, for it is more productive of *things necessary for the accommodation of life*, wherein all wealth consists', ibid. p. 50 (my emphasis).

First, exploitation is seen by them as an essentially agrarian phenomenon; it is the cultivator, the landless labourer stripped of his natural rights, whose product is appropriated. Secondly, both Ogilvie and Spence appear to have conceived of and explained exploitation in physical terms. This meant not only that their analysis and explanation of working-class poverty was applicable to an economy and society essentially agrarian in character but also that the analytical tools and theoretical constructs which they deployed could not easily be utilised, by them or subsequent writers, to formulate and articulate a critique of an economy characterised by a diversity of productive activity, specialisation and the use of capital equipment.

To elaborate a theory of labour exploitation in physical terms is not of course *per se* an illegitimate procedure. However, the feasibility of such an undertaking does rest upon the preparedness to make certain heroic assumptions. Thus a theory of exploitation elaborated in terms of the difference between the physical inputs absorbed by labour and the physical output resulting does assume a homogeneity of inputs and output at least in the wage-goods sector of the economy. Now in certain circumstances such an assumption may be permissible. Thus where agriculture is the sole or overwhelmingly dominant form of productive activity, i.e. where the labour force as a whole produces grain (or food) and consumes grain (or food);[30] or where it is believed that agriculture alone is capable of producing a surplus, i.e. the position of physiocratic anti-capitalists such as Charles Hall;[31] or where the wage-goods producing sector is, essentially, a one-product sector, it may be legitimate to reason in physical terms. For example, it has been argued that Ricardo in his *Essay on Profits* (1815) succeeded in formulating a theory of profits without confronting the problem of valuation by assuming that all wage-goods took the form of corn and that therefore in agriculture,

---

[30] Such assumptions may be seen as consistent with the experience of a large proportion of the labouring classes in the eighteenth century. 'Except in Westminster, in the mountains, or in the great sheep-grazing districts, men were never far from the sight of corn. Manufacturing industry was dispersed in the countryside; the colliers went to their labour by the side of cornfields; domestic workers left their looms and workshops for the harvest', E. P. Thompson, 'The moral economy of the English crowd in the eighteenth century', *Past and Present*, 50 (1971), 99.

[31] See below, pp. 69-70.

the wage-goods producing sector of the economy, 'the same commodity, namely corn, forms both the capital... and the product; so that the determination of profit by the difference between total product and capital advanced, and also the determination of the ratio of this profit to the capital, is done directly between quantities of corn without any question of valuation'.[32] Once this simplification was abandoned and wage-goods came to include manufactures, Ricardo was 'stopped by the word price'[33] and forced, in order to proceed further, to formulate a theory of value.

As, therefore, the economy comes to be characterised by an increasing diversity of productive activity; as, with its increasing contribution to the national product, the capacity of manufacture to generate an economic surplus becomes apparent and as the wage-basket comes increasingly to contain non-agricultural products, so the assumptions necessary for the formulation of a coherent physical theory of labour exploitation become increasingly unrealistic.

In 1775, of course, it may have been in some measure legitimate to work on the assumption that the British economy was predominantly agrarian, to view only agricultural labour as capable of producing a surplus which could be appropriated by others (rent) and to assume that land constituted the sole means of production. It was also understandable that in 1775 a writer might abstract from the economic lot of manufacturing labour and assume that the great bulk of the labouring classes consumed (largely) food and produced (largely) food.[34] Agriculture was throughout the eighteenth century and into the nineteenth the dominant form of economic activity. In addition, characterised

[32] P. Sraffa, Introduction to *The Works and Correspondence of David Ricardo*, Vol. 1, *On the Principles of Political Economy and Taxation* (Cambridge University Press, 1981), p. xxxi; see also J. Eatwell, 'The interpretation of Ricardo's *Essay on Profits*', *Economica*, 42 (1975), 182–7; for a contrary opinion see S. G. Hollander, 'Ricardo's analysis of the profit rate, 1813–15', *Economica*, 40 (1973), 266: 'it appears unjustified to interpret Ricardo's intentions in terms of a Corn Model'; also S. G. Hollander, 'Ricardo and the corn profit model, reply to Eatwell', *Economica*, 42 (1975), 188–202, and *The Economics of David Ricardo* (London, Heinemann, 1979), pp. 113–90.
[33] Ricardo to Malthus, 30 December 1815, *Works*, Vol. 6, p. 348.
[34] 'The labouring people in the eighteenth century did not live by bread alone, but (as the budgets collected by Eden and David Davies show) many of them lived very largely on bread', E. P. Thompson, 'The moral economy of the English crowd', p. 99.

as it was by increasing efficiency, innovation and a relatively rapid expansion of output and output per capita,[35] its capacity to generate an economic surplus was beyond question. However, between the publication of Spence's *Lecture* in 1775 and the mid-1820s when Thompson's *Principles* and *Labor Rewarded*, Hodgskin's *Labour Defended* and his *Popular Political Economy* and Gray's *Lecture on Human Happiness* saw the light of day economic developments were to occur which rendered unrealistic the assumptions which underlay the critical economic analysis of the agrarian radicals.

Where statistics are available to illuminate the magnitude of these developments they must necessarily be used with circumspection. Nevertheless, what evidence we possess does suggest strongly that it was 'in the first three decades or so of the nineteenth century [that] agriculture and manufacturing industry changed places in relative importance as measured by the numbers of jobs provided'[36] and also that the proportion of the labour force in manufacture expanded particularly rapidly in the Napoleonic War period.[37] Figures for the sectoral distribution of the national income in the early nineteenth century tell a similar story with the share of agriculture falling from 32.5% in 1801 to 23.4% in 1831, while that of manufacture, mining and building rose from 23.4% in 1801 to 34.4% in 1831.[38] In addition, there was a broadening of the base of manufacturing industry, and a dramatic growth of particular industries such as cotton and iron, many of whose products entered into the wage-basket of labourers.

It is true that the pace of economic change in the period 1775–1825 should not be overdramatised. When Thompson, Hodgskin, Gray and Owen first put pen to paper, agriculture was still of fundamental economic importance in terms of the output,

---

[35] It has been suggested that 'agriculture probably accounted for between 40% and 45% of National Income for most of the first three quarters of the eighteenth century', P. Deane and W. A. Cole, *British Economic Growth 1688–1959, Trends and Structure* (University of Cambridge, Department of Applied Economics, Monographs, 8, 1962), p. 157; on efficiency, innovation and rising productivity in agriculture see E. L. Jones, 'Agriculture 1700–80' in R. Floud and D. N. McCloskey, *Economic History of Britain*, Vol. 1, pp. 66–86.
[36] P. Deane and W. A. Cole, *British Economic Growth*, p. 144.
[37] ibid. pp. 142–3; see in particular Tables 30 and 31.
[38] ibid. p. 166.

incomes and the employment which it generated, while factory production was still in embryo and a substantial proportion of the labourer's wage would be spent on food. Nevertheless, things may be said to have changed sufficiently to render increasingly untenable the assumptions necessary for any simple physical theory of distribution or labour exploitation.[39]

By the mid-1820s, therefore, it was no longer legitimate to abstract from the diversity of productive activity and the growing importance of manufacture or to see land as the sole means of production. Nor was it acceptable when explaining labour's impoverishment to concentrate exclusively on the lot of agricultural labour or to abstract from the economic power wielded by the owners of industrial capital. By the 1820s those who wished to develop a critique of existing economic arrangements were confronted by a material reality qualitatively different from that which Spence and Ogilvie had sought to interpret. To come to terms with it required new tools of analysis, new concepts and new theoretical constructs. In these changed economic circumstances, if writers wished to explain impoverishment as a consequence of labour exploitation it became necessary to establish a common denominator in terms of which the consequences of a diverse range of productive activity could be measured. For when, even as a rough approximation, the homogeneity of inputs and outputs in the wage-goods sector could no longer be assumed, it became impossible to distinguish – except in the most general, rhetorical, non-theoretical fashion – what constituted the economic surplus produced by labour and of which labour was deprived. More specifically, without a theory of value, however crude, it became impossible to give any theoretical precision to the statement that labour was exploited. What was appropriated from labour and the extent of that appropriation were questions to which it was no longer

---

[39] 'the period of greatest structural change fell within the first three to four decades of the century', ibid. p. 169; on the growing importance of the cotton and iron industries see B. R. Mitchell and P. Deane, *An Abstract of British Historical Statistics* (University of Cambridge, Department of Applied Economics, Monographs, 17, 1971), p. 187; on the growing importance of fixed capital equipment in this period see C. H. Feinstein, 'Capital accumulation in the industrial revolution' in R. Floud and D. N. McCloskey, *Economic History of Britain*, Vol. 1, p. 130.

possible to provide a satisfactory answer couched in physical terms.

Even writing when they did, the failure to deploy a theory of value created problems for Spence, Ogilvie and Paine, particularly when they discussed what they saw as the central evil from which all others stemmed, namely the abrogation of Man's right to a share of the means by which an adequate material subsistence might be produced. For Spence, Man's access to or ownership of the means of production was primarily, though not solely, legitimised by natural right. As Spence himself realised, natural right legitimation held only so long as the means of production existed prior to and independently of human productive activity. Under certain circumstances this might be the case, e.g. where the means of production took the form of land or rather land existing in its natural state unaltered by human labour. Where, however, the land was improved or where the means of production took the form of human artefacts, then natural rights alone were not sufficient to legitimise access or ownership.

Spence confronts this problem in his *Rights of Infants* (1797) when he considers critically Paine's view as propounded in *Agrarian Justice* (1797), that Man has, by natural right, a claim upon only a tenth part of the value of landed property 'Because, says Mr Paine, it has so improved in the hands of private proprietors as to be of ten times the value it was of in its natural state.'[40] Spence accepts that the labour involved in improving land must also confer some sort of right to it but the crucial question was 'who improved the land?'[41] and to this Spence gave the answer that it was 'evident to the most superficial enquirer that the labouring classes ought principally to be thanked for every improvement'.[42] So it was the labouring classes who had rights to improved land rather than those 'proprietors' who happened to own it at present. For Spence there was no essential conflict, therefore, between natural rights and those conferred by labour. All Mankind, by virtue of its humanity, had a natural

---

[40] T. Spence, *The Rights of Infants*, p. 15.   [41] ibid.
[42] ibid. It would be wrong, therefore, to suggest that Spence attacked the Lockean idea of labour giving rights to property; see, for example, M. Beer, *History of British Socialism*, p. 107.

right to land, while the greater, labouring, part of humanity had a right to improved land conferred by their labour upon it. However, while Man's natural right to the land could be viewed, and was by Spence, as a right to an equal share of land in its unimproved or natural state, the extent of the rights conferred by labour was more difficult to specify. Thus Spence did not tackle the question of how to estimate the area or quality of land to which productive effort might entitle the labourer.

Now it could be argued that for Spence what labour did was to confer a right to an equal share of 'improved' land. All labourers would, therefore, have been entitled to an equal share of land by virtue of their natural rights and an equal share of improved land in consequence of the labour they had expended upon it. However, such an argument, while providing some sort of solution to the problem, rests upon two assumptions. First, it assumes that the labouring classes are solely employed upon the land and thus that all labourers are in some sense occupied in upgrading the quality of the soil. Secondly, the view that labour confers equal rights or rewards must assume that the productive activity of each labourer is roughly comparable in terms of its intensity, skill and duration. Again such assumptions might be tenable where the economy was essentially agrarian in character and where agriculture was the sole or predominant form of economic activity. In such circumstances the labouring classes might be seen as employed in improving the land and their labour could be regarded as roughly homogeneous in character. However, when and where diversification of productive activity arises and labour comes to perform a multiplicity of tasks other than that of working upon the land, it becomes impossible to legitimise labour's equal right to 'improved' land in this way. There is no reason, for example, why labour of an industrial or commercial kind should be seen as conferring any rights to land.

If, therefore, the argument is to be advanced that labour confers rights of access to or ownership of the means of production, it becomes necessary to find some common denominator in terms of which all productive activity can be measured. For only in this way is it possible to make defensible statements about the extent of the rights which labour does or should confer. In effect what again becomes necessary is the formulation of a theory of value which allows the productive contributions of a non-homogeneous labour force to be assessed.[43]

Ogilvie too accepted that property rights could derive from a natural right of occupancy or from labour.[44] Nevertheless, as regards land, 'the principal stock of every nation',[45] Ogilvie was adamant that the rights stemming from labour did not have the same 'sacred and indefeasible' quality as the 'original right of equal property in the land founded on [the] general right of occupancy'. Thus for Ogilvie 'a right founded in labour cannot supersede [the] natural right of occupancy'.[46]

The question then arises as to the nature and extent of the property rights actually conferred by labour. Ogilvie regarded these as being grounded in natural law and as covering the additional produce which resulted from land having been made more fertile by labour. 'It is also a maxim of natural law', he wrote, 'that every one, by whose labour any portion of the soil has been rendered more fertile, has a right to the additional produce of that fertility, or to the value of it, and may transmit this right to other men.'[47] In addition labour was also seen as conferring a right to that part of the sale price of land which was paid for the additional value given to the soil by labour.[48]

---

[43] P. M. Kemp-Ashraf, 'An introduction to the selected writings of Thomas Spence', in Anselm Schlösser (ed.), *Essays in Honour of Willie Gallacher* (Berlin, Humboldt University, 1966), p. 276, has argued that Spence 'took over the labour theory of value'. However, leaving aside the somewhat problematic question of from whom Spence took it over, it is simply not permissible to dignify vague statements concerning the productive capacities of labour as a labour theory of value. In this context it is interesting that Kemp-Ashraf does admit that Spence did not use the labour theory of value 'to explore the mechanisms of the economic system'. This writer also argues that Spence was aware of the increasing diversity of economic activity in the late eighteenth century. Thus he points out that Spence 'had before him [in Newcastle] a particularly striking example of the complex alliance of the landed interest with city merchants and large industries already run on capitalist lines'. Yet even if Kemp-Ashraf is correct, this awareness does not seem to have materially affected the form and thrust of Spence's critical analysis. Certainly he showed no awareness of the kinds of theoretical problems that the increasing diversity of economic activity created for his analysis. On this point too see G. Hardach, D. Karras and B. Fine, *A Short History of Socialist Economic Thought*, p. 5: 'Neither Spence nor Hall foresaw the necessary structural changes of developing capitalism: thus for example they both either completely neglected the industrial sector or demanded that it should be dramatically limited and even abolished.'

[44] W. Ogilvie, *Essay*, p. 35. [45] ibid. [46] ibid. pp. 39–40.
[47] ibid. p. 41. [48] ibid. pp. 43–4.

Yet neither in his discussion of the reward which should accrue from land-improving labour nor when explaining what determined the magnitude of the component parts of land's saleable value did Ogilvie have recourse to a theory of value.

With respect to land improvement, Ogilvie might believe that labour conferred an entitlement to the additional produce which resulted but he made no attempt to suggest what might determine the value of this additional produce, and in the absence of this it was impossible for him to establish the extent to which labour was deprived of its just reward. In any case it is evident that Ogilvie is thinking in terms of the physical appropriation of 'additional' agricultural produce rather than in value terms.

As regards the component parts of land's saleable value, the problem was 'solved' by arguing that the size of these could be 'accurately enough appreciate[d]' by 'men skilful in agriculture, and acquainted with the soil of the country'.[49] Thus Ogilvie circumvents a potentially knotty theoretical problem by reducing it to a merely technical or administrative one which can be easily solved by the requisite dose of practical expertise. In doing so Ogilvie is able to retain his natural rights/physical product approach to the analysis of labour's impoverishment but at a theoretical cost which severely circumscribed its application both in terms of the problems and the type of economy to which it could be applied.

In these respects Ogilvie also had much in common with Thomas Paine, who argued that Man had a natural right to land in its uncultivated state. 'It is a position not to be controverted', he wrote, 'that the earth, in its natural uncultivated state, was, and ever would have continued to be, the COMMON PROPERTY OF THE HUMAN RACE!'[50] Thus there could have been 'no such thing as landed property originally ... neither did the Creator of the earth open a land–office, from whence the first title–deeds should issue'.[51] Landed property had arisen, rather, from the improvement of the land and the resultant difficulty of disentangling the natural rights to it in its original state from those conferred by labour. Thus for Paine it was 'impossible to separate

---

[49] ibid. pp. 42–3.
[50] T. Paine, *Agrarian Justice* (1797) in M. Beer, *Pioneers of Land Reform* (London, Bell, 1920) p. 183.
[51] ibid. p. 184.

the improvement made by cultivation, from the earth itself, upon which the improvement is made'.⁵² Also, Paine believed that 'the value of the improvement so far exceeded the value of the natural earth . . . as to absorb it; till, in the end, the common right of all became confounded into the cultivated right of the individual'.⁵³ Thus loss of natural rights had arisen not from some original act of expropriation but rather as a result of neglecting⁵⁴ the increasingly difficult task of distinguishing Man's original rights from those conferred by land-improving labour.

For Paine, therefore, the problem to be solved was that of determining the relative extent of natural and 'artificial' property rights; a question which he saw as an essentially practical one amenable to a simple administrative solution. Indeed, Paine provided the solution himself, without recourse to 'skilful men', estimating the sum of money which would have to be paid to compensate those whose natural rights had been lost. Thus he advocated the creation of a National Fund which would pay £15 to each individual at the age of twenty-one for the loss of his 'natural inheritance' and 'also the sum of Ten Pounds per annum during life, to every person now living of the age of fifty years and to all others as they shall arrive at that age'.⁵⁵

Paine provided no theoretical justification for the magnitude of these sums; they obviously represent a simple rule of thumb solution to what is conceived of as an essentially practical problem. As with Ogilvie natural rights rhetoric proved an adequate medium through which Paine could elaborate his explanation of the causes of impoverishment. Yet it is adequate only because Paine reduces a theoretical problem of valuation to a purely administrative one and also because he confined his attention to the land and, therefore, thought in terms of a fundamentally agrarian economy and society.

---

[52] ibid. p. 183.
[53] ibid. p. 185.
[54] 'The fault . . . is not in the present possessors. No complaint is intended, or ought to be alleged against them . . . The fault is in the system, and it has stolen imperceptibly upon the world', ibid. p. 187.
[55] For a fuller exposition of Paine's practical solution see ibid. pp. 186–7. Spence fulminated against these 'poor, beggarly stipends which he [Paine] would have us to accept of in lieu of our lordly and just pretensions to the soil of our birth', *The Rights of Infants*, p. 3.

As the means of production increasingly assumed the form of factories, mines and machines and as these came to constitute an ever more significant proportion of the nation's productive resources, so analyses of labour impoverishment which concerned themselves almost exclusively with questions of landownership became increasingly irrelevant to the experience of the labouring classes. In these circumstances the ownership of capital threw up questions which could not be ignored and these were questions which did not prove amenable to discussion in natural rights terms. Indeed, as Thomas Hodgskin showed in his *Labour Defended against the Claims of Capital* (1825) when he attacked the classical understanding and defence of capital and capital ownership, these were questions which could only be satisfactorily tackled with the aid of a theory of value. For only with a theory of value could statements easily be made about labour's contribution to capital formation.[56]

Here again, therefore, economic developments occurring in early-nineteenth-century Britain rendered inapplicable or irrelevant the critical economic analyses of the agrarian radicals. The assumptions upon which they were based, the language and concepts used in their elaboration and the tools of analysis which they deployed, precluded them from furnishing or being used to furnish an understanding of the nature of that exploitation and impoverishment which characterised early industrial capitalism.[57] By the 1820s and 1830s the formulation of an economic critique of the status quo required recourse to value theory and the qualitatively different form of economic discourse and analysis which that entailed. Such a theory, however crude, was indispens-

---

[56] Hodgskin with the aid of value theory was able to explain capital in terms of co-existing labour, an explanation which obviously impressed Marx who discussed it at some length in his *Theories of Surplus Value* (3 vols., Moscow, Progress Publishers, 1969–72), Vol. 3, pp. 263–96.

[57] It was not just that the 'social vision' of writers like Paine could 'no longer have an immediate relevance to a population of factory workers', G. Stedman Jones, 'Class struggle and the industrial revolution', *New Left Review*, 90 (March/April 1975), 57. Indeed, the initial popular enthusiasm generated by O'Connor's Chartist Land Company gives some idea of the appeal that a vision of small, independent, agrarian producers still had as late as the 1840s. The agrarian radical explanation of poverty was displaced by that of Owen and the Ricardian socialists not so much because its 'social vision' lacked relevance as because the tools of analysis, the concepts, the rhetoric which they utilised could not be used to elucidate the contemporary economic experience of a large section of the labouring classes.

able to any discussion of labour's rights over the nation's means of production or to any formulation of a theory of labour exploitation applicable to the labouring classes *as a whole*. It was just this articulation and use of a theory of value which distinguished the political economy of the Ricardian socialists.

Just as poverty and exploitation assumed qualitatively different forms in the early nineteenth century, so did the economic insecurity and uncertainty experienced by labour, as the periodic incidence of general economic depressions changed the nature of the unemployment which it suffered. It is difficult to pinpoint exactly when the British economy began to be characterised by that periodical rhythm of slump and boom which was to be such a feature of the nineteenth century. Marx, for example, pointed to the 1820s as the period when 'Modern industry... was... emerging from the age of childhood as is shown by the fact that with the crisis of 1825 it, for the first time, opens the periodic cycle of its modern life.'[58] Engels, in the Preface to the first English translation of *Capital*, wrote similarly of the 'decennial cycle of stagnation, prosperity, overproduction and crisis ever recurrent from 1825 to 1867'.[59] For Marx and Engels, therefore, it was in the mid–1820s that the British economy began to experience those general slumps which could generate mass unemployment or underemployment for significant periods.

Subsequent writers have cast doubt on this view that the modern economic cycle and the prolonged periods of general economic depression associated with it began in 1825. Gayer, Rostow and Schwartz have argued that 'the cycle which occurred from (circa) 1788 to 1793 ... was of much the same nature as the major cycles with peaks in 1825, 1836 and 1845'. However, these writers have also stressed that the 'differences in degree between that 1788–93 cycle and those of the twenties, thirties and forties are impressive',[60] a point echoed by Deane who has written that 'the nineteenth-century English cycles are more pronounced, more continuous and more easily distinguished than

---

[58] K. Marx, *Capital* (3 vols., Moscow, Progress Publishers, 1974), Vol. 1, p. 24.
[59] F. W. Engels, ibid. Vol. 1, p. 17.
[60] A. D. Gayer, W. W. Rostow and A. J. Schwartz, *The Growth and Fluctuation of the British Economy* (2 vols., Oxford, Clarendon Press, 1953), Vol. 2, p. 568.

the eighteenth-century cycles'.[61] Whether, therefore, it was the greater integration of national markets for both capital and goods or the increasingly interdependent nature of economic activity[62] or the 'growing relative importance of capital investment'[63] or, in more general terms, 'the increased industrialization of the British economy' which yielded 'more clearly marked major cycles',[64] most commentators seem agreed that the generality of the economic cycle and the length and intensity of the economic suffering which it caused do seem to have altered between the eighteenth and nineteenth centuries. Economic depression did affect more people, it did last for a longer period of time and it did affect most of those whose livelihood depended upon productive activity.[65] In addition, labour was more vulnerable to economic fluctuations when they did occur; for while, in a pre-industrial economy, a depression in manufacturing industry organised along domestic lines might be compensated for by work on the land or a depression in agriculture might be compensated for by increased labour at the loom, the more specialised nature of wage-labour in the nineteenth century meant that such occupational mobility, even when employment was available, was becoming less feasible. Economic depressions increasingly involved complete unemployment with correspondingly disastrous consequences.

So radical writers in the early nineteenth century were faced with a 'new' economic phenomenon. Those who wished to explain the poverty of labour had to come to terms with something which affected not just this or that section but the labouring classes as a whole. In such circumstances, it might be

[61] P. Deane, *The First Industrial Revolution*, p. 244.
[62] T. S. Ashton, for example, contrasted the nineteenth- with the eighteenth-century economic cycle when 'The fluctuation of the diverse parts of the economy did not always coincide', *Economic Fluctuations in England 1700–1800* (Oxford, Clarendon Press, 1958), p. 138.
[63] A. D. Gayer, W. W. Rostow and A. J. Schwartz, *Growth and Fluctuation*, Vol. 2, p. 571.
[64] ibid. p. 569.
[65] 'Industrialisation made for greater variations in the level of unemployment attributable to changes in business demand conditions', P. K. O'Brien and S. L. Engerman, 'Changes in income and its distribution during the industrial revolution', in R. Floud and D. N. McCloskey, *Economic History of Britain*, Vol. 1, p. 171; see also A. D. Gayer, W. W. Rostow and A. J. Schwartz, *Growth and Fluctuation*, Vol. 2, p. 571.

The need for a working-class political economy

argued, working-class writers or those who wrote in defence of working-class interests would necessarily be driven to abandon sectional or traditional explanations of impoverishment. Thus the impoverishment which resulted from general economic depression could no longer be explained in terms of the difficulties of a particular trade or the nefarious activities of 'bad' employers. More importantly general falls in the level of economic activity in the nineteenth century proved less amenable to explanations couched in terms of factors exogenous to the functioning of the economic system such as harvest failures, wars, plagues etc.[66] The influence of the autonomous causes of economic fluctuations did not of course cease in 1800[67] but it would be fair to say that during the course of the nineteenth century fluctuations increasingly resulted from factors endogenous to the economic system.[68] General economic depressions thus assumed a form which required an economic rather than a military or meteorological explanation. Their incidence and course came to be dictated by an economic logic and, where these 'downswings were prolonged and painful',[69] it became an economic logic which demanded the attention of radical writers.

In this context one other contrast between eighteenth- and nineteenth-century depressions should be noticed. In the eighteenth century, because they frequently originated with harvest failures, depressions were associated with dearth. They were characterised by the absence of the physical means of subsistence and the starvation and disease which resulted from this. As such they could be easily explained in physical terms. In contrast, the aspect of nineteenth-century depressions which impressed contemporaries was not the poverty in the midst of scarcity which they manifested but the fact that poverty intensified in the midst of abundance. It was not the shortage of physical produce which caused hardship in nineteenth-century depressions

---

[66] 'there were few eighteenth century cycles that were not conditioned more by political than by economic events', P. Deane, *The First Industrial Revolution*, p. 248.
[67] See P. Mathias, *The First Industrial Nation: An Economic History of Britain 1700–1914* (London, Methuen, 1969), p. 227.
[68] 'From 1815 to 1914... war became an infrequent and minor factor in setting up these pulsations, so that the rhythms inherent in the economic processes themselves were dominant', ibid. p. 228.
[69] P. Deane, *The First Industrial Revolution*, p. 254.

but rather the fact that markets were glutted with products which could not secure adequate remuneration for their producers. This situation could not be explained in simple physical terms but only in terms of concepts such as demand and supply, market price, value, wages and profits; that is, it required an explanation which necessarily required writers to avail themselves of the conceptual and analytical apparatus provided by political economy. Here again it may be argued that economic developments in the early nineteenth century posed problems which could not be solved by recourse to traditional modes of analysis and here again it was the Ricardian socialists, utilising the tools and constructs of political economy, who took up the challenge.

In explaining why those who wrote from a working-class standpoint had, increasingly, to come to terms with political economy in the 1820s and 1830s, one other important factor must be mentioned, namely the didactic zeal of the populasiers of classical orthodoxy. As early as 1808 James Mill had stressed the need to propagate the true principles of political economy and had lamented 'The great difficulty with which the salutary doctrines of political economy are propagated in this country'.[70] In the decades which followed such sentiments were constantly reiterated. Thus in 1816, for example, Mrs Marcet regretted that while political economy was 'immediately concerned with the happiness and improvement of mankind', it had 'not yet become a popular science';[71] while in the same year a writer introducing a proposed syllabus for a course of political economy lectures to be given at Cambridge complained in similar fashion that 'the many important truths which Dr Smith has established and their application to subsequent events are alike neglected and unknown due to a failure to realise the utility of their widespread dissemination'.[72] Initially, though, this diffusion of the principles of political economy was seen as having utility only within certain circumscribed social limits. Mrs B, for example, when

---

[70] J. Mill, 'Thomas Smith on money and exchange', *Edinburgh Review*, 13 (October 1808), 35.

[71] J. Marcet, *Conversations on Political Economy* (London, Longman, 1816), p. vi. This work had gone through five editions by 1824.

[72] G. Pryme, *A Syllabus of a Course of Lectures on the Principles of Political Economy* (Cambridge, 1816), p. 1.

asked by the deferential Caroline in Mrs Marcet's *Conversations* whether she would teach political economy to the working classes, gave a most emphatic 'No!'[73] and certainly the didactic treatises which proliferated in the immediate post-Napoleonic War period were aimed at an educated, middle-class readership.[74] James Mill's *Elements of Political Economy* (1821), Jean-Baptiste Say's *Catechism of Political Economy* (translated from the French by John Richter in 1816), Mrs Marcet's *Conversations on Political Economy*, and *A New and Easy Introduction to the Principles of Political Economy* (1823) by an anonymous author, were all works of that kind.

In this period too the popularisation of economic thinking among the middle classes by means of influential magazines and reviews became increasingly important. What such publications[75] did on a quarterly or a monthly basis, papers such as the *Morning Chronicle* and the *Globe/Globe and Traveller* (1822–5) did more regularly. The former, under the editorship of James Black, carried articles by James Mill, Ricardo, J. R. McCulloch and Nassau Senior, while the latter was under the control of Robert Torrens.[76] Furthermore, the sixth edition of the *Encyclopaedia Britannica* was also used to popularise the principles of the discipline with J. R. McCulloch writing a section on political economy for the 1824 Supplement.[77]

---

[73] J. Marcet, *Conversations*, p. 158.

[74] Some commentators have failed to emphasise this point; see, for example, J. H. Marsh, 'Economics education in schools in the nineteenth century: social control', *Journal of the Economics Association*, 3 (1977), 116–18.

[75] Periodicals such as *Blackwood's Magazine* began to devote significant space to a discussion of economic questions in the 1820s; see F. W. Fetter, 'Economic articles in *Blackwood's Magazine*', *Scottish Journal of Political Economy*, 7 (1960), 85–107 and 213–31. By the early 1820s the *Quarterly Review* was publishing as many articles on matters of political economy as the *Edinburgh Review*, though, like *Blackwood's*, from a very different standpoint; see F. W. Fetter, 'Economic articles in the *Quarterly Review*', *Journal of Political Economy*, 66 (1958), 47–64 and 154–70. In terms of the theoretical quality of its economic articles, however, the *Edinburgh Review* and the *Westminster Review* must be considered the most important periodicals of this period; see F. W. Fetter, 'Economic articles in the *Edinburgh Review* 1802–47', *Journal of Political Economy* 61 (1953), 232–59, and 'Economic articles in the *Westminster Review* 1824–51', *Journal of Political Economy*, 70 (1962), 576–96.

[76] J. W. Flood, 'The Benthamites and their use of the press', unpublished PhD thesis (University of London, 1974), pp. 29–31.

[77] J. R. McCulloch, 'Political Economy', Supplement to the *Encyclopaedia Britannica*, 6th edn (Edinburgh, 1824).

Universities too gave further scope for a popularisation of political economy aimed at the politically and socially influential.[78] As Nassau Senior stated in an article in the *Westminster Review*, the importance of establishing (1825) the Chair of Political Economy which he occupied at Oxford University was that it provided a marvellous opportunity 'of innoculating the minds of a class, whence, in after-life, a great portion of the governing body in this country is drawn, with the principles of so beneficial a science'.[79]

The late 1820s were, however, characterised by a changed and changing attitude to popularisation;[80] specifically, by a broader conception of the educative and social value of popularising sound principles of political economy amongst all strata of society. Fears of ignorance or false economic doctrine engendering discontent and disturbance among the lower orders had been expressed prior to 1824. S. Gray, for example, in a work entitled *All Classes Productive of National Wealth* had, as early as 1817,[81] strongly attacked Adam Smith's distinction between productive and unproductive labour as 'calculated to inflame', arguing that

---

[78] As did institutions such as the East India College at Haileybury, where T. R. Malthus was made professor of Political Economy in 1805, and the Ricardo Institution; see Preface to J. R. McCulloch's *Syllabus of a Course of Lectures on Political Economy* (London, 1825).

[79] N. W. Senior, 'Political Economy', *Westminster Review*, 8 (July 1827), 189; for Cambridge University see G. Pryme, *An Introductory Lecture and Syllabus to a course delivered in the University of Cambridge on the Principles of Political Economy* (Cambridge, 1823).

[80] Francis Place was an exception. Place saw early the importance of familiarising the working classes with what he believed to be the essential principles of sound political economy. He wrote articles on wages for John Wade's *Gorgon* (1818–19) and 'supplied the editor with much of the matter which he worked up in his own way into essays', G. Wallas, *The Life of Francis Place*, 2nd edn (London, Allen and Unwin, 1918) p. 205. In addition, Place published articles, with a neo-Malthusian slant, on the population question in the *Black Dwarf*, 12 July 1823, 3 August 1823 and 1 October 1823, as did the young J. S. Mill, 27 November 1823, 10 December 1823, 7 January 1824 and 25 February 1824; see also Place's avowed intent to use Mechanics Institutes to propagate the tenets of political economy, I. Prothero, *Artisans and Politics*, p. 201.

[81] S. Gray (alias G. Purves), *All Classes Productive of National Wealth; or, the Theories of M. Quesnai, Dr Adam Smith and Mr Gray Concerning Various Classes of Men, as to the Production of Wealth to the Community Analysed and Examined* (London, 1817), pp. 227–8; see also S. Gray, 'Remarks on the production of wealth', *Pamphleteer*, 17 (1820), 414n. It is interesting that Gray pointed to Smith rather than Ricardo as the originator of a theory of value amenable to popular perversion.

The need for a working-class political economy 59

it encouraged insubordination among the lower classes 'by representing their labour as the sole source of wealth', thus setting 'class against class as if natural enemies to one another'. The expressed need for a systematic attack upon wrong economic thinking among the labouring classes becomes more apparent at a later date. Henry Brougham, perhaps, best reflected this changed attitude when he stated in his *Practical Observations on the Education of the People* (1825) that tracts on political economy 'ought to be more extensively circulated for the good of the working classes, as well as their superiors ... I can hardly imagine, for example, a greater service being rendered to men, than expounding to them the true principles and mutual relations of population and wages',[82] while in the same year he wrote to congratulate his friend John Marshall on his *Economy of Social Life* (1825), a work avowedly written 'to explain in a clear and familiar manner, so as to be intelligible to the working classes the most important doctrines of political economy'.[83] J. R. McCulloch too called for the instruction of the working classes in those economic principles 'that most determine their condition in life',[84] while with similar propagandist intent Nassau Senior stressed the need for political economy to be 'diffused throughout the community; it must attract the notice of the mechanic and the artisan and penetrate into the cottage of the labourer'.[85] In this respect Harriet Martineau's *The Rioters* (1827), a work of fiction which aimed to establish the economic futility, economic irrationality and immorality of machine-breaking, pointed the shape of things to come.

---

[82] H. Brougham, *Practical Observations on the Education of the People, addressed to the Working Classes and their Employers* (London, 1825), Preface.

[83] J. F. C. Harrison, *Learning and Living 1790–1960: A Study in the History of the English Adult Education Movement* (London, Routledge and Kegan Paul, 1961), p. 80.

[84] J. R. McCulloch, 'The rise, progress, present state and prospects of British cotton manufacturers', *Edinburgh Review*, 46 (June 1827), 38–9.

[85] N. W. Senior, 'Political Economy', 183; see also F. Jeffrey, 'Political economy', *Edinburgh Review*, 43 (November 1825), 14, 23, who saw the dissemination of 'correct' economic ideas as an important means of sublimating the economic hostility of the labouring classes as expressed through combinations; also in this context see T. Chalmers, 'On Mechanics Schools and on political economy as a branch of popular education', *Glasgow Mechanics Magazine*, 5 (3 June 1826), 221, who saw political economy as a means of 'tranquillizing the popular mind and removing from it all those delusions which are the main cause of popular disaffection'.

In Scotland in the mid-1820s such institutions as the Schools of Art in Edinburgh and Haddington and the Glasgow Mechanics Institute[86] were used as a means of imbuing the labouring classes with sound political economy, while in England the London and other Mechanics Institutes fulfilled a similar function. In this context it is interesting to note that Thomas Hodgskin's offer, in 1825, to lecture at the newly founded London Mechanics Institute was declined in consequence of a warning given by Francis Place to George Birkbeck about the heterodox nature of Hodgskin's economic opinions, while William Ellis was invited to lecture in Hodgskin's stead.[87] As for the other English Mechanics Institutes, Brougham wrote a course of lectures on political economy in the summer of 1825 which was subsequently read in many of them,[88] while the Leeds Mechanics Institute established a course of lectures on political economy designed to point up the fallacies in 'artificial, socialist and communal systems'.[89]

[86] A. Tyrell, 'Political economy, Whiggism and the education of working-class adults in Scotland 1817–40', *Scottish Historical Review*, 48 (1969), 155–6.

[87] T. Kelly, *George Birkbeck: Pioneer of Adult Education* (Liverpool University Press, 1957), pp. 98–9; see also G. Wallas, *Life of Francis Place*, p. 268n. Eventually in 1826 Hodgskin was allowed to lecture but he gave only four in all. The opposition of Place to Hodgskin followed a bitter struggle for control over the management and finance of the London Mechanics Institute; see T. Kelly, *A History of Adult Education in Great Britain* (Liverpool University Press, 1970), p. 121, and T. Kelly, *George Birkbeck*, pp. 87–9. H. Perkin has written that the Benthamites in taking over the London Mechanics Institute 'put a stop to Hodgskin's lectures on "Labour defended against the claims of Capital", one of the classics of the working-class ideal', *The Origins of Modern English Society 1780–1880* (London, Routledge and Kegan Paul, 1981), p. 305. In fact the lectures stopped were those subsequently embodied in Hodgskin's *Popular Political Economy*. It was around 1825 too that Hodgskin was dismissed by the Society for the Diffusion of Useful Knowledge as an editor of works on political economy; a dismissal which led to a somewhat acrimonious correspondence over payment for past services rendered; see Letters of Thomas Hodgskin (1827–8) in the *College Correspondence Collection of University College London*.

[88] J. F. C. Harrison, *Learning and Living*, p. 80.

[89] For a short summary of the role played by Mechanics Institutes in popularising political economy see ibid. pp. 80–3. R. D. Altick has pointed out that while on occasion those who controlled the Mechanics Institutes might ban the discussion of anything as controversial as political economy, generally, 'the proponents of the institutes wished to encourage discussion of political and economic matters, so that under proper guidance honest workingmen would be persuaded of the truth of middle-class doctrines', *The English Common Reader, a social history of the mass reading public 1800–1900* (Chicago and London, University of Chicago Press, 1957), p. 194. In addition, as one writer has phrased it, the Mechanics Institute Movement may also be seen as reflecting 'the desires among middle-class ideologues to improve the

In the mid-1820s even the *Trades Newspaper*, set up in July 1825 by metropolitan and provincial trades delegates as a medium for the defence of trades union interests,[90] was temporarily pressed into service as a means of popularising the principles of classical orthodoxy.[91] Thus Francis Place[92] in particular used it as a means of disseminating his own brand of classical economics on matters such as trade combinations, the Corn Laws, minimum and bread-based wages, currency questions and machine-breaking.[93]

This was the kind of ideological onslaught which could not be ignored. 'Ad hominem' abuse of classical writers such as that resorted to by Cobbett was one possible response but while its entertainment value might be high, it was no substitute for reasoned and dispassionate refutation. In the post-Napoleonic War period those who wished to answer such questions as why the idle few became rich at the expense of the productive many; 'why in spite of continually protracted labour, are we [the labouring classes] still unable to procure the necessaries of life?';[94] why the labouring class 'of all classes of society [have] . . . always been involved in poverty and distress?'[95] and who wished to answer them by way of an attack upon existing economic arrangements, were confronted by a new genus of apologetics. For classical political economy claimed to have provided answers to these questions, answers derived from the principles of a new science, answers which rendered redundant both the 'old corruption' and 'natural rights' explanations of poverty advanced by writers such as Spence, Ogilvie, Paine and Cobbett and also

understanding of the connections between the advances of technology and the doctrines of political economy', M. Berg, *The Machinery Question and the Making of Political Economy 1815–48*, (Cambridge University Press, 1981), p. 146.

[90] For fuller details of the *Trades Newspaper* see the bibliography and I. Prothero, *Artisans and Politics* pp. 183–91.

[91] Particularly during the period October 1825 to June 1827.

[92] In addition to using the *Trades Newspaper* as a medium for his economic ideas Place also supported the establishment of a rival paper, *The Journeyman and Artisan's London and Provincial Chronicle*; see A. E. Musson and R. G. Kirby, '*The Voice of the People*', *John Doherty, 1798–1854, trade unionist, radical and factory reformer* (Manchester University Press, 1975), p. 39.

[93] On Place's 'indefatigable didacticism' see also W. E. S. Thomas, 'Francis Place and working-class history', *Historical Journal*, 5 (1962), 61–70.

[94] Roger Radical (pseud.), *Why are we poor? An Address to the Industrious and Labouring Classes of the Community* (London, 1820), p. 3.

[95] T. Hodgskin, *Labour Defended* p. 101.

the 'gorgeous bubbles' of Godwinian utopianism.[96] Thus for the popularisers of classical orthodoxy the working classes were impoverished, their material condition depressed, because the rate at which the population (and hence the labour supply) grew had a tendency to outstrip the rate of capital accumulation and hence the rate of growth of the wages fund which furnished the demand for labour's services.[97] Political corruption, sinecures and placemen, the National Debt and 'money juggles' might all, in their different ways, exacerbate the problem of poverty but they were not, in the final analysis, the fundamental cause. That lay in those constraints, legislative and otherwise, which obstructed the accumulation of capital[98] and in the absence of the requisite moral restraint[99] necessary to strengthen the position of the working classes in the labour market. In effect these writers provided an explanation of poverty which made the labouring classes culpable for their own misfortune,[100] and while opinions of the classical economists were more sophisticated and more carefully qualified than those of their popularisers it was

---

[96] 'Godwin's dreams were but gorgeous bubbles, destined to speedily collapse when brought into contact with the facts of the actual world', L. Stephen, *A History of English Thought in the Eighteenth Century*, 3rd edn (2 vols., London, Smith, Elder and Co., 1902), Vol. 2, p. 279. On this point, Francis Place wrote of Godwin that he 'forfeited his claims to respect by ignoring Political Economy', *Illustrations and Proofs of the Principle of Population* (London, 1822), p. 270. Had working-class writers ignored political economy they would have left themselves open to a similar charge; also, as M. Vaughan and M. S. Archer have pointed out, 'Without a new approach to economic theory, working-class demands for universal franchise and attempts at educational substitution could be rejected as impractical since they conflicted with the recognised requirements of the market economy', *Social Conflict and Educational Change in England and France 1789–1848* (Cambridge University Press, 1971), p. 85.

[97] To take but one of many similar examples, '*the rate of wages depends on the extent of the fund for the maintenance of labourers, compared with the number of labourers to be maintained*', N. W. Senior, *Three Lectures on the Rate of Wages*, 2nd edn (London, Murray, 1831), p. iv (Senior's italics).

[98] 'The principal means by which the fund for the maintenance of the labourer can be increased, is by increasing the productiveness of labour. And this may be done – first, by allowing every man to exert himself in the way which ... he finds most beneficial; by freeing industry from the mass of restrictions, prohibitions and protecting duties', ibid. p. iv.

[99] 'the condition of the labouring classes [can be] improved, only by either increasing the fund for their maintenance, or diminishing the number to be maintained ... The only effectual and permanent means of preventing the undue increase of the

The need for a working-class political economy 63

undoubtedly the ideas of their popularisers which had the greatest popular impact.[101] As one writer has put it, in the popularisation of ideas 'Gresham's Law operates in its most remorseless fashion: vulgar vulgarisation drives out subtle, just as strong ideology drives out weak.'[102]

In addition, classical political economy or at least a significant number of classical writers may be said to have appropriated the essence of eighteenth-century agrarian radicalism. Thus for many classical writers the existence of rent represented an unjustifiable exaction by the unproductive, though an exaction which was seen as squeezing profits first and hitting wages only indirectly. So political economists such as Ricardo, Senior, McCulloch and James Mill took over in effect the attack upon the economic and social position of the landowner and gave it a pseudo-scientific precision and rigour which the Spenceans might have envied, had they understood it.

To counter such 'strong ideology' in the form it assumed, it became necessary for radical writers to employ a mode of critical economic discourse which allowed them to give battle on roughly similar conceptual and terminological ground to that which the classical popularisers had come to occupy. What was required was the articulation and defence of working-class interests in the language of political economy.[103] Only thus could

---

number to be maintained, is to raise the moral and intellectual character of the labouring population', ibid. pp. iv–v.

[100] Or their suffering was seen as the inevitable consequence of a parsimonious Nature: 'want and labour spring from the niggardliness of nature, and not from the inequality which is consequent on the institution of property', *Examiner*, 26 December 1830, quoted from M. Blaug, *Ricardian Economics, a historical study* (New Haven, Yale University Press, 1958), pp. 144–5.

[101] Thus as J. M. Keynes remarked, it was 'the education stories of Miss Martineau and Mrs Marcet that fixed laissez-faire in the popular mind as the practical conclusion of orthodox political economy', 'The end of laissez-faire' in *Essays in Persuasion*, ed. D. E. Moggridge, *The Collected Works of John Maynard Keynes* (London, Macmillan, 1972), Vol. 9, pp. 279–80.

[102] P. A. Samuelson, 'Economists and the history of ideas', *American Economic Review*, 52 (1962), 5.

[103] Thus the Tory anti-capitalist Piercy Ravenstone (pseud.) wrote in 1824, 'that it was in the armory of her [political economy's] terms that tyranny and oppression found their deadliest weapons', *Thoughts on the Funding System and its Effects* (London, 1824), p. 6.

the theoretical basis for the politico-economic quietism[104] of popularised classical orthodoxy be undermined. It was on just this ground that the Ricardian socialists were prepared to wage war and it was in just this way that their contribution to a fundamental critique of existing economic and social arrangements was to prove vital.[105] In order to clarify the importance and nature of this contribution, however, it is necessary first to consider briefly the work of two pre-Ricardian socialist writers, Charles Hall and Robert Owen.

[104] 'Popularisations displayed the natural laws by which the economy and society operated, explained all social problems in terms of the violation of these laws and encouraged the view that submission to the laws led to infinite progress', M. Berg, *The Machinery Question*, p. 161. It is, however, an exaggeration to suggest, as Berg does, that 'The supreme concern of this popular political economy was the problems of production and...the absolute benefit of machinery', ibid. The primary concern of classical populariser was rather to show that the lot of the labourer was the consequence of natural economic laws and incontinent breeding rather than the result of capitalist exploitation.

[105] 'By thus fighting them [the political economists] upon their own ground, and with their own weapons, we shall avoid that senseless clatter respecting "visionaries" and "theorists", with which they are ready to assail all who dare move one step from that beaten track which, "by authority", has been pronounced to be the only right one', J. F. Bray, *Labour's Wrongs and Labour's Remedy or, The Age of Might and the Age of Right* (London School of Economics and Political Science, 1931), p. 41.

3

Charles Hall and Robert Owen: anti-capitalist and socialist political economy before the Ricardian socialists

If the sparse secondary literature on Hall indicates anything, it is that he is a writer whom it has proved singularly difficult to categorise. He has been variously described as an 'agrarian radical', a precursor of the so-called Ricardian socialists, a writer who anticipated the main lines of Ricardian socialist analysis twelve years before the publication of Ricardo's *Principles*, a 'Pre-Marxian', a writer who occupies an intermediary position in the history of socialism 'between natural law or ethical socialism and proletarian or revolutionary socialism' and someone who provided the 'first interpretation of the voice of rising Labour'.[1] If a consensus can be said to have emerged, however, it is that Hall occupies an intermediate position somewhere between agrarian radicals such as Spence, Ogilvie and Paine and the Ricardian socialists Hodgskin, Thompson, Bray and Gray. Certainly in terms of the structure of their works on the history of anti-capitalist and socialist economic thinking, that is where Hall is physically located by Beer, Cole and Alexander Gray.[2]

Nevertheless, few writers have been prepared to discuss the specific nature of this intermediate position though it would

---

[1] G. Claeys, 'Four letters between Thomas Spence and Charles Hall', *Notes and Queries*, NS, 28, 4 (August 1981), 317; G.D.H. Cole, *A History of Socialist Thought* (5 vols., London, Macmillan), Vol. 1, *Socialist Thought: The Forerunners, 1789–1850* (1977), p. 36; M. Blaug, *Ricardian Economics, a historical study*, pp. 148–9; A. Chabert, 'Aux sources du socialisme anglais: un pré-marxiste méconnu: Charles Hall', *Revue d'Histoire Économique et Sociale*, 29 (1951), 369–83; M. Beer, *A History of British Socialism*, p. 127; A. Gray, *The Socialist Tradition, Moses to Lenin* (London, Longman, 1967), p. 262.

[2] Though A. Gray lumped Hall together with Thompson, Hodgskin, Bray and Gray as the 'English pre-Marxians', *The Socialist Tradition*, p. 262.

appear to rest upon the view that his critique of early industrial capitalism had some Ricardian socialist characteristics, while his positive suggestions as to how the impoverished state of the labouring classes might be alleviated were similar in important respects to those advanced by Ogilvie, Paine and Spence.

Like Spence and Ogilvie, Hall traced the poverty of the labouring classes back to a primal act of dispossession. Originally 'no person' had 'an exclusive right to any portion of land, except perhaps to such a quantity of it as was sufficient to furnish himself and family with the necessaries of life'.[3] In the course of time, however, 'some daring spirits arose, and seized certain parts to themselves, and their conduct was imitated by others. This, probably, must be the original foundation of exclusive property in land; for what other can possibly be supposed?'[4] For Hall it was this and other[5] 'arbitrary and forcible assumptions of land' which were 'the foundation of the inequality of all other species of property, in all or most civilized countries'.[6] It was this appropriation of land which laid the foundations for the birth of modern civilisation for it provided 'the great proprietors' of land with the power to direct the labour of the dispossessed. Thus while *de jure* 'no man is compelled to work at any particular trade' *de facto* there was 'an absolute necessity, under the penalty, the heaviest of all penalties, namely the deprivation of all things that are necessary to him and his family's existence',[7] for the landless labourer to submit to the direction of others.

Thus Hall sees the causes of labour's vulnerability to exploitation in very much the same way as Ogilvie and Spence. Yet Hall does two things which Ogilvie and Spence do not. First, Hall generalises the argument so that the victims of oppression and exploitation are not simply those who labour on the land but the labouring classes as a whole. Secondly, Hall makes the point that labour is vulnerable to exploitation not only because it is denied its right to property in the land but also because of the exclusive possession by 'the rich' of cattle, corn, raw materials, tools, machinery and goods already manufactured;[8] i.e. it was

---

[3] C. Hall, *The Effects of Civilisation* (London, 1805), p. 58.
[4] ibid. p. 57.
[5] For example, the German invasions of the Roman Empire, ibid. p. 132.
[6] ibid. p. 133. [7] ibid. p. 44. [8] ibid. pp. 43–4.

the exclusive possession of fixed and circulating capital in all its many and varied forms, in addition to the exclusive possession of land, which forced the labourer 'to do the things . . . imposed upon him to do'.[9]

Labour, because it did not own these things, was forced to sell its services in order to acquire the necessaries of life. A situation was created where 'Every rich man [was] to be considered as the buyer, [and] *every poor man* as the seller, of labour' and in such circumstances it was obviously in 'the interest of the rich man to get as much of the work of the poor man and to give as little for it as he can; in other words, to get as much of the labour, and to give the labourer as little of the produce of that the labour as he can help; the less of the product of his labour, the labourer himself is suffered to consume, the more is left to his employer to take to himself'.[10] Thus Hall's explanation of exploitation embraces all labour ('every poor man') whether that labour is employed in manufacture or agriculture. Indeed, Hall goes on to make the point that even competition among manufacturers will not limit their capacity to appropriate the produce of the labour they employ. Competition did not increase 'the small proportion . . . of the produce of the labour of the poor, that is allowed them'.[11] In addition, labour in manufacturing industry was too weak even by strike action to raise the proportion of the produce they received because their poverty meant they could not hold out in a prolonged dispute. In any case 'this, the only method they have of redressing their grievances, is frequently crushed by the military'.[12]

For Hall, master manufacturers as well as landowners played an exploitative role. In explaining the existence of widespread poverty, therefore, Hall did not confine his attention to the lot of the agricultural labourer but developed a critical analysis which recognised the increasing significance of manufacture and commerce. Hall sought to explain the impoverishment of the labouring classes as a whole and he was aware that labour could no longer be seen as synonymous with agricultural labour.

[9] ibid. p. 44 [10] ibid. p. 111 (my emphasis).
[11] ibid. p. 112 [12] ibid.

Hall condemned the growth of manufactures and trade. He saw them as an unnatural economic excrescence and indicative of a fundamental misallocation of productive resources. In addition manufactures were seen as 'all injurious to the health of the body, and the improvement of the mind'.[13] They involved 'unnatural postures' which resulted in physical deformity and they confined labour to 'unwholesome atmospheres'.[14] Yet while Hall did not ignore the realities of nascent industrial capitalism, he attempted to come to terms with their exploitative consequences with very much the same physical tools of analysis as those wielded by Ogilvie and Spence. Thus looking again at Hall's discussion of the nature of exploitation, he wrote that it was in the rich man's interest 'to get as much of the labour and to give the labourers as little of *the product of their labour* as he can . . . ; the less of *the product of his labour* the labourer is suffered to *consume*, the more is left to the employer to take to himself'.[15] Approached in this way exploitation is quite obviously conceived of as the appropriation of a physical surplus, i.e. the difference between the physical inputs or consumption of the workforce and the physical output which results from the productive activity of labour.

This tendency to think in physical terms manifests itself in another aspect of Hall's reasoning, namely in his tendency to see the impoverishment of labour as resulting from the physical shortage or absence of the basic necessities of life. Such a shortage occurred, for Hall, because those who owned the means of producing directed the productive energies of the labouring classes to the satisfaction of their own demand for manufactured luxuries:

And as the quantity of the necessaries of life, that are or can be consumed by the rich, are limited, and in the purchasing of which a small part of their wealth can be expended, the surplus they are naturally inclined to lay out in procuring the conveniences, the elegancies, and luxuries of life; these are the produce of the more refined manufactures of different kinds; [and] . . . of course a greater

---

[13] ibid. p. 19; to lend force to his arguments, Hall quoted extensively from those passages in the *Wealth of Nations* where Smith discussed the kinds of mental mutilation which could result from the excessive division of labour.
[14] ibid. pp. 19–20.
[15] ibid. p. 111 (my emphasis).

proportion of the labouring hands are forced to apply their industry in the various fine manufactures, in which they only can get employ.[16]

Thus there resulted a diversion of labour away from the production of necessities towards the production of 'refined manufactures' with consequent scarcity and hardship for the bulk of the population. The growth of manufactures, therefore, far from being a manifestation of increased national wealth, was indicative rather of increasing exploitation and poverty. To the extent that labour was exploited and wealth became concentrated in the hands of a few, manufactures flourished; to the extent that the distribution of wealth became more equitable, productive resources would be switched from the refined manufactures towards agriculture which was the primary source of life's necessities. It was particularly in the act of consumption, therefore, that the necessary economic antagonism of the rich and the poor was most obviously expressed. As Hall wrote, 'what the possessor has, the non-possessor is deprived of. The situation of the rich and poor like the algebraic terms plus and minus, are in direct opposition to, and destructive of each other.'[17] Thus it was that Hall's tendency to think in physical rather than value terms almost inevitably led him to a zero-sum-game conception of economic life.

Hall did attempt to apply his essentially physical analysis to elucidate the nature of exploitation as it occurred in manufacture and commerce but his attempt is more notable for highlighting the difficulties involved in such a procedure than for its success in solving them. Thus Hall argued that 'traders or manufacturers' are able to 'share *a part of the product* of the labour of the poor' by way of 'their capital'.[18] These 'capitals of tradesmen consist of stores of such articles as they get up by means of the labour of artificers that work under them [and] . . . From those stores of goods they can supply the people that are in want of them'.[19] Now a significant market for such goods was provided by the 'owners of land' who as they are in 'possession of the necessaries of life' exchange these for the products in the hands of the

[16] ibid. pp. 44–5.
[17] ibid. p. 67.
[18] ibid. p. 70 (my emphasis).
[19] ibid. p. 71.

manufacturer–trader. So, Hall argued, these manufacturers became *de facto* owners of land. They

> may be considered as possessed of a certain share of the land, ... They have a claim on it resembling that of a mortgagee ... this capitalist, this manufacturer, is in reality a possessor of land, and, like him, has in his power and disposal a certain quantity of the necessaries of life ... The manufacturer therefore forces his workmen to work for him, and to give him a share of what the work produces, in the same manner as we have shown the *other proprietors of land* or proprietors of the necessaries of life do ... It is easily seen that the acquisition of fortunes by tradesmen is in reality nothing but a participation of landed property.[20]

Thus what Hall does when discussing the exploitation of labour by the manufacturer is to interpret the latter's economic power as deriving from his *de facto* control over land. In effect, disparate factor inputs are reduced to material subsistence (food) and the analysis proceeds in physical terms, with the manufacturer appropriating a share of the labourer's product 'in the same manner as we have shown the proprietors of land ... do'. However, while inputs can be reduced to food, manufacturing output cannot and so the idea of exploitation cannot be given any theoretical rigour or precision. Hall himself admitted as much in an ingenuously revealing passage in the *Effects of Civilization* where he wrote that

> whether or not in the very complicated state of civilization, occasioned by the intervention of money, and the great division of labour in the manufactures, we could account for and render visible the manner in which it happens, that the poor workman receives and enjoys so little

---

[20] ibid. pp. 71–3 (my emphasis); for Hall, the coercive economic power wielded by the manufacturer resided in his 'de facto' landlord status, so it is necessary to treat with care statements to the effect that Charles Hall's achievement was that of 'transmuting anti-landlordism into anti-capitalism ... thus redrawing the lines of class antagonism', J. R. Dinwiddy, 'Charles Hall, early English socialist', *International Review of Social History*, 21 (1976), 272. A similar point is made by Hall in his correspondence with Thomas Spence: 'I have suspected that those persons who receive the rents are only in part the owners of it. The tradesmen who furnish those landlords with drapery, grocery, cakes and seed etc., etc., have all a claim to a certain property (somewhat in the nature of a mortgage) on the land. *The land here is the only real property, as it is called in law, and all personal property is only property as it gives a right to the share of the land*', G. Claeys, 'Four letters between Thomas Spence and Charles Hall', p. 318 (my emphasis).

of the fruits of the labour of his own hands; nothing can be more clearly demonstrated than that he does.[21]

Here Hall overtly admits the formidable theoretical problems created by the increasingly complex character of economic activity when it comes to isolating the nature and extent of exploitation. So Hall, unable to give his arguments theoretical precision, is forced to fall back upon the assertion that the important point to grasp is that exploitation does obviously occur and must inevitably occur as long as the disparity of economic power possessed by manufacturers and labourers obstructed any possibility of a 'voluntary compact equally advantageous on both sides'.[22]

To establish as lucidly and perceptively as Hall did the economic and social conditions which rendered the industrial labourer vulnerable to exploitation was a considerable achievement but, as Hall himself seemed to be aware, this was not the same as 'account[ing] for and render[ing] visible the manner in which it happen[ed]'; to do that 'in the very complicated state of civilization, occasioned by the intervention of money, and the great division of labour in manufactures' it was necessary to formulate and utilise a theory of value.

Yet Hall, in one short paragraph, did provide an explanation of what determined – or rather, what should determine – the exchange value of commodities. Like Spence, Ogilvie and Paine he accepted that labour gave entitlement to property and he wrote that

Whatever things a man makes with his own hands, out of such things as his proportionate share of land yields, must be allowed to be his own; and these may be accumulated, if they are not consumed by the maker of them; or they may be exchanged for other things, made by and belonging to other people, of an equal value; *to be strictly estimated by the quantity of labour employed in making the things exchanged*.[23]

---

[21] C. Hall, *Effects*, p. 127.
[22] ibid. pp. 72–3; Hall also arrives at what he considers to be the all-important conclusion that the labouring classes are exploited by another, non-theoretical, route. This route was essentially statistical. Thus having arrived at a figure of £312 million for the value of the national product and £40 million for the total value of the wages paid to labour, Hall came to the conclusion that the labourer enjoyed only one part in eight of what he produced.
[23] ibid. p. 68 (my emphasis).

However, while this presages in important respects the political economy of the Ricardian socialists, Hall does not use his explanation of what should govern the exchange value of commodities as the basis for his theory of labour exploitation. Nor does he need to do so as long as he thinks and reasons in terms of physical inputs and outputs. Hall's foray into the field of value theory is not an integral part of his anti-capitalism; it does not furnish him with an analytical tool to be used for critical purposes. Rather, what he is intent on establishing in this passage, as its context makes clear, is the principle which should govern the exchange of goods once Hall's ideal of an essentially atomistic, agrarian society had been established. Unlike the Ricardian socialists he does not argue that it is as a result of the violation of this principle that labour exploitation arises.

Hall's intermediate position between agrarian radicalism and Ricardian socialism might therefore be defined in this way. Like the agrarian radicals, Hall saw impoverishment as a consequence of exploitation but this exploitation was suffered not just by landless agricultural labourers but by the labouring classes as a whole. In addition it was not just landowners who wielded their economic power in a coercive fashion, but all those whose ownership of fixed and circulating capital gave them control, directly or indirectly, over labour. Thus Hall provided an economic critique which was more applicable to the economic conditions generated by early-nineteenth-century British capitalism than that of the agrarian radicals.[24]

Yet Hall stops short of Ricardian socialism. It was not just that he looked backward to a reconstitution of an agrarian society of independent, small-scale producers; nor was it his view that manufacture and trade were, for the most part, wealth-destroying rather than wealth-creating, which prevented him from coming to critical terms with early industrial capitalism in the manner of the Ricardian socialists. The major obstacle in the way of further advance was that while Hall recognised the difficulty of elaborating a coherent theory of labour exploitation where productive activity was assuming more complex, diverse and

---

[24] Hall's 'analyses of the coercive power of capital and the exploitative nature of profit... were more sophisticated than any previously made', Dinwiddy, 'Charles Hall, early English socialist', p. 276.

specialised forms, he made no attempt to furnish the analytical tools with which the problem might be tackled. Instead, like the agrarian radicals, Hall shackled himself to an explanation of poverty that proceeded in physical terms. To strike off these shackles it was necessary to have recourse to value theory and to the concepts, categories, theoretical constructs and discourse which went with it.

In many respects Robert Owen may be seen as the antithesis of Hall. A manufacturer, involved initially in the making of cotton-spinning equipment and then in cotton-spinning itself, Owen was a living part of that ineluctable industrialisation of Britain which Hall abhorred. Owen was, of course, quick to condemn the economic and social evils of early industrial capitalism but unlike Hall he considered that the growth of manufactures laid the foundations for the transformation of Man into 'a terrestrial angel of goodness and wisdom... inhabit[ing] a terrestrial paradise'.[25] In contrast to Hall, Owen did not see the growth of industry as synonymous with human enslavement; rather, the distress and poverty which grew *pari passu* with industrial development were a function of the irrational and ignorant misuse of the enhanced productive powers which industrialisation made available. Owen did not, therefore, attack capitalism with the analytical weaponry either of those whose conception of the economy was essentially agrarian (Spence, Ogilvie, Paine) or whose aspiration was that it should once again become so (Hall).

In investigating the causes of working-class poverty Owen had to come to terms with an economy which his own experience had convinced him was, and increasingly would be, dominated by manufacture and commerce.[26] Owen could not, therefore, avail himself of the natural-rights rhetoric of the agrarian radicals or the genre of anti-capitalism purveyed by Hall. Rather, it was some of the tools of analysis and economic concepts furnished

---

[25] R. Owen, *The Life of Robert Owen written by Himself* (2 vols., London, E. Wilson, 1857–8), Vol. 1, p. xliii.

[26] Thus Owen wrote in his autobiography of a period *c.* 1815 when 'all the manufactories of the kingdom were ... freely opened to me, and I visited most of them from north to south ... *I thus saw the importance of the machinery employed in these manufactories and its rapid annual improvements*', ibid. Vol. 1, p. 112 (my emphasis).

by the classical political economists which were more suited to his purpose. In this context it is interesting that while in disagreement with them on most matters, Owen was on good personal terms with many classical writers. Thus in discussing acquaintances made in the period 1810–15 he makes mention of 'my friends... the political economists – Messers Malthus, – James Mill, – Ricardo, – Sir James Mackintosh, – Colonel Torrens, – Francis Place etc. etc. From these political economists, often in animated discussions, I always differed. But our discussions were maintained to the last with great good feeling.' In similar vein referring to a period c. 1816 he wrote of 'Malthus, Mill, Ricardo, Colonel Torrens, Hume and Place... With all these really clever... well-intentioned men, I had day by day much discussion... most frequently when breakfasting with them, and before their business of the day commenced.'[27] Now Owen was, of course, not one of life's great listeners, particularly to those whose opinions ran contrary to his own, nor is there any evidence that he studied the works of these political economists with whom he was personally familiar. Nevertheless, his acquaintance with them may well, among other things, have familiarised him with the mode of discourse they used to order and explain the economic world. Certainly, when Owen came to analyse the poverty and distress of the working classes, it was frequently in the idiom of his political economist friends.

Owen in his early writings considered critically those economic forces and social arrangements which ensured that the labouring classes were and remained economically vulnerable and he argued that competitive capitalism necessarily translated this vulnerability into working-class impoverishment. Owen had little doubt that the value and thus, for him, the remuneration of labour had fallen in the period after 1815. In 1817 he wrote, 'The immediate cause of the present distress is the depreciation of human labour'[28] and Owen saw this depreciation as something which must inevitably continue as mechanisation in industry continued to produce 'a most unfavourable disproportion between demand for and supply of manual labour', which 'will go on increasing'.[29]

[27] ibid. Vol. 1, pp. 103, 129.
[28] R. Owen, 'Report to the Committee for the Relief of the Manufacturing Poor', 1817, ibid. Vol. 1A, Appendix I, p. 54.
[29] R. Owen, 'Two memorials on behalf of the working classes', 1818, ibid. Vol. 1A, p. 220.

Unless, therefore, these expanding productive powers could be utilised in a rational, social, fashion; unless they could be applied for the collective benefit of the community, rather than in competition with the labour of the working classes for the enrichment of a few, the 'certain consequences of the undirected progress of this power will be to reduce the unchangeable value of manual labour until it falls below the means of procuring a wretched subsistence for any large proportion of the working classes';[30] the paradoxical consequence being that the labouring classes would suffer grinding poverty in a world awash with an abundance of their own creation.

Integral to the development of Owen's economic thinking was his crude formulation of a theory of value. Thus in his *Report to the County of Lanark* (1820), Owen raised the question of how to assess and fix the value of labour in order to prevent its further depreciation and he concluded that as

> the average physical power of men ... has been calculated ... On the same principle, the average of human labour or power may be ascertained; and, as it forms the essence of all wealth, its value in every article of produce may also be ascertained, and its exchangeable value, with all other values, fixed accordingly.[31]

It is difficult to fathom Owen's exact meaning here but he would seem to be suggesting that as labour is utilised in the production of all commodities and as it is possible to estimate the human labour necessary for the manufacture of every article, so it is possible to estimate what should be both the exchange value of labour and all other commodities. If such exchange values prevailed Owen believed that great economic benefits might be expected as 'Human labour would thus acquire its natural and intrinsic value, which would increase as science advanced ... The demand for human labour would be no longer subject to caprice, nor would the support of human life be made, as at present, a perpetually varying article of commerce.'[32]

Owen's labour theory of value, if such it may be called, was both crudely and inadequately articulated but the important point still remains that Owen was trying to come to terms with

---

[30] ibid. Vol. IA, p. 210.
[31] Robert Owen, *Report to the County of Lanark of a Plan for Relieving Public Distress*, (Glasgow University Press, 1821), p. 7.
[32] ibid. p. 7.

the problems of thinking and reasoning in value terms. In addition he goes on to use his value theory to explain labour's impoverishment. Thus he argued that under competitive capitalism neither labour nor anything else exchanged at their 'natural' or 'intrinsic' values or what Owen also referred to as their 'prime cost' or 'cost price'.[33] Exchange at prime cost was the basis upon which the commerce of the world should be conducted[34] for when commodities sold at a 'profit upon price' not only were the 'lower passions of human nature' brought into operation but such exchanges also led to 'a false estimate of all things' with goods, labour included, no longer valued at their 'intrinsic worth'.[35] It was when this occurred that labour suffered; it was in the process of the formation of exchange values that competitive capitalism translated labour's vulnerability into impoverishment. The solution was to ensure that a natural standard of value prevailed: 'Of...new wealth...created, the labourer who produced it is justly entitled to a fair and fixed proportion of all the wealth which he creates. This can be assigned to him on no other principle, than by forming arrangements by which the *natural* standard of value shall become the *practical* standard of value.'[36]

Thus Owen detailed the conditions and specified the mechanism which operated to deny labourers the fruits of their productive efforts and he used a theory of value so to do. As such, his approach to the poverty of labour contained many of the elements which were later to be embodied in the exploitation theories of the Ricardian socialists. Owen's emphasis on the deteriorating material well-being of labour; the stress he placed on labour as the source of wealth and as a means of estimating the value of commodities;[37] his concern with the economic repercussions of commodity prices deviating from their intrinsic or natural values: these were all salient features of the Ricardian socialist analysis of labour exploitation. Yet there is something absent from Owen's critique of early-nineteenth-century indus-

---

[33] 'The wants of the world have been long supplied through a commerce founded on a *profit upon cost price*', *An Explanation of the Cause of Distress which pervades the civilized parts of the World* (London, 1823), pp. 1–2.
[34] ibid.
[35] ibid. p. 2.
[36] R. Owen, *Report*, p. 20.
[37] 'the natural standard of value is in principle human labour', ibid. p. 6.

trial capitalism which distinguishes it from that of the Ricardian socialists. At a superficial level this difference comes across almost as one of tone; a style of writing which lacks the vital, antagonistic acerbity of Hodgskin, Bray, Thompson and the early Gray. However, the difference is more fundamental than this, for while Owen deployed some of the tools and concepts of political economy to explain the vulnerability and impoverishment of labour, Owen did not develop the idea of exploitation as a systematic process of value abstraction, consciously directed by industrial capitalists.[38] Indeed, in this respect, and in contrast to the Ricardian socialists, it is doubtful whether Owen can be said to have formulated an economic theory of labour exploitation at all.

In support of this contention a number of points can be made. First, it should be noted that Owen did tend to eschew levelling the charge of exploitation generally, against a particular social grouping or class. Rather, what Owen condemned was the abstraction of supranormal profits which he saw as consequent upon the greed and cupidity of individual employers whose characters had been corrupted by existing social arrangements. It is true that the opposition of manufacturers to the early campaign for factory legislation in which Owen had been involved undoubtedly lowered them in his estimation but even when their opposition shrivelled the fruit of Owen's labour to the husk of the 1819 Factory Act,[39] Owen was not provoked to the combative anti-capitalism which characterises the economic writing of the Ricardian socialists.[40] On the contrary, Owen was at pains to emphasise that 'the rich and the poor, the governors and the governed have really but one interest',[41] although human

---

[38] For a contrary opinion see S. Pollard, 'Robert Owen as an economist', in *Robert Owen and his Relevance to Our Times*, Co-operative College Paper No. 14 (Loughborough, 1971), pp. 29–30: 'Owen was among the first to develop an exploitation theory and to locate the point of exploitation in the sale of his labour by the worker.'

[39] On this point see M. Cole, 'Owen's mind and methods', in S. Pollard and J. Salt (eds.), *Robert Owen, Prophet of the Poor* (London, Macmillan, 1971), pp. 188–213.

[40] Though his annoyance with the opposition of the manufacturers comes across with particular force in his *Observations on the Effect of the Manufacturing System* (London, 1815).

[41] R. Owen, 'An address to the working classes', April 1819, Appendix P, *Life*, Vol. IA, p. 230.

ignorance and irrational social arrangements might temporarily conceal that fact.[42] Thus Owen asserted that if the remuneration of labourers was increased and the labouring classes allowed to 'consume a larger portion than heretofore of what they produce' this would enable 'the higher ranks of society' to secure 'a much larger surplus than they have ever yet received from the working classes'.[43] In this context, the labour-produced surplus accruing to the 'higher ranks of society' was obviously not something which Owen wished to condemn, let alone subject to the critical scrutiny which the articulation of a fully fledged labour exploitation theory would entail. So while he stressed that goods should exchange at their 'intrinsic' or 'natural' values and while profits might serve to prevent this by creating a 'false estimate of all things', where profits were at what Owen deemed to be an acceptable level,[44] he seems to have been unprepared to subject their recipients to critical attack. Thus in outlining his plans for 'Villages of Unity and Mutual Co-operation', he made clear to potential investors that under such arrangements 'labourers might be made to create all their own subsistence and repay the interest of all capital invested in the outfit of the establishments'.[45] These institutions were therefore described to potential investors as profit-making concerns; indeed Owen stressed that it would 'be in the interest of society that [their] . . . profits should be most

---

[42] For Owen 'the class struggle was . . . a transient expression of the human irrationality entailed by the times in which they lived', G. Hardach, D. Karras and B. Fine, *A Short History*, p. 12.

[43] R. Owen, *An Explanation*, p. 5.

[44] For Owen an acceptable level of profits covering 'capital and risk' seems to have been around 5%. This is certainly what he was prepared to pay shareholders in New Lanark, any surplus over and above this being 'freely expended for the education of the children and the improvement of the workpeople . . . and for the general improvement of the condition of the persons employed in manufactures', *Life*, Vol. I, p. 95; in this context it should also be noted that Owen wrote with approbation of one of his early employers, Mr McGuffog that 'he would have a *reasonable* profit upon what he sold', ibid. p. 20 (my emphasis).

[45] R. Owen, *Development of the Plan for the Relief of the Poor* (London, 1820), p. 4; see also, 'Letter published in the London newspapers', 25 July 1817, Appendix I, *Life*, Vol. IA, pp. 70, 73. Labourers would 'create that surplus which will be necessary to repay the interest of the capital expended'. Potential investors in Owen's villages of mutual co-operation were informed that their investment would not only 'remoralise the population employed' but also 'return 5% interest for the capital expended' – an obvious opportunity here for the rich man to pass through the eye of the needle.

ample'.⁴⁶ So despite fears as to the deleterious economic repercussions of profit upon cost price, there was always in Owen something of the businessman's respect for an adequate or fair return on capital invested;⁴⁷ a respect which must explain in some measure why he escaped the vials of wrath poured down by classical popularisers upon the heads of writers such as Thomas Hodgskin.⁴⁸

In addition, Owen had a tendency to explain the distressed condition of the labouring classes as a by-product of the operation of material forces for which capitalists could not be held responsible. Thus the poverty of labour was seen as resulting from the conjuncture of wholesale mechanisation and rapidly intensifying competitive pressures. It sprang from an essential ignorance of how to control rationally the productive forces which Man's inventive genius had unleashed,⁴⁹ in a situation where manufacturers to survive must steal a competitive march on their rivals. Thus the increasing emiseration of the labouring classes was a consequence of the misapplication of productive powers rather than the result of the conscious, systematic, malign exercise of economic power by any group or class. Owen tended, therefore, to separate the question of labour's depreciating value, under existing economic arrangements, from the question of

---

[46] R. Owen, *Report*, p. 20.

[47] See, for example, Owen's declaration, 'I am...a manufacturer for pecuniary profit', *A New View of Society, Essays on the Formation of Human Character* (Harmondsworth, Pelican, 1970), p. 76.

[48] At least when Owen's economic thinking was attacked by classical writers such as Robert Torrens and J. R. McCulloch it was on the basis that it was erroneous rather than because it was pernicious or socially subversive. See, for example, R. Torrens, 'Mr Owen's plans for relieving the national distress', *Edinburgh Review*, 32 (October 1819), 453–77, and J. R. McCulloch, 'The opinions of Messrs Say, Sismondi and Malthus on the effects of machinery and accumulation', *Edinburgh Review*, 35 (March 1821), 102–23; see also G. P. Scrope, 'The rights of industry – the banking system', *Quarterly Review*, 47 (July 1832), 412: 'The Owenists' doctrine, however, is at least a harmless speculation, and may even be defended with some shadow of plausibility. There is another lately broached by writers ... of a more pernicious, as well as a more monstrous character' – Scrope then goes on to cite Hodgskin's *Popular Political Economy*.

[49] See, for example, Owen's 'Letter published in the London Newspapers', 25 July 1817, pp. 68–9, in which the cause of general economic distress is determined to be the 'misapplication of the existing powers of production in the country, both natural and artificial, when compared to the wants and demand for these productions'.

which classes or social groupings stood to benefit from that depreciation. In this way Owen was able to concentrate his analytical attention upon the *general* macroeconomic causes of labour's plight, rather than pointing a finger of theoretical accusation against those who might be considered the responsible beneficiaries. In addition, emphasis in much of Owen's political economy was placed upon macroeconomic problems as something common to all classes,[50] rather than upon those economic grievances, peculiar to the working classes, which derived specifically from the nature of the economic relations which prevailed between capitalists and labourers.[51]

Engels wrote in 1844 that 'English socialism arose with Owen, a manufacturer, and proceeds therefore with great consideration towards the bourgeoisie and great injustice towards the proletariat in its methods.'[52] Such a remark would suggest that Engels had not read, at this date, the economic works of British anti-capitalist and socialist writers as carefully as Marx was subsequently to do but, nevertheless, if he had confined his strictures to Owen, they would certainly have contained a measure of truth. Perhaps it was Owen's concern to win the support of all classes for his ideas, or his continual desire to play down class antagonism and stress the ultimate harmony of class interests, or perhaps it was simply his innately benevolent disposition – but Owen did not develop the idea that the emiseration of labour was the consequence of the systematic exploitation of one class by another. When capitalists were rebuked it was for an excess of cupidity or for their irrationality or for their failure to comprehend the workings of the economy or their ignorance of the principles governing the formation of human character, rather than for their conscious utilisation of economic power to exploit the vulnerability of labour.

---

[50] This may provide one reason for Owen's failure to elaborate 'a distinctly working-class political formula for action', J. Butt, 'Robert Owen in his own time 1771–1858' in *Robert Owen and his Relevance to our Times*, Co-operative College Papers, No. 14 (Loughborough, 1971), p. 22.

[51] See, for example, the view of C. Gide and C. Rist that 'Thompson's grasp of the idea that labour does not enjoy all it produces is much firmer than Owen's', *A History of Economic Doctrines*, 2nd edn (London, Harrap, 1948), p. 254.

[52] F. W. Engels, *The Condition of the Working Class in England* (London, Panther, 1974), p. 262.

The political economy of Robert Owen did not provide a developed theory of labour exploitation upon which writers in the working-class press could draw,[53] although it may be argued that Owen provided many of the components utilised by the Ricardian socialists in the formulation of such a theory. This does, of course, raise the difficult question of Owen's influence on the Ricardian socialists, a question which will be considered in the following chapter. What can be said at this point is that, whatever his influence, the Ricardian socialists went further than Owen. They went further in their emphasis on the importance of economic theorising;[54] further in their attempt to utilise the tools and concepts of political economy to clarify the systematic form which exploitation was assuming in a rapidly industrialising economy and further too in their preparedness to isolate and condemn its perpetrators and beneficiaries. How the Ricardian socialists set about this task and with what consequences for their political economy and that of their populacrisers are the concerns of the next three chapters.

[53] This was particularly significant in a situation where 'in the 1810s and 1820s ... class and class antagonism became a fact', H. Perkin, *Origins*, p. 28. In such a situation, therefore, it would be Ricardian socialist rather than Owenian political economy which would prove influential.

[54] On this point see J. F. C. Harrison, *Owen and the Owenites in Britain and America, the quest for the new moral world* (London, Routledge and Kegan Paul, 1969), p. 67; also H. S. Foxwell, Introduction to the English translation of A. Menger, *The Right to the Whole Produce of Labour* (London, Macmillan, 1899), p. lxxxvii: 'Owen was less important as an economic theorist than many who fought under his flag.'

4

Ricardian socialists/Smithian socialists: what's in a name?

The Ricardian socialists are generally considered to be four in number. Claims have been made for the addition of Charles Hall, T. R. Edmonds, Piercy Ravenstone 'etc. etc. and four more pages of etceteras'[1] but the relative sophistication of the analysis of Hodgskin, Bray, Gray and Thompson does set them apart as a distinctive group of writers. They grasped the prime importance of formulating a theory of value to use as a foundation for their critical analysis; they saw the utility of value theory as a means of explaining the maldistribution of wealth (exploitation of labour) which characterised capitalism and they integrated their theories of value and distribution with a macroeconomic explanation of general economic depression.[2] In addition and in contrast to Robert Owen they distinguished analytically the beneficiaries of exploitation and defined them in terms of their socio-economic role. It is these things, together with a complementary recognition of the salient characteristics of nascent industrial capitalism, which set Thompson, Hodgskin, Bray and Gray apart from other anti-capitalist and socialist writers of the period.

It is unfortunate, therefore, that Bray's major contribution to socialist political economy, *Labour's Wrongs and Labour's Remedy*, was not published until 1839[3] and so lies outside the chronological

---

[1] K. Marx, *The Poverty of Philosophy* (London, Lawrence and Wishart, 1954), p. 77.
[2] See below, chapter 7.
[3] Though some of it may have been written as early as 1837; see H. J. Carr, 'The social and political thought of John Francis Bray', unpublished PhD thesis (University of London, 1942), p. 8, who mentions that a series of lectures given by Bray in Leeds, November 1837, followed closely the plan of *Labour's Wrongs*.

limits of this study. Nevertheless, some notice will be taken of aspects of Bray's contribution in so far as it may throw light on the nature of anti-capitalist and socialist political economy in the 1820s and early 1830s. It should be remembered, however, that in the period under discussion Bray's economic ideas were not available to would-be popularisers. They will not, therefore, receive in this chapter or in chapter 7 the same consideration as the economic writings of Thompson, Hodgskin and Gray.

While the lives of Thompson, Gray and Hodgskin spanned a considerable period of history, their major works of political economy were published in the period 1824–32 and the decade 1824–34 saw their greatest impact, positive and negative, upon contemporaries. After 1834 their ideas never again seem to have met with a comparable degree of popular appreciation and acceptance. Thus in the latter half of the nineteenth century, with the exception of the notice taken of their writings by Marx, they were largely forgotten. They receive no mention, for example, in Thomas Kirkup's *History of Socialism* (1892), in which a chapter entitled 'Early English [sic] Socialism' is devoted entirely to a consideration of the work of Robert Owen; nor are they mentioned in Moritz Kaufmann's *Utopias* (1879) (although here again a chapter is devoted to Robert Owen and English socialism), nor in William Graham's *Socialism: New and Old* (1890). H. M. Hyndman gave Hodgskin and Bray only cursory mention in the footnotes of *The Historical Basis of Socialism in England* (1892) while Thompson is lumped together with Carlile, Carpenter, Hunt ('Orator') and Bronterre O'Brien as one of the 'educators of the people'. Similarly, G. J. Holyoake in his *History of Co-operation* (1891) and Beatrice Potter (Webb) in *The Co-operative Movement in Great Britain* (1891) conceded William Thompson only short and critical appreciation.[4]

It was, therefore, from near historical oblivion that H. S. Foxwell rescued these writers in his introduction to Anton

---

[4] T. Kirkup, *A History of Socialism* (London, Black, 1892), pp. 55–68; M. Kaufmann, *Utopias; or schemes of social improvement: from Sir Thomas More to Karl Marx* (London, 1879), pp. 88–109; W. Graham, *Socialism, New and Old* (London, Kegan Paul, 1890); H. M. Hyndman, *The Historical Basis of Socialism in England* (London, Kegan Paul, 1892), pp. 120n, 127n, 133n; G. J. Holyoake, *History of Co-operation*, pp. 109–11; B. Potter (Webb), *The Co-operative Movement in Great Britain* (London, Sonnenschein, 1891), pp. 47–8.

Menger's *The Right to the Whole Produce of Labour* (1899),[5] since when they have at least succeeded in generating a respectable volume of secondary literature. What has rarely been considered in any depth, however, is their relation to the more mainstream elements of classical political economy and what implications Ricardian or alternative paternity might have for the form, content and policy corollaries of their political economy. Thus they have been uncritically categorised as 'Ricardian' both collectively – by writers as varied as Hovell, Carr, Gray[6] and Roll, the latter asserting that 'They all base themselves on the teaching of the Ricardian School but use the classical conclusions to point a revolutionary moral'[7] – and as individuals, with Hodgskin seen as basing his reasoning 'explicitly on Ricardo', Thompson as welding together 'the ethical philosophy of Jeremy Bentham, the labour economics of David Ricardo and the social views of Robert Owen . . . into a system of socialism' and giving a 'consistent socialist interpretation of Ricardian economy', while John Gray has been described as having 'drawn his main ideas in unadulterated form from Ricardo'.[8]

---

[5] Anton Menger's work *Das Recht den vollen Arbeitsertrag in geschichtlicher Darstellung* was first published in 1886 but as Foxwell pointed out in his Introduction, p. viii, 'It is the juristic rather than the strictly economic aspect of socialism in which he is most generally interested' and 'From first to last the enquiry proceeds from the juristic standpoint', p. xvi. It is, therefore, Foxwell's Introduction, rather than Menger's own work, which is of greatest interest to the historian of economic thought.

It is generally believed that it was in this Introduction that the epithet 'Ricardian socialist' was first coined: 'It was Ricardo, not Owen, who gave the really effective inspiration to English socialism. This was the real intellectual origin of revolutionary socialism and it was for this reason I call it Ricardian', p. lxxxiii. It is possible to point, however, to an earlier use of the term in J. Bonar, *Malthus and his Work* (London, Macmillan, 1885), p. 214: 'Hodgskin developed the 'surplus value' theory, that inevitable corollary of Ricardo's 'labour value', which since the publication of Marx's *Capital* has raised in Germany and elsewhere a Ricardian Socialism appearing like the ghost of the deceased Ricardian orthodoxy sitting crowned on the grave thereof.'

[6] M. Hovell, *The Chartist Movement*, p. 38; H. J. Carr, 'The social and political thought of John Francis Bray', p. 280; A. Gray, *The Socialist Tradition*, p. 262.

[7] E. Roll, *A History of Economic Thought* (Homewood, Irwin, 1974), p. 245.

[8] C. Driver, 'Thomas Hodgskin and the individualists' in F. J. C. Hearnshaw (ed.), *The Social and Political Ideas of Some Representative Thinkers of the Age of Reaction and Reconstruction* (London, Harrap, 1932), pp. 210–11; M. Beer, *A History of British Socialism*, Vol. 1, p. 218; E. Roll, *A History of Economic Thought*, p. 247; L. Stephen, *The English Utilitarians* (2 vols., London, Duckworth, 1900), Vol. 1, p. 262.

On the other hand, a writer such as G. D. H. Cole fought shy of using the term 'Ricardian'. Rather, Cole was at pains to say that they developed the anti-capitalist implications of Ricardian theory. He preferred, therefore, the label 'anti-Ricardian'[9] to avoid the implication that the Ricardian socialists had developed their economic thinking within the Ricardian paradigm. For Cole, the 'anti-Ricardians' derived their political economy from Ricardo in a dialectical fashion; their economic opinions represented a reaction against Ricardian orthodoxy. It was from Ricardo, nonetheless, that the Ricardian socialists drew inspiration, even if that inspiration assumed a negative form. Thus Bray's *Labour's Wrongs* was described as a synthesis of 'Owenism and anti-Ricardian economics', while Hodgskin was seen as elaborating 'very cogently a labour theory based on a *reaction to* Ricardian economics'.[10] Though he avoided using the label 'Ricardian socialist', therefore, Cole undoubtedly saw Ricardo as the father of British anti-capitalist and socialist political economy.[11]

The 'Ricardian' nature of Ricardian socialism has, on occasion, been challenged. Thus Blaug has criticised Foxwell severely for his unqualified attribution of Ricardian socialist paternity to Ricardo, pointing to Charles Hall as a writer who displayed many of the analytical attributes of the typical Ricardian socialist twelve years before the publication of the *Principles of Political Economy and Taxation*.[12] Lowenthal, though her work was entitled *The Ricardian Socialists*, saw 'nothing in either the tone of these authors or the form of their arguments which points especially to Ricardo . . . The term Ricardian socialism is probably due to the fact that Ricardo was a dominant figure of a school in which the labour theory of value was a common doctrine.'[13] In addition, Lowenthal went on to make the point that 'There is no evidence

---

[9] G. D. H. Cole, *Socialist Thought*, pp. 106–8.
[10] ibid. pp. 133 and 111 (my emphasis).
[11] Cole's position is similar to that of Marx, who wrote in his *Theories of Surplus Value*, Vol. 3, p. 238, that 'During the Ricardian period of political economy its antithesis communism [Owen] and socialism . . . [comes] also [into being] . . . It will be seen from the works we quote [Ravenstone and Hodgskin] that in fact they all derive from the Ricardian form.'
[12] M. Blaug, *Ricardian Economics*, p. 142.
[13] E. Lowenthal, *The Ricardian Socialists* (New York, Longman, Green and Co., 1911), p. 103.

that the socialists were particularly impressed by his [Ricardo's] teachings... They all of them quote Adam Smith as their authority for the labour theory of value';[14] an opinion echoed by Kimball, by Douglas, who believed that they should 'be termed the Smithian socialists, since they derive their inspiration from Smith rather than Ricardo', and by Schwartz, who has stated simply that the Ricardian socialists 'did not draw their inspiration for the doctrine of the workers' right to the whole product from Ricardo but from Smith'.[15] In similar vein, and more recently, Hollander has made out a convincing case for the Smithian paternity of many aspects of Hodgskin's anti-capitalist political economy, particularly his theory of value.[16] However, the possible implications of building on Smithian rather than Ricardian foundations have not been fully considered and in particular there has been no close comparative examination of texts to establish the manner in which the *Wealth of Nations* may have proved seminal as far as early anti-capitalist and socialist writers were concerned.

Yet the question of whether Hodgskin, Thompson, Gray and Bray may be more accurately designated 'Smithian' or 'Ricardian' is no mere academic exercise in categorisation but a question the answer to which is of fundamental importance for a correct understanding of the nature of the Ricardian socialist contribution to the development of anti-capitalist and socialist political economy in Britain. Thus it will be argued that working along 'Smithian' rather than 'Ricardian' lines led the Ricardian

[14] ibid.
[15] J. Kimball, *The Economic Doctrines of John Gray*, p. 21; P. H. Douglas, 'Smith's theory of value and distribution' in J. M. Clark (ed.), *Adam Smith 1776–1926: Lectures to commemorate the sesquicentennial of the publication of the 'Wealth of Nations'* (New York, Kelley, 1966), p. 98; P. Schwartz, *The New Political Economy of J. S. Mill* (London, Weidenfeld and Nicolson, 1968), p. 16. G. Myrdal, *The Political Element in the Development of Economic Theory* (London, Routledge and Kegan Paul, 1953), p. 30, has also argued that there was much in Smith's writing on value to provide grist for the mills of the early socialists.
[16] S. G. Hollander, 'The post-Ricardian dissension: a case study in economics and ideology', *Oxford Economic Papers*, 32 (1980), 376–89; on this point see also my 'Ricardian socialists/Smithian socialists: what's in a name?', *Faculty of Economics and Politics Research Paper*, University of Cambridge, 1976. Hollander somewhat spoils a good case by the extreme statement that 'labour writers' in general were guilty of a 'vehement anti-Ricardianism', ibid. 373. Anti-Ricardianism was certainly there in Hodgskin's writing and Ricardo was also mentioned critically by Ravenstone and Thompson but the fact is that most 'labour writers' had not read Ricardo and were not sufficiently well informed, therefore, to be vehemently

socialists to formulate theories of labour exploitation which necessarily led them in the direction of essentially reformist policy prescriptions fundamentally different from those which would have been arrived at had the Ricardian socialists, like Marx, actually established their theories upon truly Ricardian foundations. In addition, given that Thompson, Hodgskin and Gray seem to have been important sources of theoretical inspiration for writers in the working-class press, this question of categorisation also has important implications for an understanding of the explanations of labour exploitation being popularly purveyed and the solutions to labour impoverishment which these implied.[17] The question of appellation must therefore be the starting point for an examination of the exploitation theories of Thompson, Hodgskin and Gray.

In considering how the political economy of Adam Smith might lend itself to the development of a theory of labour exploitation, it is necessary to examine briefly the difficulties which Smith had in reconciling the existence of surplus value with his understanding of what determined the exchange value of commodities.[18] Smith's problem was that the existence of surplus value appeared to contradict the laws of value which he saw as prevailing at an early stage of social and economic development, when commodities exchanged according to the quantity of labour which they embodied. Thus Smith wrote:

In that early and rude state of society which precedes both the accumulation of stock and the appropriation of land, the proportion between the quantities of labour necessary for acquiring different objects seems to be the only circumstance which can afford any rule for exchanging them for one another.[19]

However,

As soon as stock has accumulated in the hands of particular persons... In exchanging the complete manufacture either for labour

opposed to Ricardianism. By contrast they all seem to have read the *Wealth of Nations* – or at least parts of it. If there was any one economist to whom they were vehemently opposed it was Malthus, not Ricardo.

[17] See below, pp. 132-59.
[18] Smith did not use the term surplus value but rather its differentiated forms of rent and profit.
[19] A. Smith, *An Inquiry into the Nature and Causes of the Wealth of Nations*, ed. R. H. Campbell, A. S. Skinner and W. B. Todd (2 vols., Oxford, Clarendon Press, 1976), p. 65.

or for other goods, over and above what may be sufficient to pay the price of materials and the wages of the workmen something must be given for the profits of the undertaker of the work who hazards his stock in this adventure'[20]

and these profits were acknowledged as something distinct from the product of any specific labour furnished by the entrepreneur. Now when commodities exchanged according to the laws of value which prevailed in an 'early and rude state of society' it was the case that 'the whole produce of labour belong[ed] to the labourer'.[21] So the question arose as to how these laws could be reconciled with a situation where the value of production in any particular period furnished an income not only for the labourer (wages) but also for the capitalist (profit) and the landowner (rent).

The answer given by Smith was that in economically and socially more advanced societies, where rents and profits existed as separate income categories, 'the quantity of labour commonly employed in acquiring or producing any commodity [is no longer] ... the only circumstance which can regulate the quantity which it ought to purchase, command, or exchange for'[22] because, in this situation, 'Wages, profit and rent', had become 'the three original sources of all revenue *as well as of all exchangeable value*'.[23] Thus the advent of a society characterised by private appropriation of land and capital had resulted in the abrogation of the previously prevailing laws of value, and with this abrogation a situation was created where 'the whole produce of labour does not always belong to the labourer'.[24]

Smith's problem arose because of a tendency to assume that the value of labour and the quantity of labour were equivalent measures of value.[25] Unlike Ricardo, who takes Smith to

---

[20] ibid. pp. 65–6.
[21] ibid. p. 65.
[22] ibid. p. 67.
[23] ibid. p. 69 (my emphasis).
[24] ibid. p. 67.
[25] 'he sometimes confuses, and at other times substitutes, the determination of the value of commodities by the quantity of labour required for their production, with its determination by the quantity of living labour with which commodities can be bought, or ... the quantity of commodities with which a definite quantity of living labour can be bought', K. Marx, *Theories of Surplus Value*, Vol. 1, p. 70.

task on this point,[26] Smith failed to make clear that, given contemporary social and economic arrangements, the expressions 'quantity of labour' and 'value of labour' were no longer interchangeable. In accepting, therefore, that in 'civilised' society goods no longer exchanged for the *value of labour* which they embodied, Smith also assumed that commodities could no longer exchange according to the *quantity of labour* which they embodied. Thus for Smith a labour-embodied theory of value had to be abandoned and replaced by an alternative which could explain why wages (the value of labour) were no longer equivalent to the value of labour's whole product. In contrast to Ricardo, therefore, who accepted that, for the most part, commodities exchanged in proportion to the quantity of labour which they embodied,[27] Smith pointed to profits and rents as indicative of the fact that they did not. For Smith, goods exchanged according to the labour they commanded rather than the labour they embodied: 'The value of any commodity, therefore, to the person who possesses it, and who means not to use or consume it himself, but to exchange it for other commodities, is equal to the quantity of labour which it enables him to purchase.'[28]

Now such lines of argument quite obviously lent themselves to the development of a particular type of labour exploitation theory. Thus Smith's views could be reformulated or interpreted in this way. In an early stage of society goods exchanged according to their natural, labour-embodied values. In such circumstances exchanges between individuals were of an equitable nature and all received their just reward, namely the full value of their product. However, in a more advanced stage of civilisation, where land had been appropriated for private use and capital had accumulated in the hands of a few individuals, the laws previously determining the exchange value of commodities no longer prevailed. Goods exchanged according to the labour they commanded rather than the labour they embodied,

---

[26] D. Ricardo, *On the Principles of Political Economy and Taxation*, ed. P. Sraffa, Vol. I, pp. 13–20.

[27] See, for example, G. J. Stigler, 'Ricardo and the 93% labour theory of value', in *Essays in the History of Economics* (University of Chicago Press, 1965), pp. 326–42; also, M. Blaug, *Economic Theory in Retrospect* (3rd edn, Cambridge University Press, 1978), p. 95.

[28] A. Smith, *Wealth of Nations*, p. 47.

the former value being greater than the latter to the extent that profits and rents formed part of the value of commodities.[29] Thus the private appropriation of land and the accumulation of capital developed *pari passu* with the violation of the labour-embodied law of value. The labourer, therefore, ceased to receive his whole product to the extent that the originally prevailing laws of value were violated, while such violations produced a more rapid accumulation of capital in private hands. It is just such lines of argument that characterise the labour exploitation theories advanced by the Ricardian socialists.

One of the fundamental characteristics of Ricardian socialist analysis was its attempt to construct a theory of labour exploitation on the basis of a labour theory of value. It was this aspect of their thought which impressed contemporaries[30] and this which appeared to link them with Ricardo, the dominant figure associated with the labour theory of value during the period when they wrote their major works. In fact, the Ricardian socialists offered a variety of formulations of the labour theory with Hodgskin and Bray coming nearest to a strict labour-embodied expression. For Hodgskin 'natural price' or 'natural value' – the concepts were synonymous – reflected the quantity of effort or labour which Nature imposed upon Man for the creation of any good. As Hodgskin phrased it, 'As all commodities are exclusively the produce of labour, there is no other rule, and can be no other rule for determining their relative value to each other, but the quantity of labour required to produce each and all of them.'[31] Bray was equally emphatic: 'It is labour alone which bestows value; for labour, as it has been truly said, is the purchase money that is paid for everything we eat, drink or wear' and 'it is labour which gives value to all material

---

[29] 'In every society, the price of every commodity finally resolves itself into some one or other, or all of those three parts [rent, wages, profit]; and in every improved society, all the three enter, more or less, as component parts into the prices of the far greater part of commodities', A. Smith, *Wealth of Nations*, p. 68.

[30] See, for example, R. L. Meek, 'The decline of Ricardian economics in England', *Economica*, 9 (1950), 43–62, who linked the decline in the support for the tenets of Ricardianism after 1830 with a contemporary belief that elements of Ricardian political economy had been exploited in an unacceptably radical manner. This view has, however, been challenged by a number of writers; see, for example, P. Schwartz, *The New Political Economy*, p. 16.

[31] T. Hodgskin, *Popular Political Economy*, p. 185.

requisites'.³² These writers did not attempt to expand such statements into a value theory of any degree of sophistication but it would be fair to interpret them as believing that commodities should exchange according to the labour time embodied in their manufacture and would do if the natural laws of value prevailed.

John Gray is more difficult to interpret. There exist in his writings many overt admissions that on questions of value and distribution it was Adam Smith whom he regarded as his mentor.³³ However, given the element of confusion in Smith's work such avowals create more problems than they solve. In this respect Gray's work bears the hallmark of the master being permeated by a truly Smithian ambivalence revealed in his adoption at different points in his writings of both value of labour and quantity of labour measures of value.³⁴

Thompson's work displays a similar confusion, adopting as he does, at different points in his *Inquiry*, three conflicting explanations of how the exchange value of commodities might be assessed. Thus for Thompson the value of goods was determined by the labour they embodied, the labour they saved and by their perceived social worth or utility.³⁵ As for providing an adequate standard or measure of value he was driven to admit the impossibility of the task, 'while desires or tastes vary as the moral and intellectual condition of mankind improves, no accurate measure of value, as applied to wealth, can be given. To seek it is to ... hunt after a shadow.'³⁶

Yet important as it is for some understanding of the confused analytical basis from which they worked, the point of greatest consequence is not the specific form which the labour theory of value assumed under their respective pens. What is of importance

---

[32] J. F. Bray, *Labour's Wrongs and Labour's Remedy*, p. 33; Bray surely had in mind Smith's statement that 'Labour was the first price, the original purchase-money that was paid for all things', *Wealth of Nations*, p. 48; J. F. Bray, *Labour's Wrongs*, p. 29.

[33] For example, J. Gray, *Lectures on the Nature and Use of Money* (Edinburgh, 1848), pp. 6, 34.

[34] J. Gray, *The Social System, A Treatise on the Principle of Exchange* (Edinburgh, 1831), pp. 18, 100.

[35] W. Thompson, *Inquiry*, pp. 7–17.

[36] ibid. p. 15; though Thompson stated that labour was the 'best approximation' to such a standard.

is first, that they recognised the need for the formulation of a theory of value, and secondly, that they believed it was through the violation of the natural laws of value, as they understood them, that exploitation was perpetrated. For these writers it was through an understanding of the specific nature of this violation that a fundamental insight could be gained into the origin of economic injustice and material impoverishment. Thus they believed that the true nature of the exploitative relationship between capital and wage labour must reveal itself through the manner in which, under capitalistic economic arrangements, the exchange values of commodities were determined.

For Hodgskin this violation of the natural laws of value was manifested most clearly in the deviation of 'social' from 'natural' prices. 'Natural' prices or values prevailed if the underlying natural laws which Hodgskin believed governed economic activity were allowed to function in an untrammelled fashion. 'Social' prices or values, by way of contrast, prevailed when natural economic laws were distorted by ill-directed, ignorant or malign human agency. Such a distortion of natural economic laws Hodgskin saw as characteristic of the 'present state of society', where the labourer was forced to 'give a good deal more labour to acquire and possess [a commodity] than is requisite to buy it from nature. Natural price thus increased to the labourer is SOCIAL PRICE.'[37]

Thompson was also concerned that 'natural' values, however defined, should prevail in the sphere of exchange, for if such values ceased to govern exchange relations then these must of necessity be 'involuntary', 'unequal' and, therefore, exploitative. In addition, for Thompson, the failure of commodities to exchange at their 'true' values produced not only the 'evil trinity' of overpopulation, overproduction and underconsumption but also the distortion of productive capacity,[38] a shortage of necessities[39] and a permanent, artificially high level of prices.

Gray too emphasised the need for an equitable exchange of equivalents if the economic ills and evils of capitalism were to be abolished. Thus he asserted at the outset of his *Lecture on*

---

[37] T. Hodgskin, *Popular Political Economy*, p. 220.
[38] W. Thompson, *Inquiry*, pp. 122–3.
[39] ibid. p. 114.

Ricardian socialists/Smithian socialists

Human Happiness that all just contracts had for their foundation the exchange of equal quantities of labour and that it was 'exclusively by barter, that the power by which individuals are enabled to tyrannize... is introduced into the world'. Also in this work Gray's greatest criticism and scorn was reserved for those 'useless' members of society such as retailers who most obviously did 'not give to society' an 'equivalent' for what they consumed. These 'unproductive members of society' had necessarily to violate the principles which should govern exchange simply to secure the means of subsistence.[40] Similarly, Gray's utilisation of the computations contained in Patrick Colquhoun's *Treatise on the Population, Wealth, Power and Resources of the British Empire* (1814), which divided society into the 'productive' and 'unproductive', shows a concern to isolate those social elements which, having failed to embody their labour in commodities, were necessarily forced to violate the natural laws of value in order to consume at all.[41]

In developing their labour exploitation theories thus, along what may be termed 'Smithian' lines, it was almost inevitable that the Ricardian socialists came to be particularly concerned with the sphere of exchange. This comes across clearly in the work of Hodgskin who also, in this connection, stated his preference for the Smithian as against the Ricardian explanation of the determination of exchange values under capitalism. Thus Hodgskin wrote that, 'Profit, being... a diminution to the labourer of the value of his produce, enhances the price of everything into which it enters, to the labourer. It is in this sense in which Adam Smith says rent and profit enhance price',[42] while in the same letter he accused Ricardo of

> want of an accurate distinction between natural price and exchangeable value. Natural price is measured by the quantity of labour necessary to produce any commodity: its exchangeable value, or what another will give or is obliged to give for that commodity when produced,

---

[40] J. Gray, *A Lecture on Human Happiness* (London School of Economics and Political Science, 1931), pp. 5, 15.
[41] ibid. pp. 16–32.
[42] T. Hodgskin to F. Place, letter, 28 November 1820, quoted in full in E. Halévy, *Thomas Hodgskin*, pp. 69–75 (p. 73); cf. Marx's view that 'In [his]... presentation Hodgskin reproduces both what is correct and confusing in Adam Smith's view', *Theories of Surplus Value*, Vol. 1, p. 88.

may or may not be equal to the quantity of labour employed in its production. Mr Ricardo has, I think, made a mistake by supposing these two things to be equal. *They are not, or the wages of labour would always be equal to the produce of labour.*[43]

Thus, for Hodgskin, Ricardo appeared to suggest as a logical derivative of his value theory, that the labourer did indeed receive the full value of his product but Smith, by accepting that profit and rent were added to the value of labour to make up or 'enhance' the price of commodities, appeared to highlight just why the labourer was not in this enviable position. Ricardo described things as they ought to be but it was Smith who made clear how they actually were. Ricardo assumed that goods exchanged according to their labour-embodied values, but how could this be the case, asked Hodgskin, when wages were not equal to the produce of labour?

It was to the act of exchange that Gray and Thompson also directed their attention when seeking the causes of exploitation and impoverishment. 'It is our system of exchange which forms the hiding place of that giant of mischief which bestrides the civilised world, rewarding industry with starvation, exertion with disappointment, and the best interests of our rulers to do good, with perplexity, dismay, and failure',[44] wrote Gray in 1831 and this concern with the system of exchange grew even stronger in his later works.[45] It was in the realm of exchange that remedy was to be sought for the exploitation of the labouring classes. 'The condition of the productive classes', he wrote, 'would be ... greatly improved by the establishment of a free system of exchange'; the problem was that there had 'never existed a rational system of exchange or a proper instrument for effecting exchanges' and it was to be expected that an 'improved plan of exchange' would rapidly eliminate 'unmerited poverty' and 'commercial difficulties of every denomination'.[46]

Similarly for Thompson it was

By unjust *exchanges* ... supported by force or fraud, whether by direct operation of law, or by indirect operation of unwise social

---

[43] ibid. pp. 74–5 (my emphasis).
[44] J. Gray, *Social System*, p. 57.
[45] See, for example, Gray's *An Efficient Remedy for the Distress of Nations* (Edinburgh, 1842) and his *Lectures on the Nature and Use of Money*.
[46] J. Gray, *Social System*, pp. 176, 19, vii.

arrangements ... [that] the products of the labor of the industrious classes [are] taken out of their hands ... It is not the differences of production of different laborers, but the complicated system of exchanges of those productions when made, that gives rise to ... frightful inequality of wealth[47]

and so it was 'in the regulation of exchanges ... that the industrious classes must depend, for realising the general proposition that "the whole produce of labor should belong to the laborer"'.[48] Without such a regulation of exchange Thompson believed that, 'the springs of this higgling [in the market] will be always kept in the hands of adepts, and they will be so regulated, that prizes there will be, and these prizes will fall into the hands of the most skilful in the higgling exchanges of competition'.[49] Thus for Thompson too, exploitation was essentially rooted in the failure to 'exchange equivalents'.[50]

Bray was equally emphatic. Wealth had 'all been derived from the bones and sinews of the working classes during successive ages ... it had been taken from them by the fraudulent and slavery-creating systems of unequal exchanges'[51] and as long as this system of unequal exchanges continued, 'The hand of every man is more or less raised against every other man – the interest of every class is opposed to every other class – and all other interests are in opposition and hostility to the interest of the working man.'[52] Thus for Bray it was 'an inevitable condition of inequality of exchanges – of buying at one price and selling at another – that capitalists shall continue to be capitalists and working men be working men'.[53] The solution was obvious: 'UNIVERSAL LABOUR AND EQUAL EXCHANGES'. Equal exchanges would mean an end to exploitation for then every exchange would be 'simply a *transfer*, and not a *sacrifice*'. 'Under equality

---

[47] W. Thompson, *Labor Rewarded*, p. 12 (Thompson's emphasis); see also, for example, remarks by Thompson to the effect that large accumulations of capital were the by-product of exchange and that it was from the 'higgling exchanges of competition' that inequality of wealth invariably arose, ibid. pp. 32, 36.
[48] ibid. pp. 12–13.
[49] ibid. p. 36.
[50] W. Thompson, *Inquiry*, p. 101.
[51] J. F. Bray, *Labour's Wrongs*, p. 57.
[52] ibid. p. 28; 'It is inequality of exchanges which enables one class to live in luxury and idleness, and dooms another to incessant toil', ibid. p. 49.
[53] ibid. pp. 48–9.

of exchanges wealth cannot have, as it now has, a procreative and apparently self-generating power.'⁵⁴

This concern of the Ricardian socialists with the sphere of exchange, which was an inevitable consequence of the formulation of their labour exploitation theories along 'profit-upon-alienation' lines, did not mean that they ignored the significance of who owned the means of production. Thus Thompson wrote:

> as long as the laborer stands in society divested of every thing but the mere power of producing, as long as he possesses neither the tools nor machinery to work with, the land or material to work upon, the house and clothes that shelter him, or even the food which he is consuming ... as long as any institutions or expedients exist, by the open or unseen operation of which he stands dependant ... on those who have accumulated these necessary means of his exertions, as long will he remain deprived of almost all the products of his labor, instead of having the use of all of them.⁵⁵

Similarly Gray showed an awareness that exchange could not be looked at in isolation from the organisation of production. Thus, replying to the accusation that he had devoted too much attention to the former and insufficient to the latter he wrote, 'I must confess ... that I am totally unable to see how any system of exchange can be rendered effectual without the co-operation of a corresponding system of production.'⁵⁶

However, while these insights were often developed in prose with an almost Marxian ring, this should not obscure the fact that the Ricardian socialists were concerned with the organisation of production and with the nature of the relations between capitalists and wage labourers, primarily in so far as these impinged upon what they conceived of as the natural and optimal relations of exchange. This becomes apparent when the solutions to the evil of exploitation, which they derived from their analyses, are scrutinised more closely.

Gray, for example, although explicitly articulating his awareness of the necessary interrelationship of production and exchange invariably worked from his analysis of exchange relations to conclusions about the manner in which production might best

---

[54] ibid. p. 109 (Bray's emphasis).
[55] W. Thompson, *Inquiry*, p. 590.
[56] J. Gray to W. Pare, letter, *Lancashire and Yorkshire Co-operator*, September 1832.

be organised. As a result he tended to see the reorganisation of production relations as important in so far as it facilitated the introduction of a rational and equitable system of exchange. Thus after an initial flirtation with Owenite communitarianism in his *Lecture*, Gray came to believe that once a stable standard of value had been established and a circulating medium introduced, the volume of which might be controlled according to certain easily understood principles of monetary management, little of evil would be left in the economic world. Certainly there would be no need for any fundamental, let alone revolutionary, reconstruction of society. Thus Gray wrote in *The Social System* that the 'system of commerce' which he wished to establish was 'consistent with individual competition in bodily and mental occupations, with private accumulation to any amount, with all forms of political government having the least resemblance to fairness or freedom',[57] while in a similar vein he was to write in a later work, 'We require no reconstruction of society, in order to increase our annual income a hundred millions or so. A few salutary money-laws are all that are wanted along with the repeal of some that are absurd.'[58] In the final analysis, therefore, what Gray sought was a means of grafting the exchange virtues of the Smithian rude state onto a mode of production which was essentially capitalist, even if this capitalism, as in *The Social System*, was of a corporatist and technocratic kind.[59]

John Francis Bray also saw the creation of a new medium of exchange as a fundamental prerequisite for any transition from the social and economic evils of existing society to the more just and rational world of his prospective small communities and joint stock companies. Money and credit had been 'the great armoury from whence the capitalists derive all their weapons to fight with and conquer the working class'[60] and it was Bray's aim to utilise this same armoury to provide the means of transforming existing economic and social arrangements. Thus

---

[57] J. Gray, *Social System*, p. 95.
[58] J. Gray, *The Nature and Use of Money*, p. 90.
[59] 'did Gray want to eliminate the capitalist and expropriate the landlord? The answers to these questions seem to be negative', J. Kimball, *The Economic Doctrines of John Gray*, p. 78.
[60] J. F. Bray, *Labour's Wrongs*, p. 146.

it was to be through the *purchase* of land and capital by labour bonds or notes that the economic millenium was to arrive.[61] Bray's ultimate aim was to create a situation where 'labour shall be universal ... [and] the land and all productive property shall be held and enjoyed in common'.[62] However, this was to be effected by a colossal act of equitable exchange. Production was to be socialised by purchase. By the same means as the capitalist exploited 'may the working classes purchase from the capitalists all those accumulations which the present system of unequal exchanges has enabled them to obtain possession of'.[63] What Bray sought to achieve was 'the purchase of the real capital of the country'.[64]

Yet perhaps the most overtly reformist, with respect to his policy prescriptions, was, paradoxically, the revolutionary *bête noire* of Francis Place, James Mill and other classical popularisers: Thomas Hodgskin. He was also in this respect the most obviously Smithian. Thus Hodgskin was primarily concerned with removing those malignly created obstructions which caused the market economy to malfunction. Free trade,[65] the elimination of monopoly power and, of particular importance, the cessation of state interference in the economic life of the nation: these were policies which would have pleased the most fervent disciple of Adam Smith and these were the policies of Thomas Hodgskin. Even Hodgskin's support for trade unions was given in the expectation that their activity would redress the disparate bargaining strength of labourers and capitalists and thus contribute to a more perfect functioning of the market.[66] Marx was undoubtedly right when he wrote of Hodgskin that he 'accept[ed] all the economic preconditions of capitalist production as eternal forms and only desire[d] to eliminate capital, which is both the basis and necessary

---

[61] cf. K. Marx, *Capital*, Vol. 3, p. 607: 'the illusions concerning the miraculous power of credit and the banking system, as nursed by some socialists, arise from a complete lack of familiarity with the capitalistic mode of production and the credit system as one of its forms'.
[62] J. F. Bray, *Labour's Wrongs*, p. 123.
[63] ibid. p. 171.
[64] ibid. p. 172.
[65] For Hodgskin, free trade was an abiding concern; see, for example, his *Lecture on Free Trade* (London, 1843) and his spell as a journalist with the *Economist*, E. Halévy, *Thomas Hodgskin*, pp. 184–8.
[66] This is the line of argument pursued in *Labour Defended against the Claims of Capital*.

consequence (of these pre-conditions)'.⁶⁷ For Hodgskin, capital could be eliminated by purging the exchange process of its pathological features.

Thompson too, particularly in the first 366 pages of the *Inquiry*, stressed the economic benefits which would accrue from more perfectly functioning markets.⁶⁸ Thus he saw 'really free competition' as a 'protecting aegis', argued for freedom in the direction of labour and 'the free interchange of the products of labor' and condemned those social and economic arrangements which obstructed the untrammelled operation of market forces.⁶⁹ Indeed, it is fair to say that in the *Inquiry* Thompson adhered to the view that most labour exploitation would cease and much greater equality of wealth distribution would be secured if the economy functioned on a more purely competitive basis.⁷⁰

In this earlier work it was Thompson's 'moral economy', his awareness of the deleterious social and ethical consequences of free competition which led him to stress the need for social and institutional arrangements from which the attrition of the market

---

⁶⁷ K. Marx, *Theories of Surplus Value*, Vol. 3, p. 260.

⁶⁸ Thompson stressed the need to remove all obstacles to what he termed 'the natural laws of distribution' which he saw as operating given the existence of 'free labor' and 'voluntary exchanges'. Thus Thompson advocated, among other things, the abolition of monopolies, bounties, guilds, apprenticeship regulations and the repeal of those 'laws or contrivances which control the rate of the wages of labor, diverting them from that standard to which the natural laws of distribution lead' such as those laws 'which aid combinations of capitalists ... to keep down the wages of labor' *Inquiry*, pp. 363–6.

⁶⁹ ibid. p. 125; also ibid. pp. 103–44 where Thompson discusses at inordinate length the adverse social and economic consequences of bounties and monopolies; also *Weekly Free Press and Co-operative Journal*, 5, 246 (1830), 4, Letter IV: 'The pretended system of competition is a gross falsehood on the very face of it; there is no freedom in it ... there is no competition at all, there is nothing but restraints ... I would make competition what it pretends to be, really free, not only between labourers ... but as between the labourers and all the rest of society.'

⁷⁰ *Inquiry*, p. 150: 'How far this approach to the blessings of equality may be carried, when all obstacles of force and fraud to the entire development of free labor and voluntary exchanges shall have been removed ... it would be hazardous to predict. *That it would approach very nearly to Mr Owen's system of mutual co-operation by common labor, there can be no doubt*' (my emphasis); see also ibid. p. 590: 'it has been proved that a strict adherence for the future to the natural laws of distribution, for labor, entire use of its products and voluntary exchange ... would ... gradually put all productive laborers in possession of the several articles, under the name of capital, which are necessary to them to enable them to gather the fruits of their industry'.

place had been purged. In the *Inquiry*, therefore, Thompson went on in the final third of the work to attack even 'really free competition', not because it would deprive the labourer of a significant portion of the produce of his labour but because it dehumanised Man by the corrosion of his social nature[71] and the debasement of all human qualities to the status of commodities – 'nothing in life is too sacred not to find its price in money'.[72]

In the *Inquiry*, therefore, Thompson's stress on the need for a transcendence of the market economy was a function of his critique of the moral and social consequences of competitive capitalism.[73] Thus as far as this work is concerned a distinction should be made between the policy prescriptions which Thompson derived from his economic critique of early industrial capitalism, prescriptions designed to create the conditions necessary for the smooth functioning of a market economy, and those derived from his moral economy, which stressed the need for communities of mutual co-operation which would foster attitudes and behaviour ethically and socially superior to those which characterised capitalism.

In *Labor Rewarded*, however, Thompson's attitude to individual competition was markedly more hostile. For, even in its purest, freest form it was seen as generating significant inequalities; dispensing rewards more often on the basis of chance than of justice, equity or merit. Thus Thompson wrote, 'The "higgling of the market" will never effect a just remuneration to all, though equal laws and equal means of knowledge prevailed', for remuneration was 'no where regulated by calculations of difficulty, hardship, unhealthiness, strength, skill, utility of the work ... but by a variety of accidents and chances, comprised in the phrase "proportion of supply to demand"'.[74] Thus in his

---

[71] 'Rivalry and distrust, the necessary effects of competition, universally prevail ... a universal fever of excitement not to increase enjoyment but to outrun each other, runs through society and ... sometimes the glaring effects of insanity are produced, sometimes self-destruction', *Practical Directions for the Speedy and Economical Establishment of Communities* (London, 1830), pp. 199–200.

[72] ibid.

[73] 'It is evidently for the interest of society, and even *more as to happiness from all other sources than from mere immediate wealth*, that as much as possible of human labor should be performed by mutual co-operation; in preference to the system of individual exertion and competition', *Inquiry*, p. 592 (my emphasis).

[74] W. Thompson, *Labor Rewarded*, p. 33.

later work the market economy had to be replaced by communities of mutual co-operation not just because they provided an environment in which salutary moral qualities could flourish but because they were the only means by which exploitation might be eliminated and the labourer guaranteed the products of his labour.

So here we have a Ricardian socialist prepared, on the basis of his economic critique of capitalism, to advocate something more than the refurbishing of the market economy. Here again, however, as with the policy prescriptions elaborated by Hodgskin, Gray and Bray, exploitation was to be eliminated via the elimination of unequal exchanges. Thus as Thompson wrote in *Labor Rewarded*,

even the unions of large numbers of the industrious possessing all the materials and implements requisite to make their labor productive, would not, if directed to the manufacture of any one article, or of various articles for sale in the common market of competition, secure to such industrious the whole products of their labor in any other articles consumed by them and acquired in exchange for ... articles ... by them fabricated ... For all other articles of their consumption they must pay the advanced cost of competition ... The profits of the grower, landlord, manufacturer, carrier and wholesale dealer they would still be compelled to pay.[75]

So, in so far as exchange continued to exist labourers would be exploited in the sense of being denied the full product of their labours. The great advantage of the fully fledged communities which Thompson advocated, therefore, was that goods, for the most part, would be produced in proportions dictated by their perceived social utility and distributed equally without the need for exchange. It was for this reason that members of co-operative communities would be free from exploitation or, as Thompson put it, free from 'the defalcations of exchanges':[76] '*In proportion to the number of articles consumed by them, which they produce and supply to each other, will be the advance which they make towards the possession of the whole products of their labor.*'[77]

For Thompson, therefore, the co-operative community was

[75] ibid. pp. 115–16.
[76] ibid. p. 103
[77] ibid. p. 116 (Thompson's emphasis).

not only to be a haven of social virtue, it was also to be an autarkic sanctuary – 'self-supplying unions of the industrious'[78] – from which the possibility of exploitation had been banished along with the need to exchange.[79] If the exchange mechanism could not be rationalised or reformed it should be abolished. Yet there was a price to be paid and this took the form of a retreat from the economic world as it existed – 'Unite in large numbers, and withdraw yourselves from the sources of misery.'[80] Thus Thompson's understanding of exploitation as 'undervaluing the thing to be acquired or overvaluing the thing to be given'[81] led on to an unshakeably optimistic political economy of autarky which more often stressed the need to borrow capital than to challenge it.[82]

Thus their particular 'Smithian' conception of exploitation as rooted in exchange led Hodgskin, Thompson, Gray and Bray to present essentially reformist solutions to working-class exploitation and impoverishment. There was no need to expropriate the expropriators; no need to seize the property of those whose wealth had been accumulated by the exploitation of labour. They did not wish to interfere 'With the profits of general society already accumulated and formed into capital'; what they wanted was to 'prevent the future growth of any such excrescences'.[83] Exploitation would cease, existing accumulations of capital would wither away and capitalists, stripped of their economic power, would be forced to labour productively for their daily bread, once the system had been set on a rational and equitable footing or once the whole need to exchange had been eliminated.

Yet why, leaving aside the inherently abstract and difficult nature of the exposition, did Ricardo's *Principles* not provide the starting point for Ricardian socialist political economy? Why did Thompson, Hodgskin, Gray and Bray not use the theoretical

---

[78] ibid.
[79] Thompson did accept that initially exchanges would have to be made with capitalist producers for necessities which could not be provided, or at least only at high cost, by the community. He looked forward, however, to a time when those exchanges which did take place were exclusively between communities on the basis of labour for labour.
[80] ibid. p. 109.
[81] ibid. p. 12.
[82] See, for example, ibid. p. 114.
[83] W. Thompson, *Inquiry*, p. 403.

foundations laid by Ricardo as the basis for the development of their own economic theories? Certainly statements to the effect that labour was 'the foundation of all value'[84] and that it was 'the quantity of labour realised in commodities' which regulated their 'exchangeable value',[85] and Ricardo's whole emphasis upon the special value-creating capacity of labour,[86] might have been expected to recommend Ricardo's political economy to those who wrote from a working-class standpoint. Indeed, at a cruder level, such statements became the stuff of popular political economy, paraphrased and regurgitated in a hundred different forms by writers in the working-class press of the later 1820s and early 1830s.[87] Similarly, Ricardo's emphasis upon distribution as a fundamental economic question[88] and the suggestion of a necessary antagonism between wages and profits,[89] which appeared to follow from his analysis, might also have been expected to endear him to writers such as the Ricardian socialists. So why, with all its superficial attractions, did British socialist and anti-capitalist writers fail to use Ricardian analysis, as Marx did, to provide the foundation for a political economy critical of capitalism?

The answer to this question would seem to be that the Ricardian socialists failed to use Ricardo because they could not easily derive from his writing on value an explanation for the contemporary existence of profit or exploitation. Ricardo in the opening pages of the *Principles* had pointed out the inconsistencies in Smithian value theory. He had lamented that:

Adam Smith who so accurately defined the original source of exchangeable value and who was bound in consistency to maintain that all things became more or less valuable in proportion as more or less labour was bestowed on their production has himself created another standard of value ... after most ably showing the insufficiency

---

[84] D. Ricardo, *Principles*, p. 20.
[85] ibid. p. 13.
[86] 'It is true that Ricardo seems to accord labour a special role in value creation – treating it as, in some sense, the source of value', S. G. Hollander, *The Economics of David Ricardo*, p. 263.
[87] See below, pp. 138-9.
[88] 'To determine the laws which regulate ... distribution, is the principal problem in Political Economy', D. Ricardo, *Principles*, p. 5.
[89] 'I have endeavoured to show ... that a rise of wages would not raise the price of commodities, but would invariably lower profits'; 'profits would be high or low in proportion as wages were low or high', ibid. pp. 127, 110.

of a variable medium such as gold and silver, [he] has himself by fixing on corn or labour, chosen a medium no less variable.[90]

In contrast, Ricardo made 'the comparative quantity of labour, which is necessary to their production, the rule which determines the respective quantities of goods which shall be given in exchange for each other'[91] and added that labour itself exchanged at its 'natural', labour-embodied value, namely, 'the price which is necessary to enable labourers ... to subsist and perpetuate their race'.[92] How then could exploitation occur when, as the Ricardian socialists desired, the labour-embodied law of value did actually prevail? Or as Marx phrased the question in his *Contribution to a Critique of Political Economy*, 'how does production on the basis of exchange-value solely determined by labour-time lead to the result that the exchange-value of labour is less than the exchange-value of its product?'[93]

It was here that Smith's inconsistencies had more to offer the Ricardian socialists than Ricardo's more rigorous analysis. What these inconsistencies did was to suggest a deviation of the real from the ideal. In particular Smithian political economy implied a change in the nature of exchange relations with the emergence of the capitalist and the wage labourer and suggested that different factors now governed the determination of exchange value from those which had determined it when, in the early and rude state, the labourer had received his whole product. To comprehend this was, for the Ricardian socialists, to understand the origins, nature and contemporary causes of labour exploitation.

It was left to Marx to show how the greater theoretical consistency of Ricardo could be used to provide the basis for a theory of labour exploitation and that even when commodities (labour included) did exchange at their natural, labour values, this did not herald the end of exploitation. As Engels put it,

The more strongly ... earlier Socialism denounced the exploitation of the working class, inevitable under capitalism, the less able was it clearly to show in what this exploitation consisted and how it arose ... This was done by the discovery of surplus value. It was

---

[90] ibid. p. 14.
[91] ibid. p. 88.
[92] ibid. p. 93.
[93] K. Marx, *Contribution to a Critique of Political Economy* (London, Lawrence and Wishart, 1971), p. 62.

shown that the appropriation of unpaid labour is the basis of the capitalist mode of production and of the exploitation of the worker that occurs under it; *that even if the capitalist buys the labour-power of his labourer at its full value as a commodity on the market, he yet extracts more value from it than he paid for.*[94]

Marx did not have to rely on a putative deviation of market prices from natural values or abandon the Ricardian theory of value to explain the origin and nature of labour exploitation. For Marx commodities exchanged at their full labour-embodied values under capitalism, yet exploitation both existed and increased in intensity. As one commentator has put it, 'The notion of exploitation in Marx does not depend on ... imperfections. The important task is to explain exploitation in a world free of imperfections however real they may be.'[95]

Marx was the only Ricardian socialist. Hodgskin, Gray, Thompson and Bray may be more appropriately designated 'Smithian'. Those commentators who have seen the Ricardian socialists as precursors of Marx[96] have mistaken a similarity of

---

[94] F. W. Engels, *Socialism, Utopian and Scientific* (London, Allen, 1911), p. 43 (my emphasis).

[95] M. Desai, *Marxian Economic Theory* (London, Gray Mills, 1974), p. 10; or as P. A. Samuelson put it, 'Marx might have emphasized the monopoly elements of distribution: how wicked capitalists, possessed of the nonlabour tools that are essential to high production ... gang up on the workers and make them work for a minimum ... the monopoly explanation he did not use, perhaps because he wanted to let capitalism choose its own weapons and assume ruthless competition, and still be able to show it up', '*Economists and the history of ideas*,' 13. The point is surely that if exploitation was simply a function of monopoly power then exploitation might be eliminated assuming a capitalist capacity for self-reform which would purge markets of their imperfections. Marx was not sufficient of a classical economist to be able to accept this.

[96] See, for example, B. Potter, *The Co-operative Movement in Great Britain*, p. 47; M. Hovell, *The Chartist Movement*, p. 31; J. Kimball, *The Economic Doctrines of John Gray*, p. 130; A. Gray, *The Socialist Tradition*, pp. 295–6; H. S. Foxwell, Introduction to A. Menger, *The Right to the Whole Produce*, pp. iii–iv; A. Briggs, 'The language of class in early nineteenth century England', in A. Briggs and J. Saville (eds.), *Essays in Labour History in Memory of G. D. H. Cole* (London, Macmillan, 1967), p. 65; E. K. Hunt, 'Value theory in the writings of the classical economists', *History of Political Economy*, 9 (1977), 322–45; E. Roll, *History of Economic Thought*, p. 250; E. K. Hunt, 'Utilitarianism and the labour theory of value', *History of Political Economy*, 11 (1979), 561. In a somewhat confusing article this writer states that Thompson wished to distinguish himself from 'those radical social critics who advocated the forceful overthrow of the capitalists property system', ibid. 569. In the aftermath of the Cato Street fiasco it would be interesting to know which social critics the writer of this article believes that Thompson had in mind.

terminology and rhetoric for a similarity of analytical form.[97] For the Smithian socialists exploitation was, fundamentally, the product of an imperfect market mechanism; for Marx even a perfect market, even really free competition, would fail to prevent economic exploitation and the impoverishment of the labouring classes.

What Marx did was to clarify the nature of capitalist productive relations. He showed that profit arose and exploitation existed not as a result of the abrogation of the natural laws of value but rather as a consequence of adherence to them in an historical situation where the labourer was alienated from the means of production and vulnerable, therefore, to the direct appropriation of the surplus value which he produced, at the point of production. Exploitation resulted not from the addition of profit and rent to the value of labour embodied in a commodity but as a result of the straightforward appropriation of unpaid labour by the capitalist.[98]

---

[97] By far the most persuasive case for seeing the Ricardian socialists as anticipating the essentials of Marxian political economy has been made by J. E. King, 'Utopian or scientific? A reconsideration of the Ricardian socialists', *History of Political Economy*, 15 (1983), 345–73. King effectively demolishes the crude Marxian accusation against the Ricardian socialists that they derived their value theory and concept of exploitation from moral arguments, thereby committing the sin of utopianism, see e.g. E. K. Hunt, 'The relation of the Ricardian socialists to Ricardo and Marx', *Science and Society*, 44 (1980), 196–7. Ricardian socialism was indeed, as King argues, more than a *mélange* of vituperative ethical pronouncements. The Ricardian socialists did have a concept of 'surplus value' (though if Hall and Ravenstone are to be included they more often deployed a concept of 'surplus produce') and they did argue that this surplus value was created by labour. However, the important point is surely that their explanation of the manner in which that surplus was appropriated was fundamentally different from that of Marx. There may be a few hints (J. E. King, 'Utopian or scientific?' 354) that on this question the Ricardian socialists were feeling their way in a Marxian direction but as King himself points out there are also numerous 'hints' which may be used to render them guilty of the charge of 'utopianism', ibid. 348. How then do we determine the 'authentic' Ricardian socialist position on exploitation? The question is obviously a difficult one but we can surely say that the concept of exploitation with which we credit them should at least be consistent with the means they suggest to eliminate that exploitation and as these were largely concerned with the rationalisation or abolition of exchange, it would seem legitimate to assume that for Hodgskin, Bray, Gray and Thompson at any rate, exploitation was located in the exchange process. One should therefore guard against confusing Marx-like flourishes with Marxian analysis.

[98] It occurred at the point of production not in the realm of exchange.

However, while Bray, Gray, Thompson and Hodgskin may be labelled Smithian, the question of the extent to which their economic thinking was influenced by Robert Owen still remains. Should they as political economists be denominated the 'Owenite socialists'?

Only a tentative answer can be given to this question. John Gray specifically discounted Owen's influence, stating that while he had read some of Owen's works, he had only done so after the essentials of his political economy had already been elaborated.[99] Indeed, in *The Social System* Gray directly criticised Owen for failing 'on the three great subjects of production, exchange and distribution, to explain his views sufficiently to make them a fair subject of criticism'.[100]

Thompson was undoubtedly influenced by Owen as regards his general approach to economic and social questions. His criticism of the narrowness of 'political' economy and his categorisation of himself as a moral economist provide one indication of his wider, Owenite approach to economic questions. Nevertheless, his *Inquiry* must be seen as an infinitely more sophisticated, detailed, cogent and sustained piece of economic writing than anything produced by Owen. In addition, Thompson's disagreements with Owen[101] show that he was very far from being an uncritical Owenite acolyte.

The influence of Owen upon Hodgskin can be altogether discounted. Hodgskin was a proponent and defender of a radical, anarchic individualism against legal, institutional, political and other constraints and Owenite or co-operative communities were as much a human perversion of the natural laws which should govern the functioning of the economic world as existing social and economic arrangements. Like Smith, Hodgskin was suspicious of those men, wise in their own conceit, who felt they could improve upon the artifices of Nature. In addition Hodgskin criticised those such as the supporters of 'Mr Owen's co-operative societies ... who have asserted that all the evils of society arise from a right of property ... I look on the right of [private]

---

[99] J. Gray, *Social System*, pp. 340–1.
[100] ibid. p. 370.
[101] For Thompson's disagreements with Owen see R. K. P. Pankhurst, *William Thompson*, pp. 170–4, and the *Proceedings of the Third Co-operative Conference* (London, 1832), reported by W. Carpenter.

property... as essential to the welfare and even the continued existence of society.'[102]

However, two aspects in particular of their theoretical approach to labour exploitation distinguish the political economy of the Smithian socialists from that of Robert Owen. First, they did not hesitate to condemn explicitly those social classes and groupings which they considered to be the instigators and beneficiaries of labour exploitation. Thus Hodgskin attacked the capitalist for growing rich not by saving 'but by doing something which enabled him, according to some conventional usage, to obtain more of the produce of other men's labour',[103] this something being the role he played as 'middleman' in 'oppressing the labourer'.[104] For Hodgskin it was the capitalists who were the main beneficiaries of the economic oppression suffered by the labouring classes; 'It is, therefore, now time that the reproaches so long cast on the feudal aristocracy should be heaped on capital, and capitalists.'[105] Profit not rent was the main burden carried by labour. It was not rent which broke 'the back, and to give it up would not break the heart of labourer. The landlord's share therefore, does not keep the labourer poor.'[106]

Thompson was equally emphatic as to the beneficiaries of exploitation:

A universal and always vigilant conspiracy of capitalists... exists everywhere, because founded on a universally existing interest, to cause the laborers to toil for the lowest possible and to wrest as much as possible of the products of their labor, to swell the accumulations and expenditure of capitalists.[107]

And he was quick to detail 'the atrocious powers of [the] combination laws, of wages regulation,... corporation and thousand other, expedients of insecurity, by which capitalists extract labor and life from the ignorant and wretched'.[108]

For Gray, capitalists were 'unproductive', living solely on the 'interest of money', this interest representing wealth taken from

[102] T. Hodgskin, *The Natural and Artificial Rights of Property Contrasted*, p. 24.
[103] T. Hodgskin, *Popular Political Economy*, p. 248.
[104] T. Hodgskin, *Labour Defended*, p. 27; see also ibid. p. 21.
[105] ibid. p. 19n.
[106] ibid. p. 6.
[107] W. Thompson, *Inquiry*, p. 171.
[108] ibid. p. 500.

its producers and 'obtained by persons who buy... labour... at one price, and sell it at another';[109] while Bray saw the capitalist as selling or exchanging 'the produce of labour for a greater sum than the labour originally costs him', thus increasing 'his store of wealth'.[110] This transaction between capitalist and producer Bray saw as 'a palpable deception, a mere farce'.[111]

Secondly, linked to this condemnation of the economic role of the capitalist went a perception of his necessarily antagonistic relation to labour. Thus Hodgskin wrote, 'Wages vary inversely as profits; or wages rise when profits fall... and it is therefore profits, or the capitalist's share of the national produce, which is opposed to wages, or the share of the labourer.'[112] Thompson similarly considered that 'the higher the profits of capital – other things remaining the same – the lower must be the wages of labor'; 'the real interest of the capitalist, as such, is always and necessarily opposed to the interest of the laborer... the object of the capitalists is not to increase the general capital of the community but to make most... profit for themselves'.[113] Likewise Bray believed that 'the gain of the capitalist and the rich man is always the loss of the workman... so long as there is inequality of exchanges'.[114]

The Smithian socialists not only outlined the general economic conditions and provided a theoretical explanation of the mechanisms which permitted and facilitated exploitation, they were also quite clear as to the identity of the exploiters. For them labour exploitation was a systematic process of value abstraction from the labouring classes and the beneficiary was the capitalist. Thus, unlike Owen, they did elaborate a clearly articulated theory of labour exploitation. Their economic writings were more acerbic in character, more aggressively critical of existing economic arrangements, more defensive of working-class economic interests and more antagonistic towards those of the capitalists than were the economic writings of

[109] J. Gray, *Lecture on Human Happiness*, pp. 26, 70.
[110] J. F. Bray, *Labour's Wrongs*, p. 47.
[111] ibid. p. 50.
[112] T. Hodgskin, *Labour Defended*, p. 5.
[113] W. Thompson, *Inquiry*, p. 241.
[114] J. F. Bray, *Labour's Wrongs*, p. 53.

Robert Owen.[115] As such their political economy was bound to have greater popular appeal in a period of increasing class hostility.

The achievement of the Smithian socialists was to fill a theoretical lacuna in the analytical weaponry available to the working classes. They explained poverty and exploitation in the language of political economy rather than the rhetoric of natural rights, money juggles, the 'Thing', pensioners, placemen and royal extravagance, which had characterised the critical economic work of previous writers. In this sense their political economy represented a marked advance on the work of Spence, Ogilvie, Paine and Cobbett. In contrast to works such as *Paper against Gold* and the *Decline of the English System of Finance*, the Smithian socialists located exploitation within the economic system rather than explaining it in terms of factors exogenous to the system's functioning. These writers provided, therefore, an economic explanation of poverty and a body of ideas and analysis which could and was taken up and counterposed to the apologetics of the classical popularisers. Thus writers in the working-class press of the late 1820s and early 1830s had to hand an alternative explanation of labour's impoverished material condition to that furnished by the classical economists and their popularisers; an explanation which had as its basis a theory of labour exploitation and which when popularly purveyed sent writers such as Martineau, Place, Knight, Ure, Tufnell and others scurrying to take up their apologetic pens with a vengeance in the early 1830s.[116]

In elaborating an economic theory of labour exploitation the Smithian socialists provided one of the two main theoretical pillars for a popular, working-class, political economy. This was a definite achievement. Yet it must be stressed once again that the form of their analysis led them to see exploitation as an aberration of the market mechanism, a distortion of the exchange process, a deviation from natural economic laws and, therefore, led them to believe that the key to its elimination lay in the rationalisation of exchange rather than any direct appropriation of the means of production.

[115] See above, pp. 77-81.
[116] See below, pp. 155-9.

5

The theory of labour exploitation and the working-class press 1816–30

The approach of the radical and co-operative press 1816–24

In order to formulate a general theory of labour exploitation, it was necessary for writers to provide answers to a number of questions. First, given the diversity of productive activity in which labour was involved, it was important to determine what constituted economic value; secondly, it was necessary to decide who or what produced it; thirdly, reasons had to be given for believing that the value input of one group of producers was not matched by their value receipts; fourthly, it was necessary to establish the beneficiaries of this; and finally, it had to be shown that the deviation of group or individual value inputs from value receipts was not a once-and-for-all phenomenon but rather part of a systematic process of value abstraction from producers.

In attempting to explain the origin and nature of labour exploitation writers in the radical press worked without any coherent theory of what produced or constituted economic value.[1] It can of course be argued that, in general terms, they regarded labour as the essential constituent of all goods and services of economic worth but what writers in the radical press tended to produce was a vindication of the noble nature or social 'value' of labour rather than a labour theory of value. In effect

[1] The one major exception being the *Gorgon*.

they elaborated a defence of the utility, dignity, status and primacy of labour and, by association, of the labouring classes; 'the real strength and all the resources of a country, ever have sprung and ever must spring, from the labour of its people'; 'there can exist no riches and no resources which they [the labouring classes] by their labour have not assisted to create ... even the land itself would be good for nothing without [their] labour'; 'it is the labour of the poor that gives currency to wealth, that originally created what we call treasure and still continues to increase it'; 'those who labour being the only productive classes in the community, [are] the creators of all wealth, whether in lands, commerce, trade or navigation'.[2]

Such general assertions seemed sufficient. These writers perceived no need to develop an economic theory of value or to draw upon those already expounded. They were not primarily concerned after all with elaborating the theoretical basis for a popular political economy but rather with giving added substance to their demand that the suffrage should be extended to the labouring classes. Labour was property and the creator of all property: 'labour is the foundation and sole foundation of all property'; 'agricultural and commercial property would be of no value whatever were it not for the labour which is bestowed on it'; 'what is property or what is the value of a dirty spot of earth before the hand of industry makes it fruitful? Is not labour then the very basis of property and has not every man a property in the labour of his hands?'[3] If property, therefore, was considered to be a necessary qualification for the possession of the franchise, its creators were surely justified in claiming their share of political power, the major share as befitted their economic role and status as property creators.

It is hardly surprising, therefore, with the main focus of attention on essentially political matters, that there was insufficient consistency in the remarks of radical writers even to allow us to

---

[2] *Cobbett's Twopenny Register*, 31, 18 (1816), col. 545, 'To the Journeymen and Labourers of England'; ibid. col. 560; *Black Dwarf*, 1, 3 (1817), col. 35; *Northern Reformers' Monthly Magazine and Political Register*, 1, 4 (1823), 136, 'Petition approved at the General Meeting of Reformers of Newcastle', Resolution 3.

[3] *Cobbett's Twopenny Register*, 34, 13 (1818), col. 386; *Medusa*, 36 (1820), 282, a contribution signed 'Radical Reformer'; *Northern Reformers'*, 1, 1 (1823), 15, reported remarks of E. MacKenzie at a 'Newcastle Meeting on Hunt's Liberation'.

assume that they had in mind something approximating to a labour theory of value. Indeed, labour was viewed very often as merely 'one of the articles of value'[4] and land was frequently considered of equal or superior value-creating importance; 'In using the term productive power, we do not mean labour which is *also* a productive power, but *the land the primary productive power*';[5] while agriculture was often considered in physiocratic terms as the only truly productive activity: 'There is no species of wealth or power, which does not spring from Agriculture, and if that perish all must perish'; 'The earth is the only barterer with whom we can always make a profitable exchange.'[6] For many radical writers, therefore, it was obviously some combination of land and labour which was productive of economic value. This cannot be dignified as a theory of value.

Yet whatever their range of views on what caused and what constituted economic value, many writers in the radical press were certainly at one in believing that the value input of the labouring classes was not matched by the economic value of their wages. Assertions to this effect were a constant theme in the columns of these papers. Cobbett, in particular, articulated such sentiments with characteristic force: 'The fruit of labour is now taken and given to unproductive labour ... This is the cause and the only cause of the miseries of the country'; 'It is the sum taken from those who labour and given to unproductive labour that has produced all our present misery.'[7] However, the idea finds expression in other papers besides the *Twopenny Register*. The *Medusa* saw 'industry' as meeting everywhere 'with starvation instead of reward', with 'sloth and pride [living] in splendour upon the fruits of industrious toil'; the *Black Dwarf* considered that it was 'the plunder of the labourer' which had produced 'the immense fortunes made at Manchester and its vicinity'; while *An Address and Petition of the Distressed Mechanics of Birmingham* stated that although,

---

[4] *Cobbett's Twopenny Register*, 34, 25 (1819), col. 767.
[5] *Republican*, 6, 19 (1822), 578 (my emphasis).
[6] *Cobbett's Twopenny Register*, 32, 5 (1817), col. 138, 'Letter to Lord Sidmouth'; *Black Dwarf*, 3, 1 (1819), col. 2.
[7] *Cobbett's Twopenny Register*, 32, 5 (1817), col. 140, 'Letter to Lord Sidmouth'; ibid. 31, 22 (1816), col. 691, 'Letter to the Luddites'.

In former times the labour of an Englishman could procure a sufficient quantity of the Good Things of Life... And we presume to believe that the Labour of an Englishman is still competent to produce a far greater quantity of the Good Things of Life than his humble Maintenance requires... some cause which we cannot understand, has deprived Industry of its Reward and has left us without Employment.[8]

This constant articulation of the fact of exploitation was important, for it undoubtedly directed the attention of working-class readers to matters and grievances economic, even if the greater part of the radical press was dominated by the discussion of more purely political or religious (anti-clerical) concerns. This repetition of the fact of exploitation pointed to the need for a popular political economy to explain it; a popular political economy which could explain that 'cause which we cannot understand' which had 'deprived Industry of its Reward'.

However, while writers in the radical press accepted the existence of labour exploitation, the absence of any attempt to formulate even a crude theory of value and distribution made it difficult for them to explain it in *economic* terms or to see it as part of an *economic* process. Thus exploitation tended to be seen as a product of factors exogenous to the functioning of the economic system rather that as endogenous to the functioning of a particular set of economic arrangements. Writers in the radical press saw labour exploitation as a product of actions and decisions made with consciously exploitative intent but extrinsic to the sphere of general economic activity, i.e. as a product of legislative or political rather than economic action.

For example, the Bank Restriction Act of 1797, which suspended the convertibility of the currency into gold and created the 'paper money system', was seen by most radical writers as a prime cause of the material depredations suffered by the labouring classes. 'What is the principal cause of that ruin and misery which now pervades the land and which makes the life of the industrious man hardly worth preserving?' asked Cobbett, answering that 'the cause is the existence of a paper system, by means of which the... earnings of the industrious, are taken from them in proportions so large as to... produce... that monster in civil

---

[8] *Medusa*, 1 (1819), 1, article by 'Probus'; *Black Dwarf*, 3, 44 (1819), col. 714; *Birmingham Inspector*, 8 (1817), 155.

society, starvation in the midst of abundance'.[9] For a correspondent to Carlile's *Republican* also, it was the case that 'the power of the Government, by the alternate issue of gold and paper, to make purchase at whatever price they please', allowed them 'progressively to become the proprietors and vendors of all the property in the country'.[10] Thus again it was the political power to juggle with the currency which was the primary cause of the exploitation of labour. Similarly the editor of the *People* believed that it was 'By Mr Pitt's paper money system [that] the labouring classes of society were deprived not only of everything like superfluity but of everything they could part with, without parting with life'[11] while the *London Alfred* asserted that it was 'a fictitious paper Currency', which had 'enabled knaves, monopolisers, forestallers and regraters, to enrich themselves out of the wages of the labour of the more honest toiling poor'.[12]

Explanations of the manner in which this exploitative 'Act' took effect varied. Cobbett believed that it resulted in the compulsion to pay in an appreciated medium of exchange (after the return to cash payments in 1819) debts contracted in terms of a depreciated currency; paying in gold what had been contracted in paper.[13] A writer in the *Medusa* saw the Bank Restriction Act of 1797 as providing for the creation of 'a false capital ... by which hellish means speculators can purchase and monopolise the staff of life' and then retail it to the public at a monopoly price, while the editor of the *People* saw exploitation as resulting from a rigidity of money wages in the face of a rise in the general level of prices precipitated by an increase in the supply of paper money. Thus the editor of the *People* considered that 'the increase and diminution of money or the circulating medium [are] equally evils to the labouring classes [for] the increase of money tends to give ... activity to employments but it always raises the price of an article before that of labour and always in a higher degree too'. It was the case, therefore, that

[9] *Cobbett's Twopenny Register*, 37, 23 (1820), col. 1568, 'Second Letter to Lord Grey'.
[10] *Republican*, 6, 28 (1822), a letter signed H. Fish.
[11] *People*, 12 (1817), 370.
[12] *London Alfred*, 12 (1819), 91, 'Address to the Prince Regent from a London Meeting on the Manchester Massacres'.
[13] Among numerous occasions when Cobbett expounded such views see *Cobbett's Twopenny Register*, 33, 6 (1818), col. 181; ibid. 34, 6 (1818), col. 167; ibid. 35, 4 (1819), col. 116; ibid. 36, 1 (1820), col. 9; ibid. 36, 3 (1820), col. 207.

'the great cause of the decrease of wages was that their normal increase did not go on so fast as the depreciation of the currency'.[14]

For these writers, therefore, it was the exogenous factors of the Bank Restriction Act and the return to cash payments which were the primary cause of the exploitation suffered by the working classes. Where such legislative machinations did not result in the direct appropriation of the products of labour they set in motion economic forces which provided ample opportunity for others so to do.

One of the major evils of this legislative interference in the workings of the economy was that it facilitated manipulation of the monetary standard of value,[15] the 'sole cement of society', 'without which no contracts can be made and no trade carried on'.[16] Such manipulation made 'everything uncertain'. 'Every contract made under a system of paper money is liable to be violated every hour, by those who have it in their power to change the value of paper.'[17] However, while the manipulation of contracts might be perpetrated by individuals and groups operating within the economic system, the opportunity for such malign manipulation was exogenously provided.

Another primary cause of exploitation whose origin was exogenous to the workings of the economy was taxation. Richard Carlile, for example, saw exploitation and taxation as effectively synonymous, so 'whatever strips industry of its produce *is* taxation'[18] and most radical writers of the period from Waterloo to Peterloo would have agreed with him. Thus Cobbett stated simply that 'all the miseries of the labouring classes arise from taxation', while a writer in the *Medusa* informed the working classes that, 'The inroads they [taxes] have made in the value of your labour is far beyond conception.'[19]

Taxation was seen as producing its deleterious consequences

---

[14] *Medusa*, 4 (1817), 28, article signed 'Homo'; *People*, 12 (1817), 370–1, 'What is to be done next?'; ibid. 3 (1817), 80, 'Plan for the Removal and Prevention of Distress, Poor Rates and Mendicity'.
[15] See, for example, *Cobbett's Twopenny Register*, 33, 6 (1818), col. 181.
[16] ibid. 34, 25 (1819) cols. 771–2; also ibid. 35, 3 (1819), col. 82, for Cobbett's belief in the need for and benefits of a stable standard of value.
[17] ibid. 34, 22 (1819), col. 687.
[18] *Republican*, 6, 11 (1821), 338 (my emphasis).
[19] *Cobbett's Twopenny Register*, 32, 33 (1817), col. 1031; *Medusa*, 20 (1819), 144.

in a number of ways. It increased the cost of food and thus reduced the real wages of the labourer;[20] it forced the labourer to 'work constantly for [his] lords and masters';[21] it reduced employment and increased labour's impoverishment by diminishing the wages fund[22] and even a constant level of taxation reduced real wages in a period of falling prices.[23] Again, however, the important point is that in the minds of popular writers exploitation in this form was a product of external factors impinging upon the realm of normal economic activity. This is further emphasised by a cursory examination of the groupings, interests and individuals listed by these writers, as primarily responsible for the exploitation of labour. For the most part, those referred to as exploiters were defined in terms of their political or institutional rather than their economic role. Cobbett, indeed, specifically discounted the idea that such groupings as employers played a significant part in lowering wages,[24] although on occasion he might castigate them for their political pusillanimity, which allowed the impoverishment resulting from the abuses of legislative power to continue.

The real exploiters were 'the various agents of the borough tyrants',[25] i.e. the fundholders, sinecurists and placemen;[26] 'Kings, priests and nobles or satellites'[27] and 'the monied Tyrants of the Stock Exchange'.[28] These were the groups and individuals who

---

[20] See, for example, *Republican*, 2, 2 (1820), 43: 'The reduction [of taxation] would lessen the price of provision and increase labour and its value. Therefore the decrease of famine and misery can *only* be found in the ratio of the decrease of taxation' (my emphasis).
[21] ibid. 4, 5 (1820), 160.
[22] *Black Dwarf*, 1, 3 (1817), col. 35.
[23] See above, p. 116.
[24] *Cobbett's Twopenny Register*, 31, 18 (1816), col. 570: 'On the subject of lowering wages... you ought to consider that your employers cannot give to you, that which they have not.'
[25] ibid. 36, 6 (1820), col. 992: 'All that he [the labourer] earns beyond the bare means of subsistence is taken away by the various agents of the borough tyrants.'
[26] ibid.: 'The Fundholders receive and live upon part of the rents, profits and earnings of the rest of the nation'; also *Republican*, 1, 5 (1819), 72, where Carlile asserted that 'one third of the profits of... labour [was] required to furnish an interest to the imaginary property of the fundholder'.
[27] *Medusa*, 8 (1819), 58: 'Kings, priests and nobles or satellites... having the power of plundering the industrious classes of society'.
[28] *Black Dwarf*, 1, 12 (1817), col. 247, article signed 'Observer' on the Funding System.

intervened in the economic game to twist the rules to their advantage without actually playing the game itself.

Once again, though, John Wade's *Gorgon* distinguishes itself from the rest of the early radical press. During the lifetime of the paper Wade, for example, made a genuine attempt to formulate some kind of value theory to use as an economic tool of analysis. His 'theory' ended up embodying both Smithian and Ricardian elements. 'Dr Smith in his *Wealth of Nations*', wrote Wade, 'says that the price of every commodity is made up of one or more of these three components, namely, rent, labour, or profit'[29] and Wade proceeded to build upon this insight his own additive explanation of what determined the value of commodities: 'For the sake of greater simplicity, we shall say that the price of every article is made up of one or more of these four elements, namely, the price of raw material, the wages of labour, taxes and the profits of the merchant.'[30] He also saw the wages of labour, in classical fashion, as being determined by the forces of supply and demand:

> the price of labour, like that of every other commodity depends solely on the demand for it ... When the supply of labourers is greater than the demand, then owing to the competition among servants for masters, will the price of labour decline; on the other hand when the supply of labourers is less than the demand, then owing to the competition among masters for a servant will the price of labour advance.[31]

Here obviously the hand of Francis Place looms large.

An element of Ricardian value theory comes to the fore, however, in the course of an interesting defence of the benefits to be expected from a high-wage economy.[32] Thus Wade used Ricardo's views on value to counter the idea that high wages must necessarily entail high prices and ultimately the loss of foreign markets and a diminution of employment opportunities. Abandoning his earlier additive approach to the determination

---

[29] *Gorgon*, II (1818), 82.
[30] ibid.
[31] ibid.
[32] Interesting in the sense that no other anti-capitalist or socialist writer or populariser used Ricardo in this way against those who argued that high wages must prove counterproductive through the ruination of British trade.

of exchange values, Wade argued that an increase in wages did not add to the value of a commodity for that was already determined by the quantity of labour which it embodied. Rather, what an increase in wages did was to increase labour's and diminish capital's share of what was received from the sale of a commodity leaving the actual value at which it sold unchanged: 'Mr Ricardo in his *Principles of Political Economy* proves very clearly that the price of a commodity does not in the least depend on the amount of wages, but the quantity of labour expended in its production.'[33] Therefore, 'if wages advance then profits must fall, but the trade of the country is not at all effected [sic]; for it does not in the least alter the market price of commodities'[34] and similarly, if 'the price of labour were reduced one half, our merchants, neither in the home nor in the foreign market, would sell their manufactures a farthing cheaper'.[35] In effect Wade made explicit what he took to be the logical corollaries of Ricardo's labour theory of value[36] in order to substantiate his case for higher labourers' wages, while seemingly unconcerned that this contradicted his earlier championing of Smith, for whom a rise or fall in wages would have had a comparable effect upon prices.

Wade's emphasis on the distress produced by the exploitation of labour was certainly 'unclassical'[37] but his explanation of why labour failed to receive payment equal to its true value would have been accepted by most classical writers. Exploitation was seen by Wade as resulting from those factors which hindered the smooth functioning of the market. Sometimes these factors were external to the market such as the 'unjust laws which restrain[ed]

---

[33] *Gorgon*, 17 (1818), 132.
[34] ibid. Wade does not attempt to argue from this that the interests of capitalists and labourers are necessarily antagonistic though he does accept that 'an increase in the wages of journeymen is attended with a proportionate decrease in the profits of masters'.
[35] ibid.
[36] Of course Ricardo would have argued that whether the relative prices of particular products rose or fell when wages rose depended upon the proportions of fixed capital and labour used in their manufacture. If the proportion of capital to labour was relatively high then the price would fall, if it was relatively low then the price would rise, D. Ricardo, *Principles*, pp. 43–7.
[37] See, for example, *Gorgon*, 10 (1818), 80: 'we know that throughout the counties of York, Lancaster and Nottingham the wages of manufacturing industry are not only much less than formerly, but they do not in spite of the lengthened toil of the poor artisan afford the means of a comfortable subsistence'.

the free disposal of labour',[38] more often Wade drew the attention of his readers to those intrinsic to the functioning of the market economy itself. In 1818, for example, Wade considered that there existed 'a great demand for labour but no advancement in the price owing to a tacit agreement, combination, esprit du corps, or something else which prevailed among the masters'.[39] These combinations of masters were viewed as 'keeping labour below that price, to which it would naturally have risen' and employers were condemned for acting in this economically coercive fashion. Thus it was to the malfunctioning of the labour market that Wade pointed as the source of labour's exploited and distressed condition.

This suggestion that exploitation could be endogenously generated by the malfunctioning of the market led on to a consideration of the specifically economic role actually played by the exploiters. Thus it was the masters, manufacturers and combinations of masters who were seen as extorting 'exorbitant profits'[40] and it was further argued in the *Gorgon* that it was employers and masters who were responsible for 'the greatest encroachment on the labouring classes... the gradual extension of the hours of labour'.[41] In addition it was combinations of masters which prevented the market from ensuring that labour received adequate remuneration for its productive endeavours, 'keeping labour below that price to which it would naturally have risen'[42] and employers who robbed 'their workmen of that fair reward for their labour, which both justice and humanity assign'.[43]

Despite the articulation of such sentiments it must be said that the *Gorgon* throughout its life displayed the influence of Francis Place and the imprint, therefore, of popularised classical orthodoxy. In many ways the *Gorgon* was a child, if on occasion

---

[38] ibid. 26 (1818), 202; see also ibid. 17 (1818), 155, where Ricardo is approvingly quoted: 'Like all other contracts, wages should be left to the fair and free competition of the market and should not be controlled by the interference of the legislature.'
[39] ibid. 17 (1818), 130.
[40] ibid. 14 (1818), 112.
[41] ibid. Wade believed that what the labouring classes wanted was 'to share with them [manufacturers] the exorbitant profits they derive from their labour'.
[42] ibid. 13 (1818), 101.
[43] ibid. 17 (1818), 131.

an errant child, of classical political economy. Exploitation did exist but it might be eliminated if only individuals were allowed to function as free economic agents immune from state or collective coercion. The theory of labour exploitation here developed is thus in no way antagonistic to the classical paradigm. Adam Smith was as outspoken in his condemnation of the consequences of employers' combinations as was John Wade in the *Gorgon*.[44]

With the solitary, though important, exception of the *Gorgon*, exploitation as understood by writers in the radical press of the period 1816–24 was essentially the product of factors exogenous to the functioning of the economy such as money juggles, taxation and *ad hoc* individual expropriations. In effect, radical writers perceived the economic world as an aquarium in which all goes on swimmingly, or would except for the constant presence of a cat which periodically dips a paw to extract those material delicacies which best suit its palate. This rather than the permanent presence of sharks in the aquarium itself was the cause of those disturbances which continually agitated the water. Economic ills and disturbances were not interpreted by radical writers as originating within the economic system; rather, they had their origin outside it. Such an analysis may have given material substance to attacks upon the political status quo but it did not contribute much in theoretical terms to the formation of a popular, working-class political economy. Where the analysis of exploitation increased in sophistication, as in the *Gorgon*, its classical foundations served to constrain, though not altogether obscure, the radical nature of the insights which resulted.

The two co-operative papers of this period[45] also devoted space to an analysis of the causes of labour's emiseration. For writers in these papers it was labour which was the primary means of production, 'the real and only power of production beyond the spontaneous gifts of nature, is the labour of man ... Capital, then, so far from being the power or source of production, is itself the product of labour.'[46] Additionally labour, in conjunction with the capital which it created, also generated

---

[44] A. Smith, *The Wealth of Nations*, p. 84.
[45] *The Economist* and the *Mirror of Truth*; see bibliography for details.
[46] *Economist*, 7 (1821), 103.

a large surplus from which it derived little, if any, benefit. As one writer put it: 'the surplus wealth, created by useful inventions and skilful combinations of labour, has never been equitably distributed ... productive powers which are capable of producing more wealth than the world can consume, have not afforded one ounce of additional plenty to the poor'.[47] Labour was, therefore, denied its deserved reward and denied because the competitive nature of existing economic arrangements, among other things, produced an incorrect or inequitable market valuation of the worth of labour and other commodities. Owen's complaint, that the practice of putting 'a profit upon price for individual gain' led to 'a false estimate of all things ... everything [being] valued by its cost instead of its intrinsic worth', was quoted approvingly by the *Economist*,[48] the editor of which (George Mudie) had previously expressed a desire to establish 'not what the money price' of a good was, 'but what the real value is to society'.[49]

Such aspirations and such an understanding of exploitation in value terms led on naturally to a concern with the optimum standard of value and how the prices of goods were determined in the market. Owen was quoted by a writer in the *Economist* on the advantages of establishing a new standard of value, the writer believing that such a standard might eliminate the 'slavery' of an 'artificial system of wages',[50] and Owen's belief that the surplus produce of co-operative communities should be exchanged through the medium of labour notes rather than by means of money was also discussed. In addition the paper reproduced the Report of the Co-operative and Economical Society which, among other things, stressed the need for 'the fair exchange of produce for produce'.[51] These papers accepted Owen's belief that it was in the course of competitive exchange that the economic vulnerability of the labouring classes was made

---

[47] ibid. 2 (1821), 23; see also ibid. 5 (1821), 67: 'at present ... a day's labour is scarcely worth a day's subsistence and in many cases it is not worth that'.
[48] ibid. 32 (1821), 94.
[49] ibid. 30 (1821), 61: 'with reference to the new arrangements, [at Orbiston] it is exceedingly fallacious to estimate any of the products by their money value. We are to see not what the money price is, but what the real value is to society.'
[50] ibid. 10 (1821), 152, letter from 'J.F.'
[51] ibid. 3 (1821), 47.

manifest but the paper did differ from Owen to the extent that it emphasised the role of capital in exploiting that vulnerability. If exchange was the mechanism through which labour was exploited, it was capital which utilised it: 'when capital is rapidly accumulating it continually manifests a disposition to exact very great exertions of industry for a scanty remuneration'; 'Capital ... will traffic even in the blood and slavery of human victims, furnished by a whole quarter of the globe for the sake of its unrighteous increase.'[52]

However, if capital in the abstract was condemned for its exploitative activities, those who owned it seldom received the same acerbic treatment in the co-operative press. Thus writers in the *Economist* went out of their way to deny any hostility to landowners, manufacturers and merchants and to confirm their rights to rent and profits.[53] Owen's plans for co-operative communities were purveyed, for example, as designed not only to alleviate working-class distress but also to ensure that 'landed proprietors and capitalists may obtain full interest and ample security for all the money they advance'. Thus in such enterprises 'every individual will enjoy, or possess the undivided fruits of his own labour, *except that portion which may be paid as rent or interest of the capital advanced for him* ... and the sums which may be required by the state, in the shape of taxes'.[54]

This analysis of labour's impoverished material lot certainly benefited by way of quotation and inspiration from the economic writings of Robert Owen. With Owen as a source co-operative writers could explain working-class poverty as an endogenous function of a competitive market economy and do so using some of the categories and concepts of political economy. Yet unlike Owen there is a measure of acerbity and a preparedness to single out capital as the agent which took conscious advantage of the economic vulnerability of labour. All that was necessary for a

---

[52] ibid. 38 (1821), 194; ibid. 36 (1821), 160.
[53] The only group which came in for particularly severe criticism was the retail trade, who were considered guilty of the cardinal sin of manipulating the exchange mechanism for their own economic ends. They were also condemned for the unproductive nature of their calling, ibid. 28 (1821), 31, and for 'wringing ... not less perhaps in the shape of profits upon the necessaries of life than twenty millions annually from impoverished hands', ibid. 28 (1821), 32.
[54] ibid. 38 (1821), 193; ibid. 20 (1821), 305 (my emphasis).

fully developed theory of labour exploitation was an overt linking of the economic category 'capital' to a particular social class or grouping but the preparedness to forge this final link, with all its attendant connotations of class hostility and antagonism, was rare. As such, the treatment of labour exploitation was decidedly low key. The antagonism of economic interests was a theme that was hardly touched upon, let alone developed. The conception of exploitation was, in purely theoretical terms, more profound and cogent than that of the contemporary radical press but the rhetoric in terms of which this conception was articulated was certainly less aggressive. In the final analysis early co-operative political economy reflected the moderate tones and ameliorating influence of Robert Owen.

The 'Trades Newspaper' and the co-operative press 1825–30

As one of the most important papers through which working-class opinion found expression in the late 1820s, the *Trades Newspaper* acted not so much as a melting pot for a variety of economic opinions (this would falsely imply the emergence of a uniformity in working-class economic thinking) but rather as a theatre of ideas, with differing conceptions of exploitation periodically dominating the stage before making their exits to be replaced by others.

Despite the initial influence of Hodgskin, contributors to the *Trades Newspaper* did not advance far in resolving the question of what constituted the sources of economic value. Nevertheless, his work obviously influenced those early editorials which argued that capital added nothing to the value of a commodity except to the extent that it was the product of previous labour: 'What they [the political economists] call capital is but the representative of that capital of which you [the labouring classes] are the possessors ... the only real capital is human labour and without that no society can subsist a single day.'[55] Capital itself was incapable of adding value to a commodity without the assistance of labour: 'Not only are all instruments and machines the produce of labour but they can effect nothing whatever without the application of labour.'[56]

[55] *Trades Newspaper*, 4 (1825), 150.
[56] ibid.

Such opinions did represent a clearer expression of the idea that labour was the sole source of economic value than anything which had previously appeared in radical or co-operative papers. In particular, the specific denial of the productivity of capital represented an advance on previous discussion of the value-creating capacities of labour. By implication, too, the owners of capital were condemned as unproductive and therefore undeserving of the reward which accrued to them by virtue of their ownership. Also, these early issues of the paper display a clearly expressed awareness of the need to resolve the problem of why the value input of labour did not match its value receipts: 'It is a question now of much importance', wrote the editor of the *Trades Newspaper*, 'for whose benefit do our people labour so excessively . . . and at the same time receive such a very small portion of what they produce?'[57] It was a question too made all the more pertinent by the fact that, if Hodgskin was to be believed, 'no adequate explanation has yet been given of the circumstances which cause the labourer in the progress of society to obtain a less and less share of his own produce'.[58] It was also a question which in this period was being thought about in terms of more purely economic concepts and categories: 'Wages, let me remind your readers, have no reference whatever to the quantity [of goods] produced by the labourer. At present all produce belongs in the first instance to landlords and capitalists and wages is the sum that they must give for labour.'[59] Further, this sum, 'the natural price of labour', was 'usually defined to be the price which is necessary to enable the labourers to subsist and to rear up as many labourers as the owners of all the produce of a country choose to pay or employ'.[60] Thus while this writer in the *Trades Newspaper* may not have possessed a coherent theory of value and distribution it was in the elementary terms of value and a tripartite division of the product of labour that he was considering the question of labour exploitation.

Given the range of opinions expressed in the *Trades Newspaper* during the comparatively long period over which it was published, it is difficult to make any general statements about

[57] ibid. 12 (1825), 177.
[58] ibid. 29 (1826), 452, letter from Thomas Hodgskin.
[59] ibid. 14 (1825), 214, letter from 'A Labourer'.
[60] ibid.

what contributors saw as the main causes of exploitation. However, three basic sets of causes can be distinguished. First, there were those advanced by Francis Place and other classically inspired contributors. These believed that the main factors adversely affecting labour were the product of market imperfections which might be eliminated by the removal of deleterious state interference with the system's functioning. Secondly, there were those in the *Trades Newspaper* who believed that exploitation was the consequence of a partial freeing of markets which removed legislative protection from the labourer in the labour market while retaining it in other markets (corn) for the benefit of other social classes (landowners). Thirdly, there were those who doubted, even if trade was made generally free, whether the market of itself could ensure a just remuneration for labour.[61]

The position of the second group of writers was well expressed by the author of an article on the silk trade who asked how 'the value of wages could find its natural level, if an artificial value was given to every other description of property'[62] by legislative protection. Thus he pointed out that even the 'necessaries of life on which the labourer subsists were ... not suffered to find their own level'.[63] More numerous, however, was the third group which argued that the existing distribution of economic power tended to prevent an equitable bargain being struck between employer and employed, even when all markets were freed of legislative interference. The fact was that the labourer's material circumstances militated against the possibility of genuinely free bargaining:

Is labour free for the operative to fix the value of his labour? ... no, for although he is not compelled by the law of the land to work for what is not a living price, yet he is compelled by necessity ... poverty renders him dependent ... his master's will is law.[64]

[61] There were no significant differences of opinion between groups two and three which were comprised of silk weavers and representatives of other metropolitan trades. Both swam hard against the tide of history in arguing for the legislative protection of wages. The arguments of the third group do embody, however, a more general critique of a free market economy and thus, by implication, of early industrial capitalism.
[62] *Trades Free Press*, 3, 143 (1828), 289,
[63] ibid.
[64] *Trades Newspaper*, 52 (1826), 828–9, 'Petition of the Macclesfield Silk Weavers'.

These writers argued that 'although produce ... can be warehoused and kept from market until it will fetch its price, hunger can neither be warehoused or bottled, but will force labour into the market at any price'.[65] Further, labourers could not expect to strike a just bargain in a market where 'A few or even the whole of operatives employed by ... grinding masters, cannot by leaving [their] employ oblige [them] to be contented with the general rate of profits, because in every trade there is a redundancy of hands.'[66] The free trade and free markets advocated by the classical economist might seem fine in theory but in practice they impoverished whole sectors of the workforce and this was so because of the 'immense power which the capitalist has over the labourer'.[67]

In addition it was argued that while definite economic benefits might accrue from trade liberalisation it would not be the labouring classes who reaped them. On the question of repealing the Corn Laws, for instance, John Gast wrote:

No man can dispute that the wages of labour rest exclusively in the hands of the employer ... It was consequently nothing more than might have been expected that the price of labour should not keep pace with the price of provisions and I should like to be informed ... what guarantee the poor have that the reduction of wages shall not keep close to the heels of the reduction in the price of bread.[68]

Gast's fears were echoed by others. Thus 'A Constant Reader' wrote, 'I am persuaded that in proportion as the price of provisions is reduced so will the unprincipled manufacturer reduce the wages of his journeymen.'[69]

For the second group of writers who saw labour's impoverish-

---

[65] ibid. 2, 60 (1826), 59, a letter from 'A Labouring Oar'.
[66] ibid. 16 (1825), 241, a letter of William Longson quoted from a Leeds newspaper where it was originally published.
[67] ibid. 28 (1826), 440: 'A free trade in this commodity [silk] may possibly bring, in the end, plenty of employment and bread; but it ought not surprise us that simple men view with suspicion and distrust, a benefit which is heralded by starvation and death'; ibid. 31 (1826), 487, letter from 'A Labourer'; while agreeing in general terms with free trade aspirations this correspondent wrote that its advocates 'overlook the immense power which the capitalist has over the labourer ... They also have in general this radical evil at the bottom of all their systems. They consider man as a machine and the labourer as a commodity.'
[68] ibid. 31 (1826), 487.
[69] ibid. 2, 80 (1827), 218.

ment as the consequence of the selective withdrawal of legislative protection, apposite legislation could provide a solution. Legislation could be used to protect labour as it did every other species of property.[70] Only legislation could prevent 'the rapacious and unjust master' from exploiting his workforce.[71] What was needed was a legislative confirmation and defence of the economic rights of labour in particular trades in order to guarantee, primarily, a fair level of prices and wages. The exploitation of labour was the consequence of its absence. Such views almost invariably led on to that particularist defence of labour's interest that has already been commented upon with respect to the silk weavers and framework knitters.[72]

What distinguished the third group of writers from the second was not the solutions to the economic ills of labour which they advanced, for this group also stressed the importance of legislative protection. Rather, they were distinguished by their more general appreciation of the economic vulnerability of the working class as a whole and their more general critique of the intrinsically exploitative nature of competitive capitalism. This general critique found its clearest expression in the early issues of the paper when Hodgskin's views, as expounded in *Labour Defended*, were also being reprinted with approbatory comment. Thus, for example, the then editor, John Robertson, wrote of the control which the 'fortunate few' had over 'The natural riches and capabilities of the country', which had 'given them the means of determining ... how much or how little labour should be expected from each individual';[73] 'it is evidently [the] command over the rude materials which constitutes the chief claim of the capitalist to the large share which he engrosses of the national produce'.[74] Such statements are very much in harmony with Hodgskin's work. They reveal a perception of exploitation which

---

[70] See, for example, the case made out for minimum wages legislation on this basis, ibid. 48 (1826), 763–4, letter from J. P. Grove; this view comes across particularly clearly in reports by the paper of what was said at meetings of workers (for example, the broad silk weavers of Spitalfields) called to press for a Wages Protection Act.

[71] ibid. For details and discussion of the campaigns to secure legislative protection for wage rates see I. Prothero, *Artisans and Politics*, pp. 222–4.

[72] See above, pp. 36–9.

[73] *Trades Newspaper*, 6 (1825), 81–2.

[74] ibid. 8 (1825), 113.

is not encompassed by legislative interference or the absence of legislative interference in the workings of the market. Rather, the whole market economy free or otherwise was skewed in favour of those who possessed the 'natural riches', the 'capabilities', the 'rude materials' necessary for production. The articulation of such opinions was largely confined to the early life of the paper but they do represent an attempt to give popular expression to the theoretical substance of a distinctively anticapitalist political economy. Here were the makings of a popularised theory of labour exploitation which explicitly held the capitalist responsible for labour's distressed material lot.

These opinions were, however, soon swept aside in the torrent of Placian political economy which followed the removal of John Robertson as editor of the paper. For Place the major cause, together with incontinent breeding, of the economic ills of the labouring classes was state interference in the workings of the market and in particular the Corn Laws. The arguments elaborated by Place and like minded writers were simple if not always consistent. Either free trade would raise real wages to their 'natural' level by forcing down the price of food and other commodities purchased by labour or it would raise them by increasing profits (through lower labour costs and increased demand for lower-priced products) which by enlarging the wages fund would increase the demand for labour; 'an actual rise [in wages] after a very few months' was also seen as the necessary outcome of Corn Law repeal because 'the additional demand from abroad will create more work at home'.[75] However, whatever the process by which it occurred the material well-being of labour would be substantially improved. Place was the major exponent of these lines of argument but it must also be said that those who explained the inadequate remuneration of labour in terms of the absence of free trade were undoubtedly representative of a definite strand of working-class economic opinion in the late 1820s. They were also firmly within the classical fold.

For the Placians the major exploiter was the state. However, for many other writers in the *Trades Newspaper*, exploiters were located within the economic process. Boroughmongers, taxeaters,

---

[75] ibid. 39 (1826), 612, an anonymous letter.

sinecurists, placemen, tyrants, kings and priests were replaced by master manufacturers, employers, capitalists; those defined according to their vested political interests were replaced by those defined in terms of their economic role, as major exploiters of the labouring classes. Master manufacturers came under particular fire for their combinations to reduce wages, 'The education of the masters together with the smallness of numbers enabl[ing] them to carry on a combination with secrecy and effect'[76] and for having 'generally proved themselves to be mischievous middlemen who stand between the producers and the consumers'.[77] 'Employers' were accused of 'enriching themselves by a grinding and oppressive system',[78] while John Gast stated that there was little doubt that the power to determine the wages of labour rested 'exclusively' in their hands,[79] the implication being that the employers were, therefore, exclusively responsible for labour's wretched state. Similarly 'capitalists' were attacked for engrossing a 'large share of the national produce', for sharing with taxation 'the greater part of what our productive classes produce'[80] and for the fact that 'The machinery, by which 95 parts of the labour out of every 100 are produced, is worked by the labourer, not for his own gain, but for the capitalist who labours not at all.'[81]

The early issues of the *Trades Newspaper* suggest, therefore, that by the mid–1820s capitalists, master manufacturers and employers were becoming, for some writers in the working-class press, the dominant incubi in the working-class demonology of exploiters. As well as detailing the conditions which made exploitation a fact of economic life, these writers were also clear as to the major beneficiaries and the economic role which they played.

Contributors to the co-operative press of this period showed

---

[76] ibid. 1 (1825), 2, the reported remarks of James Ashton made at a dinner of operative cotton spinners.
[77] ibid. 2 (1825), 18.
[78] ibid. 2, 66 (1826), 107, letter signed 'S.W.'
[79] ibid. 41 (1826), 635; by way of contrast see Francis Place, ibid. 43 (1826), 675, who absolved masters and employers from such blame: 'wages are not and cannot be regulated by the will of the masters'; also Place's attack upon the idea of minimum wage legislation in which he argued that wages could be raised only by the efforts of the working people themselves, ibid. 44 (1826), 689–90, 'On Wages'.
[80] ibid. 8 (1825), 113; ibid. 12 (1825), 177.
[81] *Weekly Free Press*, 5, 210 (1829), 2.

a continuous concern with the question of what determined the exchange value of commodities. In all, four basic answers emerged. First, there were those who believed that economic value was a joint product of land and labour inputs: 'The source of production is the land ... the real and only power of production beyond the spontaneous gifts of nature, is the labour of man.'[82] Secondly, there were those who formulated a more precise labour theory of value: 'the real cost of all commodities is the amount of labour employed in preparing them for use', some attempt also being made to define what could be considered comparable units of labour.[83] Those who adhered to such a view dismissed 'capital' as 'nothing but the produce of labour saved'[84] and 'of no use till it is converted, by labour into the luxuries of life';[85] 'labour and not mere capital is everything'.[86] Severe criticism was also levelled against those who 'observing that the productive powers of society are always put in motion ... by capital ... erroneously conclude that capital is the true and only power of production'.[87] Thirdly, there were those writers who believed that while labour was, or at least should be, the determinant of value, its own value, like that of all other commodities, was in fact governed under competitive capitalism by the forces of supply and demand; 'labour is a direct article of commerce and liable to the same fluctuations in its value, as every other purchaseable commodity. Thus the value of labour depends on the demand for it and upon the amount of supply to meet that demand.'[88] Finally, there were those writers in the co-operative press who hinted that the utility yielded by a commodity was what made it valuable: 'things only become wealth, which are wanted by different individuals to afford them comfort and enjoyment'.[89]

However, while there existed differing conceptions of what

[82] *Birmingham Co-operative Herald*, 2 (1829), 6.
[83] *Co-operative Magazine*, 2, 11 (1827), 509, Report of the Committee of the Brighton Co-operative Fund Association. Here units of labour were considered to be of equal value if they were equally necessary to the support of human life – hardly a helpful definition.
[84] *The Co-operator*, 8 (1828), 2, William King.
[85] ibid. 6 (1828), 3, William King.
[86] ibid. 8 (1828), 2, William King.
[87] *Birmingham Co-operative Herald*, 2 (1829), 6.
[88] ibid. 19 (1830), 75.
[89] *British Co-operator*, 4 (1830), 85, review of an anonymous pamphlet on emigration.

determined the exchange value of commodities, a certain uniformity of opinion emerged in the co-operative press as to why the labouring classes did not receive the full economic value of the commodities which they produced:

> it is easy to account for the never-varying poverty of labourers in most parts of the civilised world. To do this we must draw forth to view and scrutinize the spell that rules the exchanges and the production of wealth ... the barrier that checks the producing energies of every industrious people; the bane of human virtue and human happiness – PROFIT upon COST PRICE. To obtain this is the great object of competition among the holders of money; and not to obtain a share of the labour offered for sale.[90]

This opinion was constantly reiterated in the pages of the co-operative press where it assumed the form of a general concern with the whole process of exchange. Thus 'the process usually adopted in exchanging the various sorts of wealth, affords to one portion of society the means of exempting itself from useful exertion without apparent injustice' and 'it is evident that it is the manner in which ... necessary exchanges are made; that produces want and poverty; for we have just seen that *if no commercial exchanges were made at all, no injustice in ... distribution could occur* ... In other words it is the present system of commercial exchange that deprives Britain's labourers, in some way or other of 38/40 of the produce of their industry'.[91] These writers also emphasised 'the enormous profits which the working classes are daily giving away to other people *by not marketing for themselves*. Other people grow rich upon these profits and all the riches of the world are in fact got out of them.'[92] Thus the economic relationship between capital and labour was seen in terms of exchanges where 'the capitalist has the power of buying at the lowest possible price and realising splendid fortunes by selling it dear to others'.[93]

This understanding of exploitation as a function of commodity price deviations from labour costs almost inevitably focused

---

[90] *Associate and Co-operative Mirror*, 2 (1829), 6.
[91] ibid. 2 (1829), 5; *Co-operative Magazine*, 3, 3 (1828), 60 (my emphasis).
[92] *The Co-operator*, 10 (1829), 3 (my emphasis).
[93] *Weekly Free Press and Co-operative Journal*, 6, 272 (1830), 4, correspondent 'L', 'A Challenge to the Political Economists'.

analytical attention upon the malfunctioning of the exchange mechanism. Under existing economic arrangements exchange values were determined in an additive fashion by the additions of profits, commissions, interest and rents to labour cost.[94] It was through the elimination of these additional elements of price, through a rationalisation of the process of exchange, therefore, that the poverty resulting from exploitation could be eliminated. Such views are exactly those which might have been expected from writers who looked to Owen and the Smithian socialists as their mentors.

This particular concern with exchange can be seen in the desire to establish a correct and equitable standard of value and in the attention given to the nature and functions of money. Thus many contributors to the co-operative press believed that:

The general use of money, as a conventional measure of value, has tended to deprive the producers of wealth of that knowledge of the real cost, the cost of producing commodities, which would influence them in exchanging one thing for another. Money-price being substituted for the knowledge of cost price . . . The process of exchanging goods is simplified but . . . a strong inducement is held out to buy as cheap and sell as dear as possible.[95]

Or as William King put it, 'Money seems to have been an instrument of great mischief, and has bewildered all our ideas of what constitutes real wealth.' As a result labourers had 'exchanged large quantities of labour for small quantities of money. They had thus constantly made disadvantageous exchanges.'[96]

Some commentators advocated the return to a currency backed by gold; others suggested that the value of commodities might be estimated by reference to a corn standard,[97] while some wanted a paper currency denominated in units of labour.[98] What they all desired was an acceptable medium of exchange which would enable the exchange value of goods to reflect their 'true value' or 'social worth'. It was this that led Edward Garner to

[94] See, for example, *The Co-operator*, 4 (1828), 4.
[95] *Associate and Co-operative Mirror*, 2 (1829), 6.
[96] *Weekly Free Press and Co-operative Journal*, 6, 264 (1830), 5; ibid. 5, 245 (1830), 4, letter from William King.
[97] *Co-operative Magazine*, 6 (1826), 179, letter from 'C.E.'; ibid. 4 (1826), 122, letter from Hector Campbell.
[98] *British Co-operator*, 6 (1830), 124–7, Edward Garner, 'Money and Labour Notes'.

state that the value of commodities could 'only be considered in relation to the common consent of mankind'.[99]

This is not to suggest that writers in the co-operative press ignored the queston of who owned the productive means of the nation. Like Thompson, Owen and Gray, they considered the possession by the labouring classes of capital and, in particular, land, as fundamental to their future material well-being. As Charles Fry put it in his 'Practical Hints for Co-operators', 'The difference between the workman and the master is, that one possesses the labour the others capital, labour without the aid of capital... avails nothing. Capital commands labour. Capital is the grand desideratum for the labourers.'[100] Such writers believed that the possession of capital would shield the labouring classes from 'the ever recurring fluctuations of the markets for labour'[101] and also that they would be able 'possessing Capital, to maintain [their] ground against the encroachments of other Capitalists'.[102] Under the pen of William Thompson such ideas assumed much greater precision:

> One of the greatest difficulties in the way of your securing to yourselves the whole produce of your labour, is the difficulty of acquiring capital; or in other words of acquiring the possession and the proprietorship of lands and houses on and in which you live and labour, of the tools, implements and machines with which you labour; and of the materials on which you labour.[103]

However, it must be remembered that most writers in the co-operative press of the late 1820s believed that the labouring classes could ultimately secure ownership of the means of production, if only exchange relations were first placed on an equitable footing, for this would allow labour to retain and accumulate that profit upon labour costs that had previously passed to 'capitalists', 'distributors' and 'middlemen'. Thus, for example, through the medium of co-operative trading societies, 'the wealth producers will be brought into immediate contact with each other without the intervention of any middlemen to

---

[99] ibid. 6 (1830), 122.
[100] *Weekly Free Press and Co-operative Journal*, 6, 264 (1830), 4.
[101] *Associate and Co-operative Mirror*, 1 (1829), 3.
[102] ibid. 7 (1829), 43.
[103] *Co-operative Magazine*, 4, 3 (1829), reprinted letter by William Thompson; see also *Belfast Co-operative Advocate*, 1 (1830), 11.

levy a tax upon their interest in the shape of profit, commission or interest'.[104] By means of such institutions the labourers could ensure a reciprocal and direct exchange of their labour[105] either by barter or by way of 'a note signifying... the value of so many days or months of labour'[106] and this, for many co-operators, was the key to securing that accumulation of wealth, to securing 'all the profits of their labour' which would allow the working classes 'to purchase land' and to 'set up manufactures'.[107] Fair and equitable exchanges were regarded, therefore, as a sufficient condition for the working classes to secure the ownership of all the necessary factors of production[108] and this in turn would ultimately ensure and preserve the maintenance of free and equitable exchanges. It was by these means that those intermediaries who had previously exploited by the addition of profits to labour cost price would be circumvented and eliminated. So existing accumulations of capital could be ignored once equitable exchange relations had been established. Thus the important question is not whether co-operative writers considered ownership of the means of production to be important – this they undoubtedly did – but how these commentators considered the labouring classes might secure their possession. To such a question they would have replied unhesitatingly, 'By equitable exchanges'.

[104] *Birmingham Co-operative Herald*, 16 (1830), 68, letter from John Finch.
[105] See, for example, *Co-operative Magazine*, 3, 1 (1828), 12, 'The Causes of Poverty': 'The poverty of the labouring people may be summed up indeed in one short sentence... They do not possess the full value of their labour and that benefit they can never as a class derive, *unless by a reciprocal and direct exchange of the products of their labour*' (my emphasis).
[106] *Belfast Co-operative Advocate*, 1 (1830), 11.
[107] ibid. 1 (1830), 14.
[108] In this context see George Mudie's defence of the 'United Interests Society for the Mutual Support of the Members During Sickness and Old Age; and their Permanent Employment', *Advocate of the Working Classes*, 7 (1827), 115–17, whose object was 'The emancipation of the working classes from poverty through the slow accumulation of capital by the exchange of members' products exclusively among themselves until the labourers eventually possessed all the capital of the country', G. Claeys, 'George Mudie's *Advocate of the Working Classes, 1826–7*', *Bulletin of the Society for the Study of Labour History*, 44 (Spring 1982), 42–3.

6

The theory of labour exploitation and the working-class press 1830–34[1]

It can be seen, therefore, that the working-class press of the early 1830s did not initiate the popularisation of the notion that labour was, in some manner, the source of economic value. Nor can any of the contributors to working-class papers in this period be said to have clarified the exact nature of the causal relationship which existed between labour and the value of commodities. Certainly there is no theoretical advance in the discussion of this matter, upon what had already been written in the co-operative press of the late 1820s. Thus the relation between labour and value was still expressed in terms characterised by the generality of what they denied rather than the precision of what they asserted: 'labour and only labour is property... what is land?... so much dirt and dust... without labour what is everything else, valueless without labour'; 'labour is the only true wealth, nothing is produced without it'; 'There is no species of wealth or in other words no article of real and substantial value that is not more or less the product of labour'; 'of all species of property, LABOUR is infinitely the most valuable, in as much as it is the prime producer'.[2] In many respects these assertions are not markedly different from many to be found in the early radical press.[3] Yet two points must be made. First, these

[1] *The Poor Man's Guardian* ran from 1831 to 1835; some material from issues of the paper published in 1835 has been used but only when it clearly highlights economic opinions and arguments which had previously found expression in the paper. The same practice has been adopted in chapter 8.
[2] *Penny Papers for the People*, 12 February 1831, p. 2; *Crisis*, I, 2 (1832), 7, a letter; *Carpenter's Political Magazine*, July 1831, p. 21; *Midland Representative*, I (1831), I, 'To the Readers'.
[3] See above, pp. 112–13.

statements on the origins of economic value were, in the early 1830s, more widely and more frequently disseminated than had previously been the case. Secondly, and more importantly, they were not left as isolated assertions but provided a starting point for a variety of attempts to formulate a genuinely economic analysis of labour's ills. In this sense they were integrated into an anti-capitalist and socialist political economy rather than into a radical political discourse.

For the writers who made these statements, it was a short step from avowing that labour was the source of value, to the assertion that it was in terms of labour that the value of commodities, contributions to the productive process and economic rewards should be assessed. Exploitation, therefore, came to be seen as a function of the failure to ensure that this occurred and that everything exchanged at its correct labour value. It was this incorrect or unjust valuation of both commodities and labour which explained why contributions to output were not always matched by comparable rewards.

Many writers in the working-class press of the early 1830s, like those in the co-operative press of the later 1820s, believed that under existing economic arrangements additions were made to the labour value of commodities. Market prices contained more elements than labour costs. As one writer in the *Poor Man's Advocate* put it:

The value of all commodities is the amount of human labour it has taken to procure them ... But the merchant or agent between buyer and seller, being able to conceal the real state of the transaction, contrives with scarcely any labour to charge ... one quarter *above the value* which he calls profit.[4]

In the circumstances labour must necessarily be undervalued with respect to all commodities and thus effectively exploited. The essence of this perception of exploitation is again clearly revealed in a much quoted poem, 'On Wages', in the *Poor Man's Guardian*:

> Wages should form the price of goods,
> Yes wages should be all,
> Then we who work to make the goods,
> Should justly have them all.

[4] *Poor Man's Advocate*, 1 (1832), 8, 'The Value of Commodities'.

> But if their price is made of rent
> Tithes, taxes, profits all,
> Then we who work to make the goods,
> Shall have just none at all.[5]

Under existing economic and institutional arrangements exchange value was determined in an additive manner which reflected the economic power of certain social groupings and vested interests to add to the labour value of commodities. Rent, tithes, taxes and profits were added with the result that labour failed to receive the full reward for its services. Thus labour was effectively exploited in the process of the determination of exchange value. Thus 'master manufacturers' had the power to 'double their profits by doubling the price of everything they sell',[6] while the 'capitalist' was seen as having 'too much within him the power to enhance prices and reduce the retribution [sic] for human labour'.[7]

Along with this conception of exploitation went the complementary belief that if goods could be exchanged at values equal to the labour they contained or the labour costs which they embodied, then profits, rents, taxes, tithes and the social classes and interests which lived upon these categories of income would all be swept away: 'if wages were the whole value of work, how could the master take the work to market, sell it for more money than he gave for it, and grow rich upon the profit, while the workman grows poor upon the wages';[8] 'Wages should form the price of goods, yes wages should be all, then we who work to make the goods, should justly have them all.'[9] For these writers exploitation would be ended when goods exchanged according to the value of labour which they contained. Under existing arrangements exploitation was integral to the formation of exchange value.

---

[5] *Poor Man's Guardian*, 28 (1832), 222, article signed 'One of the Know Nothings'; see, for example, P. Hollis, *Class and Conflict in Nineteenth Century England 1815–50* (London, Routledge and Kegan Paul, 1973), p. 50, and P. Hollis, *The Pauper Press*, pp. 220–1, though Hollis fails to discuss the possible theoretical and practical significance of this understanding of the determination of exchange value.

[6] *Poor Man's Guardian*, ibid.

[7] *Pioneer*, 3 (1833), 20, article signed 'Concord'.

[8] *Poor Man's Guardian*, 142 (1834), 21, a letter signed 'Unteacher'.

[9] ibid. 28 (1832), 222.

Labour, too, should exchange at its natural value. It was, indeed, a common accusation of writers in the working-class press that labour was exploited because it was ignorant of its intrinsic worth: 'So little have you estimated the value of your labour that you have allowed it to be bought at one price and sold at another by every man who had the presumption to offer it in the market.'[10] Thus until labour became aware of its true value it would remain ignorant of the extent to which it was 'robbed of the fruit of [its] ... labour'.[11] For these writers it was the difference between labour's intrinsic value or worth and the price paid for labour by those who purchased it, 'bought at one price and sold at another', which constituted the essence of labour exploitation and capitalist profit. As one put it, capitalists lived 'solely on the difference between the money price of labour and what the labour is really worth'.[12]

Given the parallel nature of their analysis of labour exploitation, it is not surprising that like the 'Smithian socialists', from whom undoubtedly some drew inspiration, writers in the working-class press were particularly concerned with the process of exchange, the medium of exchange and the nature of exchange relations. It was, therefore, the market and market-related economic phenomena which attracted much of their analytical attention. Thus William Pare expressed the view of many more than his fellow co-operators when he stated that, 'With our amazing facilities for creating all kinds of wealth and the *horridly defective system of exchanging that wealth*, the working classes must continue to be ground down.'[13] In addition exploiters were often seen in terms of and castigated for the function which they performed in the process of exchange. As a result, 'middleman', a term which was used to categorise groupings as diverse as master manufacturers, merchants and retailers, was invariably applied in a condemnatory fashion: 'They [middlemen] get their living by buying your labour at one price and selling it at another'; 'Remember friends and brethren, that you and you alone produce

[10] *Crisis*, 1, 24 (1832), 96.
[11] *Herald to the Rights of Industry*, 10 (1834), 76, reported remarks of Mr John Knight to a meeting of operatives in Yorkshire; also in the *Voice of the West Riding*, 46 (1834), 365.
[12] *Poor Man's Guardian*, 154 (1834), 113.
[13] *Lancashire and Yorkshire Co-operator*, Supplement (1832), p. 17 (my emphasis).

all the real wealth of the country ... middlemen ... trick you out of the greater part of the wealth which you create.'[14] The 'non-producer', the 'monied man', the 'trader' and the 'capitalist' were all seen as fulfilling this type of exploitative economic role: 'Hitherto the non-producer or the monied man has been the general receiver of your produce, and he has retailed this produce amongst you, always retaining a part of the produce for himself in every transaction'; 'the *capitalist or mere trader*, has hitherto without producing anything, derived immense profits from mere exchange'.[15]

Thus the fundamental economic antagonism for these writers was that which existed between the distributors or exchangers of products in their many guises as manufacturers, 'shopocrats', capitalists, employers, traders, monied men etc. and the actual producers of those products, the labouring classes. In this context it is interesting to note Proposition 9 of the 'Propositions for the Consolidation of the Productive Classes' printed in the *Poor Man's Guardian*, which stated:

The present mode of making the distributors the employers and the producers the employed, is an inversion of the natural order of things and is equally injurious to the consumers and the producers. Its consequences are, that the labour of the producers is made an article of commerce and as such liable to all the consequences of competition; while the articles of consumption etc. undergo the imposition of several unnecessary profits to the great injury of the consumers.[16]

The dividing line between exploiters and exploited lay between those who possessed the economic power to exchange and distribute commodities and those who brought only their labour to the market. Significant space was devoted, therefore, to discussing how exchange-derived, profits-upon-alienation might be eliminated.

As with the Smithian socialists, there emerged in the work of these popular writers a definite belief that if the sphere of exchange could be rationalised; if the mechanism and medium

---

[14] *Poor Man's Guardian*, 80 (1833), 641; ibid. 4 (1831), 25.
[15] *Crisis*, 1, 2 (1832), 7, a letter; ibid. 3, 3 (1834), 19, contribution from a correspondent signed 'Austin' (my emphasis).
[16] *Poor Man's Guardian*, 163 (1834), 222, 'Propositions for the Consolidation of the Productive Classes'.

of exchange could be properly altered to ensure that both commodities and labour exchanged at their true or natural values, then the opportunity to exploit via the power to manipulate market prices would be removed. Thus O'Brien in the *Poor Man's Guardian* exhorted his readers to 'promote mutual exchange of labour for labour, on the competitive principle, so as to intercept the profits of trade in addition to the wages of labour'[17] and it was the general belief that exploitation was rooted in the process of exchange that led writers in many papers to throw their support behind Exchange Banks and Equitable Labour Exchanges: 'We say to all the industrious classes, exchange your labour for equal value of labour through the medium of Time Notes of Equitable Banks of Exchange and you will be *at once emancipated from poverty and after from all manner of oppression.*'[18] Equitable labour exchange 'would certainly give to every industrious and able workman, the means of enjoying his share of [the] . . . sum of comfort' and would 'secure' to the labouring classes 'the full value of their labour'.[19] Given the necessary institutional arrangements, producers could exchange labour-valued commodities with producers, and distributors and exchangers, the exploiters of labour, would lose the opportunity to add profits and other exactions to labour costs.

The nature of this understanding of exploitation also explains, in some measure, the extraordinary interest which writers in the working-class press of the early 1830s displayed in money and the functions which it performed. For money was often viewed as the means by which a natural standard of value (labour) was replaced by an artificial means of denominating the value of commodities. This, it was believed, gave scope for a manipulation of the exchange process to the detriment of the labouring classes. The need to replace money both as a standard of value and as a medium of exchange was, therefore, a common theme in the popular political economy of the working-class press. The editor of the *Ballot*, for example, while criticising Owen's attempts to replace money by labour notes as a means of exchange, nonetheless accepted that, 'The desideratum certainly is to show, in

[17] ibid. 126 (1833), 350.
[18] *Crisis*, 1, 19 (1832), 75 (my emphasis).
[19] *Birmingham Labour Exchange Gazette*, 1 (1833), 3.

every article of traffic, the value of labour – whether of the head or the hand – which was bestowed in the raising of it. Something therefore of intrinsic value is required to effect that object.'[20] In the absence of such a medium of exchange possessed of 'intrinsic value', it was believed by many that labour exploitation would continue unabated, for money as it then existed

has ... been the instrument by which legitimate and illegitimate fraud of every kind has been effected. Money is the medium through which the working classes in all ages have been deceived, robbed, degraded and impoverished. Money alone is the thing which gives the unproductive classes their power over the producer and which enables the idle to abstract from the industrious the fruits of their toil.[21]

Thus the 'monetary system of society [had] become a cunningly devised arrangement to deprive the actual producers of wealth out [sic] of the rightful fruits of their industry and to make the working-classes the slaves of the useless and non-producing classes'.[22]

Money obfuscated the fact that all value derived from labour: 'With regard to the producers, money prices only tend to confuse and bewilder all their ideas', confusing indeed what writers in the working-class press, through their forays into the field of value theory, had attempted to clarify. Consequently many believed that if only 'the productive mass of society' could be made 'fully to understand the nature of MONEY', all confusion as regards the exclusive, wealth-creating role of the labouring classes would be swept away and the labourers would 'instantly feel that the whole power of the country is in their hands'.[23] It was for these and other reasons that William King exhorted labourers to 'ease aside your money calculations and look to fair equivalents of labour for labour'.[24]

Money also permitted the purchase of labour and commodities with what was sometimes referred to as a 'fictitious capital'. This belief lay behind the 'shadow and substance' rhetoric much

---

[20] *Ballot*, 89 (1832), 3, an editorial discussion of the respective strengths of the currency reform proposals put forward by William Cobbett and Thomas Attwood.
[21] *Pioneer*, 13 (1833), 98.
[22] *Crisis*, 1, 15 (1832), 58.
[23] *Pioneer*, 11 (1833), 84; ibid. 13 (1833), 98.
[24] *Exchange Bazaars Gazette*, 1 (1832), 9, a letter from William King.

favoured by some popular writers, with labour being seen as the substance and money the shadow of value and wealth. The exchange of labour for money capital was, therefore, the exchange of substance for shadow. Thus O'Brien considered 'Capital, in the money sense of the word [to be] ... *a fiction and a fraud*. It is not wealth, but the means of abstracting wealth for others. It is but an instrument in the hands of certain classes, by virtue of which, these classes contrive to appropriate to themselves the *real capital* of the country at the expense of those who produce it'[25] and in consequence, 'those who ... monopolize the representative, can monopolize the wealth and, in effect, do monopolize it'.[26]

If that exploitation which resulted from the use of money was to be eliminated, then a new medium of exchange was required. What was needed was 'the introduction of a perfect medium of exchange of wealth to supersede the present and unjust standard of value'; 'What is now principally wanted is a good medium of exchange on the principle of labour for labour',[27] or as another writer put it in question and answer form:

How do you propose to do away with the many serious evils which arise from an artificial currency which so often robs the producer of the fruits of his industry and fills the pockets of the speculative non-producer? By introducing a correct and perfect circulating medium.[28]

Many suggestions were made respecting the form which this 'perfect circulating medium' should take, the most popular being the labour note.[29] However, it is more important to notice the general belief that much of the poverty and exploitation suffered by the labouring classes would cease with a reformation of the monetary medium, than the variety of forms it was believed such a reformation should take. For, once again, it highlights the extent to which the attention of working-class readers was

---

[25] *Poor Man's Guardian*, 198 (1835), 416 (my emphasis).
[26] ibid. 207 (1835), 538.
[27] *Crisis*, I, 13 (1832), 50; *Lancashire and Yorkshire Co-operator*, October 1832, p. 8, William Pare.
[28] *Pioneer*, 2 (1833), 14.
[29] One writer in the *Belfast Co-operative Advocate*, I (1830), 12, went so far as to suggest that 'Competition might be made shift with so long as the circulating medium took the form of labour notes.'

directed to exchange and exchange relations as the source of their ills. To eliminate profit-upon-alienation or exploitation-in-exchange, it was of fundamental importance to sweep away the medium through which it occurred by the substitution of a new medium of exchange which could accurately translate the intrinsic worth or natural value of a commodity into its representative exchange value. In fact, one of the most frequently expressed aspirations of those who articulated the need for a new monetary medium was that it could be made to reflect the intrinsic or use value of a good. Exchanges would then, it was believed, be made for the consumption of use-values rather than for the accumulation of exchange values. As one writer in the *Lancashire and Yorkshire Co-operator* put it:

the great difference that would exist between buying and selling as at present practised and the exchange of labour through a labour bank would be as follows; in the latter we should produce to consume ... In the former we produce to SELL ... only in such a way as shall produce a profit on the capital of the money-mongers.[30]

Production for consumption rather than the accumulation of profits; decisions to produce determined on grounds of utility rather than exchange value; production oriented to the provision of goods of high social worth rather than high market price; these were the economic goals to be achieved through the introduction of a new medium of exchange and the accompanying rationalisation of the exchange process.

Thus the theoretical understanding of labour exploitation of much popular political economy of the early 1830s rested upon an additive conception of the determination of exchange value under capitalism and this in turn fostered a corresponding concern to purge exchange value of its additive elements and to eliminate those factors which helped to create and maintain them. In these respects writers in the working-class press of this period would seem to be the true heirs of the Smithian socialists. Natural value or intrinsic worth was the Holy Grail which they sought, their search producing an obsession with the reform or abolition of money, an equitable standard of value, fair exchanges and the general rationalisation of the exchange process. It was in the exchange relations which characterised capitalism that exploita-

---

[30] *Lancashire and Yorkshire Co-operator*, June 1832, p. 10, a pamphlet signed 'K'.

tion was rooted. It was through the creation of equitable exchange relations that it was to be abolished.

This is not to say that writers in the working-class press neglected the question of who owned the means of production and who dominated the social relations of production. These writers, as did their Smithian socialist mentors, concerned themselves with the social mode of production which characterised capitalism and they were quick to point out the causal relationship which existed between unequal accumulations of capital and holdings of land and the exploitation of those with only their labour to sell. It was understood, for example, that as 'The producer cannot work without land to work upon, nor without the means of living during the period of reproduction... he cannot live without land or capital.'[31] The landowners and capitalists who possessed these types of property had also 'the power of appropriating to themselves the productive industry of the country': 'as the monopolists command production... in consequence of their being in possession of that land, and the houses, and ships, and the machines, or what is the same thing money... the poor... could all be starved outright, at least so far as they depend on the monopolists'.[32] In this context it was recognised that the defence of the 'sacredness of property' had become a defence of 'the sacredness of one man to appropriate to himself, through the instrumentality of capital, the fruits of another man's industry'.[33] So it was necessary that labourers should become possessors of land and capital if they were ever to ameliorate their depressed material condition: 'Without land or capital we say... the working classes can never enjoy the fruits of their earnings'; 'I hesitate not to say that the condition of the workmen will never be permanently enhanced until... they make themselves capitalists as well as labourers and employ themselves upon their own capital for their own benefit, instead of labouring upon the capital of others.'[34]

Their concern with the need to own land and capital does indicate an awareness of the sources of economic power inherent in the capitalist mode of production which may be said to

[31] *Poor Man's Guardian*, 220 (1835), 639.
[32] *Belfast Co-operative Advocate*, 1 (1830), 11.
[33] *Poor Man's Guardian*, 142 (1834), 17.
[34] *Voice of the People*, 25 (1831), 196; *Midland Representative*, 36 (1832), 3, a letter from 'A Friend to the Labourers'.

anticipate aspects of Marxian political economy. Yet, it must be stressed that when writers in the working-class press came to explain how the labouring classes should set about obtaining ownership of the means of production, their theoretical understanding of labour exploitation led them back to the market and the relations of exchange. For, if commodities and labour could be exchanged at their natural values then labourers individually (through labour banks and labour exchanges) or collectively (by means of co-operative communities and co-operative trading societies) could begin to accumulate the economic surplus which their productive efforts generated. Thus the accumulation of capital by labourers was seen as essentially a function of equitable exchanges. The ultimate aim of labour bazaars and labour exchanges was, therefore, 'to render the labourers essentially altogether independent of the capitalists by immediately commencing and perseveringly continuing the creation of a capital for the exclusive benefit of the labourers *out of their own transactions in the exchange bazaars*'.[35]

This explains in large measure why many writers in the working-class press played down the economic importance of the existing distribution of productive means. For by way of labour exchanges, co-operative trading societies etc. the material well-being of the labouring classes could be significantly improved without impinging directly upon existing accumulations of wealth and capital. As George Mudie stated in the *Exchange Bazaars Gazette*, through the rationalisation of exchange relations which such institutions brought about, 'the Wages of the Productive Classes or the reward of their labour could be increased more than fourfold *without injuring the interests of the other classes of the people*'.[36]

However, two other elements of the popular analysis of labour exploitation contributed to this tendency to underplay the significance of the existing distribution of productive means. First, given that labour was the prime or even the sole factor responsible for the creation of economic value, it seemed reasonable to suppose that the labouring classes could free

---

[35] *Exchange Bazaars Gazette*, 5 (1832), 53 (my emphasis).
[36] ibid. 1 (1832), 1 (my emphasis); see also ibid. 1 (1832), 12: 'the reward of labour may be very greatly increased even without injury to the pecuniary interests of the rich'.

themselves from their dependence on capital merely by the decision to labour, henceforward, for their own benefit and exchange their products with those of similarly emancipated producers. In consequence, the existing accumulations of master manufacturers and others could be dismissed as 'a humbug. Their wealth is solely the creation of the workmen's labour. They have got it; let them keep it. The workmen don't grudge it to them'; for 'labour . . . the sole foundation of wealth must prevail in the end. And why? because labour can beget capital but not capital labour'; 'labour and capital much less fictitious capital, is the source of wealth'.[37]

It seemed legitimate to these writers to draw from the statement 'capital is created by labour' the corollary that labour must, therefore, be independent of capital. The existing distribution of capital might be rendered inconsequential, if only labour was put in a position to realise its potential independence as the source of all value. The power of existing accumulations of capital could be by-passed or even short-circuited merely by labour's decision to produce for itself.

Secondly, there was a tendency among writers in the working-class press to equate capital and money. Capital, in the minds of these writers, assumed therefore the qualities and failings of money and so it and its power became 'fictitious' and 'illusory'; 'Capital, in the plain English is money and money is the representative of wealth and . . . the medium through which men make exchange of the fruits of labour.'[38] What could be dismissed as a mere 'medium through which men exchange' was also likely to be considered unimportant when a new medium of exchange might be immediately introduced by the labouring classes to replace it; in such an eventuality existing accumulations of capital would be rendered valueless and their owners economically powerless.

By the early 1830s, therefore, and particularly in the period 1832–4, there had emerged, in consequence of the proselytising activities of the working-class press, not only key elements of a distinctively working-class approach to the discipline of political economy but also one of the major theoretical pillars upon which a popular, anti-capitalist or socialist political economy must rest.

[37] *Poor Man's Guardian*, 135 (1834), 421, 'On Masters'; ibid. 135 (1834), 422.
[38] ibid. 173 (1834), 268.

There had emerged a popularised theory of labour exploitation which can be viewed as a heterogeneous amalgam of the themes discussed and which embodied and utilised at least some of the constructs and concepts of political economy; a theory of labour exploitation which deployed a primitive theory of value and distribution and which located the springs of labour's impoverishment within the functioning of competitive capitalism.

This does not mean that there was *one* theory of labour exploitation to which popular writers had reference any more than there was one definitively working-class approach to the discipline of political economy itself. To begin with, the more analytical, economic approach to the causes of poverty which characterised many working-class papers in the early 1830s did not entirely sweep away the traditional, radical explanation of working-class economic ills purveyed by writers such as Cobbett and Carlile, nor did it entirely sweep away the remnants of Spenceanism.[39] Assertions of the primary exploitative importance of taxation,[40] money juggles and the abrogation of natural rights to land still found expression in a variety of papers: 'As the National Debt had been the cause of all the poverty of the country, so its abolition would be the restoration of riches and prosperity'; 'the fruits of our labour are by means of taxes on everything we consume withheld from us'; 'My conviction is that taxation is the sole cause of all the country's evils that press us to the earth'.[41]

However, while statements such as these found expression in many working-class papers of the early 1830s, as they had in the

---

[39] P. Hollis, *The Pauper Press*, p. 8: 'the "new ideology" gained ground, though it never displaced more generalized radicalism'; on the longevity of Spenceanism see T. Parsinnen, 'The revolutionary party in London 1816–20', *Bulletin of the Institute of Historical Research*, 45 (1972), 282; though as this writer has pointed out, 'Aside from Thomas Evans and his son, none of the revolutionaries was an ideologue. None ever published a pamphlet', ibid. 275.

[40] See, for example, a characteristic Cobbettian assertion in the opening issue of his *Twopenny Trash*, I, 1 (1830), 12: 'the chief object of this work is to explain to the people at large HOW IT IS THAT THEY ARE MADE POOR ···[the] immediate cause is ENORMOUS TAXATION, co-operating with laws making changes IN THE VALUE OF MONEY'.

[41] *Poor Man's Guardian*, 37 (1832), 291, reported remarks of Mr Preston at a meeting of the National Union of the Working Classes; *Republican (Sovereignty of the People)*, 19 (1831), 4, anonymous letter on the poor rates; *Herald to the Trades Advocate*, 22 (1831), 344, a letter from Robert Wallace, member of the Glasgow Reform Association.

radical press of the immediate post-Napoleonic War period, two points should be made. First, opposition to the traditional view that taxation was the primary form of exploitation was much greater than it had been prior to 1830. This opposition was voiced particularly by co-operative writers, with taxation being seen as 'a trifle in comparison with the tax laid on the working classes by monopolists, in the shape of profit upon capital'.[42] In addition, it was argued that whatever limited economic benefits might accrue from the reduction of taxation were not destined to benefit the working classes: 'There are a hundred ways besides the government taxation by which the products of labour are wrested from the hands of the producer... Who does not see that the reduction of taxation to any considerable extent would end in benefitting the capitalist merely.'[43]

Yet it was not just co-operative papers which deprecated the idea that taxation was the primary form which the exploitation of labour assumed. Thus for O'Brien in the *Poor Man's Guardian* and the *Destructive* taxation was 'but a mole-hill to Mont Blanc, compared to the exactions which we endure from the profit-men'; 'Talk of tithes and taxes indeed... what signifies the parson's plundering or the taxeaters compared with that of the remorseless capitalist'; 'if tithes and taxes were abolished to-day, it would be the middle rather than the working classes who would monopolize the entire benefit'.[44]

O'Brien believed that the popularisation of the view that it was the capitalist rather than the taxeater who was the primary exploiter of labour had done much to change working-class perceptions of what caused their material impoverishment. 'Before the editor of the *Guardian* appeared as a writer', wrote O'Brien by way of self-congratulation, 'it was generally fancied by the people that the taxes were the main cause of distress. This was a very foolish idea, but considering what very eminent men held that opinion... considering that Paine and Cobbett were amongst its promulgators, it is not surprising that the people believed it.'[45] O'Brien's claim that the *Poor Man's Guardian* had alone precipitated this revolution in working-class thinking can

---

[42] *Crisis*, 2, 22 (1833), 175, a letter from 'One of the Productive Classes'.
[43] *Carpenter's Political Letters*, 12 February 1831, contribution from William Pare.
[44] *Destructive*, 40 (1833), 314.
[45] ibid. 176 (1834), 289.

be questioned, but what cannot be doubted is that those who saw taxation as the main cause of economic distress were, in the early 1830s, under intense critical fire. They certainly no longer dominated the pages of the working-class press as they had done in the immediate post-Napoleonic War period.[46]

An economic theory of labour exploitation had emerged and while it might assume a variety of forms, these forms possessed fundamental and distinctive common elements. The theory was characterised by a general concern with the market and its malfunctioning as a consequence of the malign exercise of economic power by those who possessed it; by the critical attention directed towards the existing medium of exchange and standard of value; by a desire to discover and establish the natural value of commodities and by a belief that this could be done through alterations in the relations of exchange. For many writers in the working-class press, as for the Smithian socialists, the problem of exploitation was essentially a problem of a defective method of exchange that permitted incorrect valuation or pricing of commodities. Further, the establishment of correct, just or natural prices meant for many not simply the elimination of economic injustice but also a significant step along the road to the 'New Moral World'. Thus George Mudie was one among many who saw labour bazaars as a 'bridge over which all human society ... [was] to pass from a very wretched to a highly prosperous state'.[47]

The nature of these common elements would also suggest that the treatment of labour exploitation in much of the working-class press owed its inspiration directly or indirectly to Smithian socialist political economy and to a lesser extent to that of Robert Owen. It is true that the older, radical approach to the problem continued to find expression but if the ghost of Paine had not been entirely exorcised, it haunted with less vigour than before.

In addition, this economic theory of labour exploitation provoked a direct and vigorous response from classical popularisers of a kind that the older radical analysis had not. For

---

[46] As H. Perkin has pointed out, the decline in official patronage from the 1780s onwards and the shrinking of the pension fund meant that this traditional explanation of impoverishment had less substance by the 1830s than previously, *Origins*, p. 313.

[47] *Exchange Bazaars Gazette*, 4 (1832), 45.

this theory of labour exploitation, among other things, gave some kind of theoretical substance to the view, inimical to the whole spirit of classical political economy, that the interests of the working classes and those of the capitalists were necessarily and fundamentally antagonistic. As one writer put it to his own logical satisfaction, once it had been show that

> rents, tithes, taxes, interest on money, profits on labour, profits on trade . . . are all thrown in to the price of the necessaries of life and that these various imposts combined with the wages of the working people form the real price of every species of goods, or of every article which the people have to purchase for their use; and like wise that in exact proportion as these rents, tithes, taxes and other profits increase, so must the wages of the working people be always reduced [it had been] . . . pretty clearly proved that not only the shopkeepers or middlemen, but the interest of everyone who lives by rent, tithes, taxes and other profits, which they impose upon the purchase of the people's industry, is directly opposed to the interests of those who labour.[48]

Wages and profits tended to be portrayed by such writers as two elements of an economic zero sum game. Wages and profits could not 'in relation to each other be both high and low . . . on the contrary like the two ends of a balance beam, in proportion as the one is high the other must be relatively low'; 'High wages involves [sic] low rates, low profits, low usury, low taxes, low everything that is levied on industry'; 'the increase of pauperism is a proportionate increase of wealth to the great'; 'every increase of any kind of profit is equal to a reduction . . . of wages to the same amount as the profit advanced'.[49]

Indeed it was very much against the tide of opinion that in this period Owen criticised the editor of the *Pioneer* for engendering a

---

[48] *Poor Man's Guardian*, 23 (1831), 179, article signed 'One of the Know Nothings' (note the additive approach to the analysis of labour exploitation). For one example of the rhetoric of class antagonism, see the headline in the *Pioneer*, 21 (1834), 165: 'War!! War!! War!! Labour has declared war against Capital'.

[49] *Poor Man's Guardian*, 31 (1832), 243, a letter signed 'One of the Know Nothings'; ibid. 142 (1834), 18; *Crisis*, 3, 8 (1833), 56; *Poor Man's Guardian*, 23 (1831), 179, article signed 'One of the Know Nothings'; ibid. 66 (1832), 530; here indeed was evidence of that increasingly 'bitter debate between the manufacturers and those in their employ, concerning the proper division of that fund from which these profits and wages are derived', which J. P. Kay mentioned in *The Moral and Physical Condition of the Working Classes employed in the Cotton Manufactures in Manchester* (Manchester, 1832), p. 9.

spirit of class antagonism: 'You have drawn a line of opposition of feelings and of interests between the employers and the employed in the production of wealth which, if it were continued, would tend to delay the progress of the great cause'[50] and as if to substantiate Owen's accusation the same issue of the paper categorised the disputes in which many trade unions were then involved as 'the war of labour and skill on the one hand against capital and artifice on the other'.[51] Such sentiments were also given particularly forceful expression in the *Poor Man's Guardian*: 'It ought to be well understood that every master lives out of the profits of his workmen'; 'The prosperity of a middleman means the accumulation of a fortune out of the fruits of your [labourers'] industry ... In the first place the word prosperity has two distinct meanings ... one for the master and another for the man'; 'the interest of employers and employed ever should be irreconcileable under the existing order of things'.[52] However, while vigorously expressed in the *Poor Man's Guardian* the belief that 'the kindly feelings that once existed between the employer and the employed have been destroyed'[53] was shared by many other writers in the working-class press. 'What a dreadful distance', wrote one commentator, 'have the last ten years placed between master and man. Wages sinking down to a degree below subsistence, profits rising to the overflowing of the cup.'[54]

The new, political economy of the working-class press provided the theoretical basis for such sentiments. This located the antagonism of economic interests within the economic system and defined them as antagonisms between groups and classes fulfilling an essentially economic role. This antagonism, expressed through and mediated by the market, was enunciated in the language of the political economists and, whatever the popularity of the popular political economy of which it was an integral part, it certainly succeeded in provoking a response from the populariser of classical doctrine. By the early 1830s the

[50] *Pioneer*, 19 (1834), 49, letter from Robert Owen; the great cause referred to was the emancipation of *all classes* from the old competitive, irrational, poverty-ridden system of society.
[51] ibid.
[52] *Poor Man's Guardian*, 31 (1832), 242, a letter from 'One of the Know Nothings'; ibid. 143 (1834), 27, a letter signed 'Political Corrector'; ibid. 169 (1834), 235.
[53] *Voice of the People*, 5 (1831), 37, 'The State of Feeling between Rich and Poor'.
[54] *Poor Man's Advocate*, 5 (1832), 40, letter signed 'W.M.'

popularisation of sound political economy was seen as imperative rather than salutary. Classical populariser in this period were certain that they were involved in a vital struggle for the minds and allegiance of the labouring classes and the ideological nature and intent of popularisation is clearly articulated. Andrew Ure, in his *Philosophy of Manufactures*, gave voice to the fear which underlay the activity of the populariser when he wrote:

> the factory operative, little versant in the great operations of political economy, currency and trade, and actuated too often by an invidious feeling towards the capitalist who animates his otherwise torpid talents, is easily persuaded by artful demagogues, that his sacrifice of time and skill is beyond the proportion of his recompense, or that fewer hours of industry would be an ample equivalent for his wages.[55]

And for Ure and others there was a surfeit of such demagogues abroad. Charles Knight, for instance, claimed that there existed at the time many 'pretended teachers of political economy, who [were] ranting in popular assemblies about the unequal allotment of riches',[56] while James Mill complained similarly of such 'rascals at work' and fulminated against writers like Thomas Hodgskin who propagated 'with the zeal of perfect fanaticism' the 'mad nonsense' of 'the rights of the labourer to the whole produce of the country'. Mill believed that such ideas must be immediately countered for 'if they were spread ... [they] would be the subversion of civilised society, worse than the overwhelming deluge of Huns and Tartars'.[57] Even the Home Office was moved to ask Francis Place to produce a pamphlet giving 'a brief plain exposition of wages' to counter erroneous doctrines.[58]

What was required was a forceful and persuasive counter-attack upon perniciously false economic notions which engendered class antagonism and threatened social disruption. As William Empson

[55] A. Ure, *The Philosophy of Manufactures; or, an exposition of the Scientific, Moral and Commercial Economy of the Factory System of Great Britain*, 3rd edn (London, Bohn, 1861), p. 279.
[56] C. Knight, *Passages in a Working Life during half a century* (3 vols., London, 1864–5), Vol. 2, p. 169.
[57] A. Bain, *James Mill, A Biography* (London, Longman, 1882), pp. 63–4; Charles Knight also saw Hodgskin's ideas as subverting civilisation and precipitating a return to a savage state where the 'ministers of desolation would be able to sing their triumphant song of "Labour Defended against the claims of Capital" amid the shriek of the jackal and the howl of the wolf', *Passages*, Vol. 2, p. 171.
[58] G. Wallas, *The Life of Francis Place*, p. 354; these writers were approached in the period November–December 1833.

stressed in a review of the works of Mrs Marcet and Miss Martineau, the age of original theoretical speculation was dead and the 'missionary era' had now begun; the emphasis must now be placed upon preaching the economic gospel 'to all classes more especially the poor'[59] and to this end a large number of popular economic works directed specifically at the working classes were forthcoming in the period 1830–4. Mrs Marcet, having obviously abandoned her belief that political economy should not be taught to the labouring classes, published for the 'uneducated generally' *John Hopkins's Notions of Political Economy* (1833).[60] Harriet Martineau's multi-volumed *Illustrations of Political Economy* appeared in the years 1832–4, disseminating the correct principles of classical political economy in a palatable fictional form, while Charles Knight's *Results of Machinery* (1831) was 'especially addressed to working men' at a time of 'great national alarm, when a blind rage against a power supposed to interfere with the claims of labour was generally prevalent'[61] – a great national alarm which may also have accounted for the anonymous publication of *A Plain Statement with respect to Wages* which rapidly went through three editions and *A Short Address to Workmen on Combinations to raise Wages*, published 'under superintendance of the Society for the Diffusion of Useful Knowledge'. Knight's *Results of Machinery* was quickly followed by his *Rights of Industry* (1831) which was applauded by George Poulett Scrope for having 'performed a valuable service ... by exhibiting in a popular form the great truth, that the security of

---

[59] W. Empson, 'Mrs Marcet – Miss Martineau', 8: 'Political Economy, we rejoice to think, has apparently nearly waited its appointed time. The mysteries and abstractions have retired for a while into the inner sanctuary; whilst, amongst the ministers of the outer courts, and throughout even the surrounding multitude, there are symptoms of movement which bespeak the arrival of the missionary era.'

[60] ibid. Mrs Marcet remarked in the Preface to her work that it was 'for the improvement of the lower classes. It will be obvious to the reader that it is for that rank of life that this little work is intended', *John Hopkins's Notions of Political Economy* (London, 1833).

[61] C. Knight, *Capital and Labour including the Results of Machinery* (London, 1873), Preface; the enthusiastic reception which the works of Marcet and Martineau received from political economists such as McCulloch and Say and political figures such as Brougham and Althorp, as well as historians and divines, gives some indication of the strength of the perceived need for such popularisers in the circumstances of the early 1830s; see G. Routh, *The Origin of Economic Ideas* (London, Macmillan, 1977), pp. 182–9.

property is the first and most precious right of the labourer',[62] while in 1832 the *Political and Moral Magazine* was established as 'a vehicle' by means of which the ubiquitous Place hoped 'to promulgate the true principles of politics, political economy and morals'.[63] From this period also date the origins of a jesuitical concern to inculcate in the young sound principles of political economy by means of schoolbooks,[64] and Richard Whately, who was intimately connected with this educational crusade,[65] also added to the flood of popular political economy addressed to the labouring classes with *A Letter to his Parishioners on the Disturbances which have lately occurred* (1830) and his *Village Conversations in Hard Times* (1831).[66]

The overwhelming impression is, therefore, that in the period 1830–4 classical popularisers consciously geared themselves for a vigorous and, as they saw it, vitally important ideological struggle. It was undoubtedly true, of course, that the agricultural riots of 1830, the heightened class antagonism in the aftermath of the passage of the Great Reform Act, the Ten Hours

---

[62] G. P. Scrope, 'The rights of industry – the banking system', 414. Scrope correctly identified this work as a specific counterblast to the 'pernicious' and 'monstrous' claim 'which has been set up in the name of the labourer for the whole produce of industry, and the denial of the right of the capitalist and landowner to any portion of it', ibid. 412. The work was also seen as a direct attack upon Hodgskin by a reviewer in the *Midland Representative*, 33 (1832), 4, who wrote, 'It appears, however, that certain lectures delivered at the Mechanics Institute in London and certain publications on "Popular Political Economy", have advanced the doctrine – that the capitalist has no right to charge an interest or profit on capital with which he supplies the labourer ... For the refutation of doctrines of this cast the work is especially compiled.' This onslaught in turn provoked Hodgskin to publish a second edition of his *Labour Defended* in 1831. On this point see T. Kamata, 'The life and thought of Thomas Hodgskin up to the first parliamentary reform (1832)', paper presented to the *Ninth Conference of the History of Economics Society*, 25 May 1982.

[63] G. Wallas, *The Life of Francis Place*, p. 338.

[64] J. M. Goldstrom, 'Richard Whately and political economy in schoolbooks 1833–80', *Irish Historical Studies*, 15 (1966–7), 137.

[65] See, for example, R. Whately, *Easy Lessons on Money Matters, Commerce, Trade, Wages etc. etc. for the Use of Young People as well as Adults of all Classes* (Dublin, 1835); 'The general tenor of the *Lessons* is to show the essential fairness of the economic system, especially the way it allocated income'. G. Routh, *Origins*, pp. 186–7.

[66] Whately in his *Introductory Lectures on Political Economy* (London, 1831) exhorted others to follow in his literary footsteps and in addition used the *Saturday Magazine* (1833) to popularise political economy for the benefit of children and the poor; see M. Berg, *The Machinery Question*, pp. 293–4.

Movement, the general agitation connected with the 1833 Factory Act and the burgeoning of trade unionism in the period 1833–4 gave this struggle its peculiar importance and intensity in the eyes of writers like Whately and Martineau, but the emergence of a popular political economy founded upon an economic theory of labour exploitation, exuding class antagonism and disseminated widely by the working-class press, was a major factor determining the form which the ideological struggle took. The acolytes of classical political economy had to contend with an alternative and hostile economic faith; a conflicting set of doctrines which they must declare anathema. The new bellicosity was nicely captured by Mountifort Longfield when he wrote in 1834:

> It is daily becoming more important that the notions which are generally entertained [about political economy] should be correct, since they now lead so directly to action. *No person can now remain altogether neutral and avoid such topics*... Opinions, whether true or false, will no longer remain inactive; they both immediately affect legislation, and exercise immense influence on a class of people powerfully removed beyond the reach of such discussions... I allude to the labouring classes.[67]

Political economy had become a battlefield where there was no longer a place for conscientious objectors. Economic ideas were perceived as leading directly to action and the fear of wrong action precipitated by wrong doctrine had grown greatly. In this context it is interesting to note Marx's view that 1830 was the date which marked the end of 'scientific bourgeois economy'. After that date

> It was... no longer a question, whether this theorem or that was true, but whether it was useful to capital or harmful, expedient or inexpedient, politically dangerous or not. In place of disinterested inquirers, there were hired prize fighters; in place of genuine scientific research, the bad conscience and evil intent of apologetic.[68]

In one sense this remark has undoubted validity. The popularisation of an economic theory of labour exploitation in the

---

[67] M. Longfield, *Lectures on Political Economy* (Dublin, Milliken, 1834), pp. 16–17 (my emphasis).
[68] K. Marx, *Capital*, Vol. 1, p. 25, Afterword to the second German edition.

early 1830s certainly helped to provoke an historically unique proliferation of hired prize fighters. Yet a theory of labour exploitation was only one of the pillars upon which working-class political economy rested in the early 1830s. It highlighted certain deficiencies and inequalities inherent in existing economic arrangements; it did not of itself, however, call into question the longer-term macroeconomic viability of such arrangements. To do this it was necessary to formulate a theory of general economic crisis and it is to this aspect of the political economy of anti-capitalist and socialist writers that reference must now be made.

7

Early socialist political economy and the theory of capitalist crisis[1]

Classical economists did not deny the possibility of short-lived periods of economic difficulty characterised by unsold commodities, idle capital and redundant labour.[2] Even James Mill, ever prone to outbursts of intellectual frustration with those who failed to grasp the tautological nature of his formulation of Say's Law,[3] accepted the possibility of partial gluts. Yet for Mill, the overproduction of one commodity implied the underproduction of another. A surfeit of capital and labour applied to the production of one good necessarily entailed a deficiency of capital and labour in some other productive sphere: 'It is . . . impossible, that there should be in any country a commodity or commodities

---

[1] This chapter is primarily concerned with the political economy of Thompson, Owen and Gray, though the work of a number of lesser writers is noticed. Thomas Hodgskin cannot be said to have formulated a theory of general economic crisis, though certain passages in his economic writings hint at an explanation for general depression similar to that articulated by early socialist writers and some notice will be taken of these.

Throughout this and the following chapter 'crisis' will be used in the general, non-technical sense in which it would have been understood by early-nineteenth-century anti-capitalist and socialist writers and not in the specific sense of the turning-point between boom and slump.

[2] 'The classical economists were never guilty of the absurdity sometimes attributed to them of denying the existence of depressions, unsold goods and unemployment', T. Sowell, *Say's Law: an historical analysis* (Princeton University Press, 1972), p. 51.

[3] 'The doctrine of the glut seems to be disproved by reasoning perfectly conclusive'; 'How complete soever the demonstration may appear to be, that the demand of a nation must always be equal to its supply, and that it can never be without a market sufficiently enlarged for the whole of its produce, this proposition is seldom well understood and is sometimes expressly contradicted', J. Mill, *The Elements of Political Economy*, 3rd edn (London, 1826) in D. N. Winch (ed.), *Selected Economic Writings of James Mill* (Edinburgh, Oliver and Boyd, 1966), pp. 334, 329.

158

The theory of capitalist crisis 159

in quantity greater than the demand, without there being to an equal amount, some other commodity or commodities in quantity less than demand.'[4] Such partial gluts must, therefore, be temporary phenomena disappearing when the movement of capital and labour reoriented the nation's productive base to match the prevailing structure of demand.

Ricardo also accepted the existence of temporary economic disequilibria when, for example, the too rapid accumulation of fixed capital produced a redundancy of labour. Possibly influenced by John Barton's *Observations on the Circumstances which Influence the Condition of the Labouring Classes of Society* (1817),[5] Ricardo added a new chapter, 'On Machinery', to the third edition of his *Principles* (1821) in which he suggested that an initial diminution in the demand for labour might occur where circulating capital, representing the demand for labour, was reduced to allow more rapid application of fixed capital to the productive process. In such a situation there would 'necessarily be a diminution in the demand for labour, population will become redundant, and the situation of the labouring classes will be that of distress and poverty'.[6] Ricardo did, however, argue further that labour would not long remain redundant, for the enhanced profitability produced by the productivity gains of mechanisation would increase the rate of capital accumulation and hence the demand for labour.[7]

Ricardo also attempted to reconcile the economic fact of the post-Napoleonic depression with the full employment implications of classical theory, by highlighting the redundancy of capital and labour which could result from 'Sudden Changes in the Channels of Trade'.[8] Thus in the transition from war to peace the structure of output might cease to match the structure

---

[4] ibid. p. 235; see also J. R. McCulloch, 'The opinions of Messrs. Say, Sismondi and Malthus on the effects of machinery and accumulation', 118–9: 'The fault is not in producing too much, but in producing commodities which do not suit the tastes of those with whom we wish to exchange them ... It is the wrong application of productive power, the improper adaptation of means to ends, that is in every case the specific cause of gluts.'
[5] See S. G. Hollander, 'The development of Ricardo's position on machinery', *History of Political Economy*, 3 (1971), 105–35.
[6] D. Ricardo, *Principles*, p. 390.
[7] ibid. pp. 396–7.
[8] ibid. pp. 263–72.

of demand and in such a period manufacturers would take time to adjust to the changing demands of consumers and 'during the interval when they are settling in the situations which new circumstances have made the most beneficial, much fixed capital is unemployed . . . and labourers are without full employment.'[9]

Yet it was J. S. Mill who most explicitly articulated the view that Say's Law, unless reduced to a mere tautology,[10] did not imply the theoretical impossibility of a general glut of commodities and hence a general depression in the level of economic activity. Thus in an essay written in 1830 but not published until 1844, J. S. Mill drew attention to the fact that if money performed the function not merely of a numeraire or medium of exchange but was also demanded for the utility which it yielded as a store of value, then a general glut of commodities could theoretically exist when the demand for money was greater than the supply:

Now the effect of the employment of money, and even the utility of it, is that it enables . . . [the] one act of interchange to be divided into two separate acts or operations; one of which may be performed now, and the others a year hence, or whenever it shall be most convenient . . . The buying and selling being now separated, it may well occur, that there may be, at some given time, a very general inclination to sell with as little delay as possible, accompanied with an equally general inclination to defer all purchases as long as possible. *This is always actually the case, in those periods which are described as periods of general excess.*[11]

Thus where money was demanded for the satisfaction which it yielded as a commodity in its own right and where the community wished to increase its holdings of it (i.e. where it

---

[9] ibid. p. 265; such disproportionate production was seen by J. R. McCulloch as a consequence of entrepreneurs miscalculating the scale of demand for particular products, *The Principles of Political Economy* (Edinburgh, 1825), p. 188.

[10] Proponents of Say's Identity like James Mill assumed an identity of the aggregate supply price and the aggregate value of all commodities demanded. Any increase in the value of commodities supplied would be matched by an identical increase in demand, i.e. goods were effectively seen as exchanging against goods with money serving the sole function of a convenient numeraire or medium of exchange: 'no man wants money but in order to lay it out either in articles of productive or articles of unproductive consumption', J. Mill, *Elements*, p. 329. For a fuller exposition see M. Blaug, *Economic Theory in Retrospect*, pp. 154–6.

[11] J. S. Mill, *Essays on Some Unsettled Questions of Political Economy*, p. 70 (my emphasis).

wished to increase its cash balances), there would exist a general inclination to sell without a comparable inclination to buy and, therefore, a general glut of commodities. However, while recognising the theoretical possibility of such an occurrence, classical economists like Mill believed that movements in the price level would ensure that such general gluts, should they occur at all, would be short-lived. A general depression in the level of economic activity was not regarded, therefore, as a practical problem requiring serious attention. There were mechanisms and forces inherent in the economic system which would ensure the effective maintenance or rapid return to a situation where the aggregate demand for goods was sufficient to take up the aggregate supply.

Thus classical economists did, for the most part, qualify the rigid formulations of Say's Law beloved of their populalarisers[12] and such qualifications negated the simplistic belief that in no circumstances could a simultaneous excess of capital, labour and commodities exist. However, writers like J. S. Mill did tend consciously to minimise the capacity of competitive capitalism to generate significant periods of macroeconomic disequilibrium. Indeed, to mention that there existed such a capacity was for Mill something to be avoided. Thus in a letter to John Nichol written in 1834, Mill expressed himself 'anxious that in your article on the theory of a "glut of capital", you should avoid the phrase "glut" or any other which will bring you into seeming collision ... with my father's and Say's doctrine respecting a general glut'.[13]

In addition, the constant reiteration of Say's Identity by writers such as James Mill and populalarisers like Harriet Martineau[14] must

---

[12] See, for example, H. Martineau, *Illustrations of Political Economy*, No. 25, *The Moral of Many Fables* (London, Fox, 1834), p. 128: 'Though the respective commodities of no two producers may be exactly suitable to their respective wishes, or equivalent in amount, yet, as every man's instrument of demand and supply is identical, the aggregate demand of society must be precisely equal to its supply. *In other words a general glut is impossible.* A partial glut is an evil which induces its own remedy; and the more quickly the greater the evil' (my emphasis).

[13] J. S. Mill to John Pringle Nichol, 14 October 1834, in F. E. Mineka (ed.), *Collected Works of John Stuart Mill*, Vol. 12, *The Earlier Letters of J. S. Mill* (Toronto University Press, 1963), p. 236. This may in part explain why Mill's *Essays on Some Unsettled Questions of Political Economy* was not published until 1844 by which time the intensity of the general glut controversies of the 1820s and 1830s had abated.

[14] See above, n. 12.

have produced a strong contemporary impression that classical political economy was bent upon the theoretical repudiation of one of the objective features of early-nineteenth-century economic life,[15] an impression undoubtedly reinforced by statements to the effect that 'Production is the cause and the sole cause of demand. It never furnishes supply without furnishing demand both at the same time and to an equal extent.'[16] Every classical economist may have been aware of the depressions of 1818, 1825, 1829 and 1836,[17] but for most such phenomena did not loom large in their political economy[18] and indeed, in the case of J. S. Mill, the theoretical possibility of their existence was best ignored for fear of providing a stick with which to beat classical political economy. The essence of classical orthodoxy, in both its pure and popularised form, was its stress on the transient or ephemeral nature of macroeconomic disruption and on the inherent tendency of the economic system to an equilibrium where productive resources would be fully utilised. So general economic depression tended to be explained away in terms of disproportionate supply, working-class ignorance of the laws of political economy, frictional problems generated by factor immobility or simply the unfortunate propensity of the labouring classes to increase more rapidly than the artefacts necessary for their employment or the subsistence necessary for their support.[19]

[15] Perhaps we have here another area where some classical economists 'were...reluctant...to abandon their hard won generalisations as a result of new and conflicting evidence', A. W. Coats, 'The classical economists and the labourer', A. W. Coats (ed.), *The Classical Economists and Economic Policy* (London, Methuen, 1971), p. 148.
[16] J. Mill, *Elements*, p. 329.
[17] 'We know that every one of the classical economists was aware of the occurrence of business depressions', M. Blaug, *Economic Theory in Retrospect*, p. 159.
[18] The major exception being Malthus in Book 2 of his *Principles of Political Economy* (London, 1820).
[19] Thus 'honest' John Hopkins lamented the fact that 'we are too many by half for all the mills and factories of the kingdom' and concluded, 'The fault lies in there being more people...than there is food to maintain, clothes to cover or houses to lodge them', Mrs Marcet, *John Hopkins's Notions of Political Economy*, p. 140. Trade unions were also seen as a cause of general distress. Thus E. C. Tufnell wrote of Sheffield, 'the town exhibits the extraordinary spectacle, the inevitable result of successful combinations...a decaying trade and a destitute population', *The Character, Object and Effects of Trades' Unions* (London, Ridgway, 1834), p. 84. The Corn Laws were also viewed in the same light as an obstacle which prevented the price of labour falling sufficiently to ensure a high demand for its services.

The classical approach to the possibility of general economic depression was, therefore, an obvious butt for early-nineteenth-century writers critical of capitalism and all its works[20] and their assault upon the idea that competitive capitalism tended to a golden mean of prosperity provided the macroeconomic counterpart of their labour exploitation theories.[21] For, while a theory of labour exploitation furnished the microeconomic foundations for a critique of capitalism, a theory of capitalist crisis or general economic depression provided the basis for an attack on the rationality, stability and viability of the capitalist system as a whole. A theory of labour exploitation or undervaluation might focus attention upon some of the inequitable and negative aspects of contemporary capitalism but a theory of general economic breakdown was necessary to prevent this degenerating into petty moralising and to show that inherent in this unjust and inequitable economic system were elements inimical to its continued stable functioning. While a theory of labour exploitation provided an explanation of the material impoverishment suffered by the labouring classes, a theory of general economic crisis implied the necessary, eventual dissolution of the economic system which allowed such impoverishment to occur. Leaving aside, therefore, any Marxian conception of general depression as a key component in the dialectic of historical development, a theory of general economic breakdown allowed writers such as Thompson, Gray and Owen to emphasise the mutability and hence, for them, the historical transience of capitalism.[22] Capitalism would not, of course, be forcibly overthrown but ultimately its inherent tendency to macroeconomic dissolution would necessitate its conscious replacement by more just and rational economic arrangements; in particular, for Owen,

---

[20] Most would have agreed with K. Rodbertus's view that 'the school of Ricardo and Say endeavour... to prove, in the midst of the woes of "overproduction", that no such thing can take place', *Overproduction and Crises* (English Translation, London, Sonnenschien, 1898), p. 129.

[21] In Owen's case his theory of general economic depression represented the macroeconomic counterpart of his explanation of labour's undervaluation.

[22] This may have been another factor heightening the combative ardour of classical popularisers in the late 1820s and early 1830s. As J. Robinson has remarked, 'if the possibility of changing the system is once admitted, those who hope to gain and those who fear to lose... are immediately ranged in opposite camps', *An Essay on Marxian Economics* (London, Macmillan, 1949), p. 1.

Thompson and Gray, by arrangements which had as their foundation an equitable system of exchanging labour and commodities.

In addition a theory of general economic depression allowed these writers to highlight the discrepancy between the actual achievements of capitalism and the claims made for it by its apologists. Thus the simultaneous existence of idle capital, redundant labour and glutted markets was counterposed to the claimed allocative efficiency of competitive capitalism to highlight its fundamental failings, and in this way socialist writers were able through their theories of general economic crisis to give substance and confirmation to previously vague assertions that existing economic arrangements could not hope to satisfy the material needs and aspirations of the labouring classes.

Also, once a popularly intelligible theory of general depression had been formulated and disseminated among the labouring classes, the economic world ceased for them to be an inexplicable chaos of human misfortune. More importantly, the economic distress resulting from prolonged unemployment could no longer be viewed as a collection of purely personal tragedies resulting from individual deficiencies or moral failings. Rather such a theory enabled those amongst whom it was disseminated to see unemployment and generalised distress as a characteristic feature of the contemporary economic order for which individual labourers could in no sense be held responsible.

For these reasons a theory of general economic depression or crisis was a fundamental component of the political economy of early socialist writers and it is the purpose of this chapter to establish first, its essential theoretical components; secondly, to highlight some of its theoretical deficiencies; thirdly, to discuss the consequences of those deficiencies for the nature of the early socialist critique of capitalism; and finally, to suggest that despite the many perceptive critical insights which early socialist writers provided into the manner in which the capitalist system functioned as a whole, their macroeconomic analysis was insufficient of itself to furnish them with anything more than reformist policy corollaries. In this context it will be argued that the theories of general economic depression formulated by Owen, Thompson, Gray and other lesser writers did not imply the need for any fundamental, direct alteration in the existing pattern of ownership of the nation's productive means. This is not to suggest that their political economy prevented them from challenging the justice of the existing distribution of property but rather that their theories of general crisis, by emphasising certain aspects of the problem (e.g. the nature and role of money) implied that it was the rationalisation of exchange rather than the appropriation of existing accumulations of capital which would provide the solution to economic depression.

As with their analysis of labour exploitation it was to the malfunctioning of the market that Owen, Gray and Thompson looked for an explanation of the causes of general economic breakdown. Of importance in this context was the distinction which they frequently made in their writings between exchange or market value and use value and the attendant belief that production decisions made with reference to the former, i.e. production carried on for the realisation and accumulation of exchange value rather than for the creation of use values contained within them the seeds of inevitable economic convulsion. This idea was developed with differing degrees of sophistication but at its simplest it emerged as a belief that overproduction and glutted markets resulted, at least in part, from the wrong type of goods being produced. Thus for Thompson, one of the reasons why co-operative communities or groups of co-operative communities would never suffer from a general glut of commodities was that their productive capacity was oriented to the provision of goods with a high use value, and that production would be halted or at least relaxed once the demand for really 'useful' goods had been satisfied. In such communities, wrote Thompson, the

Demand ... [and] supply of all articles necessary to health must be commensurate [for] ... such a community would be very careful how it directed its surplus labor to the production of any articles, however glittering the immediate profit, for which the *real and regular wants of society at large*, did not guaranty [*sic*] something approaching to a permanent equality of demand.[23]

So by directing the community's productive powers to the manufacture of useful articles such as foodstuffs, dwellings and

[23] W. Thompson, *Inquiry*, pp. 424–5 (my emphasis).

clothing, 'the tremendous evil of want of employment and consequent wretchedness [would] . . . be absolutely banished . . . supply and demand [would] . . . be strictly and eternally commensurate'.[24] If the purpose of production was the satisfaction of need then demand was unlimited and supply, whatever its extent, must be matched by a comparable demand.

This distinction between production for use and production for profit was also a persistent theme in the economic writing of Robert Owen:

a very large part of our artificial or mechanical agency is employed to produce *that which is of little real value to society, and which, in the act of production, entails innumerable evils . . . [producing] a misapplication of existing powers of production in the country, both natural and artificial, when compared to the wants and demands for these productions.*[25]

Thus, for Owen, it was impossible under existing arrangements to match supply and demand because demand conceived of in terms of 'wants' was not taken into account by those who controlled the nation's productive powers. Rather the powers of production were misapplied to supply goods of 'little real value'. Supply and demand would only be equated, therefore, and the productive powers of the nation cease to be misdirected when production was for the direct satisfaction of actual wants. In this way Owen, like other socialist writers of the period, exploited the ambiguity of concepts such as value, want and demand which possessed both an economic and a moral dimension. Where classical economists tried to imbue them with a kind of scientific neutrality, Owen and others used them as both ethical imperatives and economic constructs condemning simultaneously the economic rationality and moral legitimacy of capitalism.[26]

It was also the case, for Thompson in particular, that the bias in favour of the production of luxury goods, which he saw as following from an obsession with production for exchange and profit rather than use, did increase the vulnerability of an economy to macroeconomic breakdown. For while luxuries

---

[24] ibid. p. 425.
[25] R. Owen, 'A letter published in the London newspapers', 25 July 1817, *Life*, pp. 68–9 (my emphasis).
[26] This was particularly true of the term 'natural' as used in connection with value and price.

were 'liable to the changes of fashion'[27] and thus demand for them was 'irregular and uncertain, depending on the caprice or variations of the fortunes of the rich',[28] the demand for necessaries was regarded as 'constant ... almost invariable'.[29] For Thompson, therefore, co-operative communities were seen as possessing an inherent economic stability stemming from their bias towards the production of those articles for which demand was relatively inelastic. Thus one of the major attractions of co-operative communities was that 'Very uncommon and very short would be the occasions, in which the capacity to labor would not meet with an adequate demand for its exertion.'[30] The nature of their productive activity allowed them to offer an autarkic security free from the disequilibria which so adversely affected the markets for goods in the outside world.[31] They provided a relatively stable economic environment where demand would remain commensurate with output to whatever extent it was expanded, where demand would be 'constant almost invariable' and where labour and other productive resources would, of necessity, be fully utilised.

At one level, this aspect of the early socialist explanation of the origin of general economic depression implied that a general glut might be avoided by the production of high use value commodities, a conclusion in some respects not greatly different from the classical view of gluts as the product of disproportional production, i.e. the production of the wrong sort of goods.[32]

---

[27] W. Thompson, *Inquiry*, p. 204; Thompson went on to argue that, 'There consists ... in the very nature of things, a constant source of caprice in the demand for all those extra articles of luxury called for by excessive wealth', ibid. p. 207.

[28] ibid. p. 206.   [29] ibid.   [30] ibid. p. 424.

[31] This explains in some measure the 'artificiality of the closed economy, which was a tacit assumption in Owenism and most early socialist thought', R. G. Garnett, *Co-operative and Owenite Socialist Communities in Britain and America 1825–45* (Manchester University Press, 1972), p. 10. Thus communities were seen as offering *'permanent asylums* which will for ever place us beyond the influence of distressing cares and anxieties', R. Owen, *The Address of the Working Classes of Devonshire* (Exeter, 1830). It was this autarkic conception of communities as 'asylums' of economic stability which permitted the assumption of a closed economy.

[32] See, for example, Anon., *Vindication of Mr Owen's Plan for the Relief of the Distressed Working Classes* (London, 1820), p. 43, who argued that a rational division of labour amongst communities would allow '*a due proportion of every kind of wealth* [to] ... *be produced instead of occasionally glutting the markets with some commodities*' (my emphasis). Such a remark embodies an essentially classical conception of depression.

However, at another level, by emphasising the instability inherent in an economic system dominated by the need to realise exchange values, socialist writers highlighted, if unconsciously, that salient characteristic of capitalist production recognised by J. S. Mill as making the general overproduction of commodities a theoretical possibility. Thus they pointed to the fact that under capitalism the purpose of production was the realisation of exchange values rather than the appropriation of use values and that goods were not bartered directly against each other but were exchanged for money thus separating the actions of purchase and sale and introducing the possibility of general gluts.

On occasion classical writers would disregard this possibility by reducing money to the sole function of a medium of exchange: 'Productions are always bought by productions... Money is only the medium by which exchange is effected.'[33] Thus, in effect, money became a numeraire and the exchange process was reduced to one of barter, with no desire on the part of individuals to separate the act of purchase and exchange and, therefore, no possibility of a general glut occurring. To do this was, however, to strip capitalism of its distinguishing features. As Marx put it, 'In order to prove that capitalist production cannot lead to general crises, all its conditions and distinct forms all its principles and specific features – in short *capitalist production* itself – are denied.'[34] So by emphasising the distinction between production for use and production for exchange and profit, Owen and Thompson were indirectly highlighting those specific characteristics of capitalism which rendered it vulnerable to general economic depression and, indeed, they point in their writings to a mode of commodity exchange from which these distinguishing features have been removed. For what is the retreat to the autarky of co-operative communities and the organisation of labour bazaars and exchanges but the creation in microcosm of a barter economy where use values are exchanged against use values by way of a labour numeraire and where the validating conditions of Say's Identity are formally established. In this sense it was by abolishing the distinctive features of commodity exchange in a capitalist economy that early socialist writers such

---

[33] D. Ricardo, *Principles*, pp. 291–2.
[34] K. Marx, *Theories of Surplus Value*, Vol. 2, p. 501 (Marx's emphasis).

as Thompson and Owen hoped to eliminate the possibility of general depression and make communities 'permanent asylums which will forever place us beyond the influence of the distressing care and anxieties which are now ... arriving'.[35]

This recurring emphasis on the need to produce useful goods would seem to entail the conclusion that it was impossible to overproduce necessities and certainly some passages abstracted from the works of Thompson, Owen and other socialist writers would bear that interpretation. Yet such a conclusion was rejected. Thus, for example, Thompson wrote in his *Inquiry* that, 'As of late in Ireland ... [there had been] privation of dwelling, of clothes, of food, disease, death; and all this not only in the midst of a capability to produce but of an absolute surplus produce of food, the producers dying of want, the products of their labor unsaleable.'[36]

The fact was that under existing economic arrangements a glut of necessities was a possibility and this was so because capitalist producers required a certain intensity of demand for their products; an intensity of demand sufficient to produce a level of prices which would cover profits, rents and other additions to labour costs. If the demand for commodities was of sufficient intensity to generate such exchange values then the market would be cleared and entrepreneurs would continue to produce. However, should the market price of goods fall below that required by capitalists then, regardless of any 'demand' for goods in terms of wants or need, a general glut of markets would ensue and production would cease. As the Owenite Dr McCormac of Belfast put it, 'such production of wealth as would be conducive to the welfare of society ... is only permitted when it will procure a profit for the capitalist or in other words when it will enable him to have in return a means of buying more of the produce of labour, than the article cost'.[37] Hodgskin too saw

---

[35] R. Owen, *The Address of the Working Classes of Devonshire*.
[36] W. Thompson, *Inquiry*, p. 424.
[37] H. McCormac, *An Appeal in Behalf of the Poor* (Belfast, 1831), p. 16; see also J. Gray, *Social System*, p. 59, 'the quantity that can be *sold at a profit*, not the quantity that can be *made* ... is the present limit to production' (Gray's emphasis); or as Owen succinctly phrased it, 'The existing arrangements of society permit production and consumption to proceed only through profit upon price', *An Explanation of the Cause of Distress*, p. 4.

the capitalists' need to secure a profit as a possible limitation upon the scale of productive activity. Thus he argued that labourers were simply not employed unless their employment yielded what their employers regarded as an adequate return: 'Capitalists becoming the proprietors of all wealth of society... never... suffer labourers to have the means of subsistence unless they have a confident expectation that their labour will produce a profit over and above their own subsistence',[38] and, for Hodgskin, this ruled out much productive activity which would in fact have furnished an adequate material standard of well-being for the labourer and his family.[39] Thus, productive activity was stopped short of what the untrammelled operation of natural economic laws would have allowed.[40] The capitalist demand for profit therefore hindered the full development of productive forces creating an 'artificial check to production and population'.[41]

Yet what Hodgskin does not argue either in *Labour Defended* or in his *Popular Political Economy* is that this lust for profit actually precipitated a general economic crisis where there existed a fundamental imbalance between aggregate supply and aggregate demand.[42] Indeed, this is nowhere argued in Hodgskin's major works, though such a line of argument can be found in an article in the *Mechanics Magazine* (1823). Here Hodgskin specifically attacked the idea of supply creating its own demand:

It is a maxim of the political economists, that products always create their own market; but this market is derived from the supposition that

[38] T. Hodgskin, *Popular Political Economy*, p. 52.
[39] The demand for profit 'extinguishes all that labour which would only procure the labourer his comfortable subsistence', ibid. p. 246; 'Infinite are the undertakings which would amply reward the labour necessary for their success, but which will not pay the additonal sums required for rents, profits, tithes, and taxes', T. Hodgskin, *The Natural and Artificial Rights of Property Contrasted*, p. 150.
[40] T. Hodgskin, *Popular Political Economy*, p. 238, 'the practice of stopping labour at that point where it can produce, in addition to the subsistence of the labourer, a profit for the capitalist, seem[s] opposed to the natural laws which regulate production'.
[41] ibid. p. 246; thus there is here some anticipation of Marx's view that 'the capitalist mode of production which, if viewed from the other premise, [i.e. social need] would... have been altogether inadequate... comes to a standstill at a point fixed by the production and realisation of profit, and not the satisfaction of requirements', *Capital*, Vol. 3, p. 258.
[42] Though there is the implication that the necessity of profit reduces the number of employment opportunities.

no man produces but with the intention of selling or enjoying, and it does not therefore hold good with our labourers who are compelled to produce but not permitted to enjoy.[43]

It has been argued by one writer that this represents a more explicit statement of ideas contained in *Popular Political Economy*[44] but this would not seem to be a valid interpretation. What Hodgskin appears to argue in *Popular Political Economy* is that certain opportunities for productive activity are eliminated because too high a rate of return is demanded; there is no hint of a general economic depression precipitated by underconsumption. Indeed, at points in his 1827 work Hodgskin comes close to the articulation of the view that supply does actually create its own demand. Thus he wrote that 'the commodity produced by one labourer, the shoes for example, constitutes in reality and ultimately, the market for the commodities produced by other labourers; and they and their productions are mutually the market for one another',[45] a view consistent with Hodgskin's understanding of money as purely a medium for exchange: 'All trade, though nominally transacted by money, is in fact the exchange of one commodity for another.'

Thus while the passage from the *Mechanics Magazine* suggests an underconsumptionist explanation of depression this is not developed further in Hodgskin's later work and in so far as that work does contain a theory of economic crisis it was one formulated in terms of the deleterious economic consequences of harvest failures in the absence of free trade and the disastrous repercussions of changes in the value of money.[46] As with labour exploitation, therefore, the solution for Hodgskin was to free economic life from those 'social regulations' which, by obstructing the free operation of natural economic laws, delayed the advent of material prosperity.

---

[43] *Mechanics Magazine*, 6 September 1823.
[44] J. E. King, 'Perish commerce! Free trade and underconsumption in early British radical economics', *Australian Economic Papers* 20 (1981), 247.
[45] T. Hodgskin, *Popular Political Economy*, p. 116.
[46] Thus free trade 'instead of causing, as is usually stated, alternations of prosperity and decay' tended 'to raise it [the economy] above all such fluctuations, and even to secure it against the effects of variations in the seasons', ibid. p. 173; it is something of an over-generalisation to suggest, therefore, that, 'For the radical critics of orthodox political economy, underconsumption and indifference or hostility to free trade went hand in hand', J. E. King, 'Perish commerce!', 236.

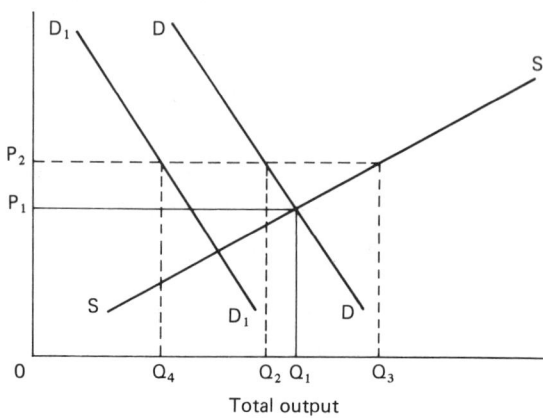

Figure 1

While Hodgskin suggested, therefore, that the need for profit could obstruct the expansion of productive activity he did not develop this idea along the lines which characterise the work of socialist writers such as Thompson and Owen, who argued that though capitalists produced only with the expectation of profit and while, therefore, goods were necessarily offered in the market at prices which reflected this, the demand necessary to ensure such prices would not and could not be forthcoming. Two factors made this certain: on the supply side the addition of profits to the labour cost of commodities and on the demand side the exploitation or undervaluation of labour.[47] These together ensured that the aggregate value of commodities demanded would be less than the aggregate supply price of the commodities produced. Their line of argument may be represented diagrammatically as in figure 1.

Let us assume an equilibrium exists where, in the absence of any undervaluation or exploitation of labour or any other distorting influences, the prices of commodities are equal to their natural, labour values. In this situation most early socialist writers would have argued that the demand for commodities would be equal to their supply at a natural, equitable, general level of prices of P_1. However, before supplying to the market the goods which they produce, capitalist entrepreneurs value them at a

[47] See above, chapters 3 and 4.

The theory of capitalist crisis 173

price higher than that which would be generated if the natural laws of value were allowed to prevail. Capitalists, in effect, make an addition to the labour values at which commodities would and should naturally exchange. Let us say that this raises the general level of prices from P_1 to P_2.

Faced with these overvalued (wages + profits and possibly + rents) commodities, demand proves insufficient and a glut of commodities (Q_2Q_3) results.[48] In addition, let us assume that labour is now exploited or undervalued and receives less than its true worth or natural value (however defined). This will cause a reduction in *the* important component of aggregate demand (i.e. the demand of the labouring classes)[49] and thus a fall in demand from DD to D_1D_1 further increasing the glut of commodities from Q_2Q_3 to Q_4Q_3. Thus on the supply side overpricing or overvaluation of commodities produces a glut of magnitude Q_2Q_3 while the undervaluation/exploitation of labour produces a glut of Q_4Q_2.[50] In consequence, 'Till this condition of profit to capitalists can be complied with . . . and from the depressing competition of laborers amongst themselves', 'labor though teeming with the capabilities of making millions happy, must lie eternally dormant'.[51] It was this absolute impossibility of a profitable demand which condemned to 'idleness as to useful production . . . more than one half the human race'.[52] In the words of Owen, 'It is want of a profitable market that alone checks the successful and otherwise beneficial industry of the working classes.' This could be secured 'only when the demand is equal to, or exceeds supply'

---

[48] 'profit upon price cannot henceforth be generally obtained'; 'nor is it likely that a profit upon price can be again procured', R. Owen, *An Explanation*, pp. 2–3.
[49] See below, p. 187 n. 95.
[50] For Thompson, Gray, Owen and their popularisers it was not a question of 'Underconsumption *or* overproduction?', P. Hollis, *Class and Conflict in Nineteenth-Century England 1815–50*, p. 65 (my emphasis). Rather for these writers the underconsumption of exploited or undervalued labour and the overproduction of overvalued commodities were two sides of the same coin of general glut. Ms Hollis's view that 'the orthodox economists saw the working-man only as a producer *and the problem only as overproduction*', 'Introduction', *Poor Man's Guardian* (4 vols., London, Merlin, 1969), Vol. I, p. xxxv, is also wide of the mark. Where classical economists did recognise the theoretical possibility of general gluts (e.g. J. S. Mill), they saw them as the consequence of a general desire to increase money balances.
[51] W. Thompson, *Inquiry*, p. 374.
[52] ibid.

and 'under existing arrangements of commerce', this was not likely to be forthcoming[53] and so, argued Thompson, capitalists were driven to make labour redundant, 'forcing [the]... community... to starve, whenever... the exercise of their industry does not... yield such a return as will not only give ordinary support to the laborers, but also that quantum of the products of the labor to themselves, under the name of profits on capital, which they have been accustomed... to look upon as their due'.[54]

For John Gray too, 'Effectual demand... [was] the only thing wanting to cause houses to be built, clothes to be manufactured and food to be produced in quantities without any known or comprehensible limit.'[55] However, in *The Social System* Gray saw the deficiency of effectual demand as resulting essentially from a money supply which failed to increase *pari passu* with production. What was required, therefore, was some system whereby each unit of output automatically created the money necessary for its purchase at a price which included 'the cost of the material... the wages of labour; and thirdly... such a percentage or profit, as shall be sufficient to ensure a gradual and sufficiently rapid increase of capital'.[56] This was to be achieved by a National Chamber of Commerce acting in conjunction with a National Bank to determine what should be the prices of commodities and expand the circulating medium accordingly. In this way Gray believed 'it would be by no means difficult to place the commercial affairs of society on such a footing, that production would become the uniform and never failing cause of demand',[57] as James Mill and others suggested it already was. Thus for Gray the problem of glutted markets and overproduction was not the consequence of the addition of profit to labour cost but the result of a 'constant deficiency of money' in circulation, and the solution lay in ensuring that 'the quantity of money in circulation would at all times be exactly equivalent to the nominal or money value of the property in store'.[58]

---

[53] R. Owen, *Report*, pp. 3–4; *An Explanation*, p. 3.
[54] W. Thompson, *Inquiry*, p. 422.
[55] J. Gray, *The Social System*, p. 195.
[56] ibid. p. 33.
[57] ibid. p. 16.
[58] ibid. pp. 59, 66.

Their understanding of the causes of general economic depression also led Owen, Thompson and other lesser socialist writers to attach particular importance to the macroeconomic role of money. If general glut and economic crisis resulted from distorted exchange values then this required a particular analytical concern with the means by which exchanges were effected. This in turn led on to the belief that what was needed was a new medium of exchange which would not have the deleterious macroeconomic consequences of existing money. This new medium of exchange was to be based upon a new standard of value, the crucial quality of which was to be its immutability because, as Gray pointed out, it was 'only by the adoption of an immutable standard of value that goods continuing to cost the same labour in their production can continue to maintain the same price in the market',[59] or as Robert Owen put it, only if the new 'circulating medium' was 'unchangeable in its value' could it ensure that goods exchanged according to their 'intrinsic' worth. By contrast the existing gold and silver 'standard of value' had 'altered the *intrinsic* values of all things into artificial values'.[60]

In addition, the new medium of exchange based upon an immutable standard of value should be in sufficient supply to guarantee the purchase of commodities once their values had been accurately assessed. Thus for example, Owen, like Gray, believed that 'in the midst of wealth, and surrounded by the means of increasing it to an unlimited extent...want of this medium [had produced]...the evils...which poverty generates'; 'thousands and millions of our fellow men [are] ...unemployed, in poverty, in ignorance, and many actually starving for want of the common necessaries of life, solely because there are not sufficient quantities of certain metals...to circulate as artificial money'.[61]

---

[59] ibid. p. 85; 'the value of money is continually liable to change, and if weights and measures were subject to the same kind of variation, greater confusion and mischief would not be the result', ibid. p. 61.

[60] R. Owen, *An Address to All Classes in the State* (London, 1832), p. 7; *Report*, p. 5 (Owen's emphasis).

[61] R. Owen, *An Address to All Classes*, p. 7; *The Revolution in the Mind and Practice of the Human Race* (London, 1849), p. 52. S. Pollard, 'Robert Owen as an economist', pp. 31–2, has stressed the important role which Owen saw money playing in the expansion and contraction of the demand for commodities; on this point see also J. F. Bray, *Labour's Wrongs*, pp. 181–2.

The solution was the creation of a labour standard of value[62] and the introduction through labour banks and exchanges of the labour note or some equivalent as the new circulating medium. This would ensure not only that commodities were correctly valued but could also be expanded *pari passu* with output:

> We should always recollect that supply and demand must keep pace with each other, therefore, to avoid the evils of over-population and overstocked markets... let us open labour banks... make arrangements for exchanging your labour with each other, as by doing so you will become self-producers, self-employers, self-consumers and lay the foundation whereby you will better your condition.[63]

Or, as Benjamin Warden saw it, this new medium of exchange would 'create at the same time a greater demand for labour: for an increased consumption will take place in proportion as the wants of the people can be readily supplied by the aid of this new medium of exchange'.[64] Owen believed similarly that the requisite 'change in the standard of value would immediately open the most advantageous domestic markets, until the wants of all were amply supplied, nor while this standard of value continued, could any evil arise in the future from want of markets'; 'society would be immediately benefitted... to an incalculable extent, by making labour the standard of value. By this expedient, all the markets in the world, which are now virtually closed against offering a profit to the producers of wealth, would be opened to an unlimited extent.'[65]

Labour banks, labour exchanges, labour notes facilitated the exchange of labour equivalents. They permitted, in effect, goods

---

[62] 'labour will be the standard of value'; 'the natural standard of value is, in principle, human labour', R. Owen, *Report*, pp. 6, 51.

[63] W. King, *The Workings of Capital, at present represented by money* (London, 1831), p. 1 (N.B. This William King is a different person from Dr William King of Brighton). See also, for example, the resolution passed at a meeting addressed by William Pare in Limerick, 1833, to the effect 'that the system of Labour Exchanges as now developed by Mr Pare is eminently calculated to benefit the labouring classes by furnishing them with permanent productive employment and creating markets co-extensive with production', quoted from R. G. Garnett, 'William Pare, co-operator and social reformer', *Co-operative College Paper* No. 16 (Loughborough, 1973), p. 16.

[64] B. Warden, *The Rewards of Industry* (Bovington, 1832?), p. 1.

[65] R. Owen, *Report*, pp. 7, 21.

to be exchanged directly against goods[66] without the possibility of overvaluation or the opportunity for exploitation. Aggregate supply could thereby be made eternally commensurate with aggregate demand; indeed, these writers' perceptions of the labour note as simply a numeraire or medium of exchange established a formal equivalence between the two. Thus with labour at last receiving its true value, with the possibility of buying at one price and attempting to sell at another eliminated, with commodities exchanging at their natural labour values and with a money supply which would expand automatically 'as substantial wealth increases',[67] a demand commensurate with the supply of commodities would always be forthcoming.[68] As J. F. Bray was to put it in *Labour's Wrongs*, once the circulating medium had been appropriately regulated, once money had become an accurate, equitable and immutable numeraire, 'There could be no confusion – no gluts – no want of employment – no poverty; but production, and accumulation, and distribution, and consumption, would be naturally adjusted to each other, and would harmoniously work out their common results.'[69]

For these early socialist writers who saw general economic depression as intimately connected with the nature of money, its elimination need have no revolutionary consequences, nor did it necessitate any fundamental challenge to existing property rights and accumulations of capital. As Gray put it, a system of commerce based upon an immutable medium of exchange, which could be expanded and contracted in line with output, 'has nothing to do with any speculative theories upon the perfectibility of man... it requires merely a conventional plan of exchange, and a rational species of money', 'a rational system of exchange, or a proper instrument of effecting exchanges', 'an improved method of buying and selling'.[70] For Owen too, 'This simple expedient' alone would, 'it is evident, have the immediate

---

[66] 'The genuine principle of barter [is]... to exchange the prime cost of, or value of labour, in one article, against the prime cost, or amount of labour contained in any other article.' ibid. p. 20.

[67] ibid. p. 21.

[68] 'labour will be the standard of value, and as there will always be a progressive advance in the amount of labour... there will be, in the same proportion, a perpetually extending market or demand for all the industry of society', ibid. p. 51.   [69] J. F. Bray, *Labour's Wrongs*, p. 148.

[70] J. Gray, *The Social System*, pp. 25, 19, 158.

effect of securing to every individual the fruits of his own industry, and will create, at the same time, a greater demand for labour; for, an increased consumption will take place in proportion as the wants of the people can be supplied by the aid of this new medium of exchange'.[71] Thus were the gorgeous bubbles of Godwin wafted aside by these more prosaic visions of utopia which drew their inspiration from the prospect of 'rational money' and a better way of buying and selling.

It is tempting, in some respects, to interpret this concern with money as an inevitable by-product of the general interest in monetary phenomena generated by the furore of the currency debates and the actual deflationary policies which preceded and followed the restoration of cash payments by the Bank in 1819; and indeed, it has been suggested, with particular reference to Owen, that it was these debates that increasingly led him to disseminate the view that the form of exchange and the nature of the circulating medium were at the root of the economic miseries suffered by the labouring classes.[72]

Certainly these economic debates, the reality of deflation and the definite popular impact of the writings of Attwood, Muntz and others of the Birmingham School[73] were important factors

[71] R. Owen, *An Address to All Classes*, p. 7.
[72] M. Beer, *A History of British Socialism*, p. 177: 'The truth appears to be that Owen was caught in the whirlpool of the currency controversies in the years 1816–19 without having been able to extricate himself'; S. Pollard also points to the immediate post-war period as that when Owen became obsessed with the economic problems created by the existing medium of exchange and the economic benefits which might follow the introduction of a new one. Writing of the period 1815–19 Pollard states, 'It was to that time that Owen's suspicion of gold and silver currency, his preference for labour notes, and his hostility to the National Debt, can be traced', 'Robert Owen as an economist', 32.
[73] As W. H. Oliver has pointed out, there was sufficient rough correspondence between the ideas of Owen and other socialist or co-operative writers and those of the Birmingham School on money, for the ideas of the latter to be given a sympathetic hearing by the former: 'the two agree that the flaw in the actual economic system was a defect in distribution; both ascribed this defect to a false and inadequate circulating medium which hampered rather than facilitated the exchange of commodities', 'The labour exchange phase of the co-operative movement', *Oxford Economic Papers*, 10 (1958), 366; E. M. J. Yeo has also shown that in Birmingham, 'this very similarity of views on the need for a more elastic currency was enough to bring several leading Political Union figures like Attwood, Muntz and Edmonds onto Owenite platforms to support the establishment of a Birmingham Equitable Labour Exchange', 'Social science and social change 1830–80', unpublished PhD thesis (University of Sussex, 1972), p. 26; for the influence

engendering a popular interest in all that pertained to the influence of money upon the material circumstances of the population. However, it must also be stressed that an abiding concern with money was an inevitable feature of a political economy which so strongly emphasised the deleterious consequences of deviations of 'social', 'money' or 'market' values from those considered 'natural'. For while many causes might be and were advanced to explain such deviations, money itself was an obvious scapegoat for any failure to translate labour values into their money exchange value equivalents.

In addition, money was important to early socialist economists because it symbolised the existence and application of a standard of value which appeared to give no weight to the relative social utility of commodities. It was for this reason, among others, that Owen wanted the 'surplus produce' of one community to be exchanged 'for the surplus produce of other similar communities, by estimating the value of such surplus produce *in labour*, and *not in money*'.[74] Similarly, William King anticipated that one of the advantages of labour exchanges would be that 'goods so bartered would be valued by the exchanges in proportion to the relative utility they bore each other'.[75] Thus it was hoped that goods exchanged in and by these institutions, because they were free of the distorted valuations which money produced, would exchange according to their true social worth or utility. In effect, what these writers wanted, as Marx pointed out with respect to John Gray, was to ensure that even if goods were produced as commodities they would not be exchanged as such; rather their exchange would be socialised and their value expressed in terms of social utility not money.[76]

It is true that writers like Gray and Owen who regarded money as a major precipitant of economic depression did not stop at recommending labour exchanges or alterations in the medium of exchange. As Marx again pointed out with reference to Gray, the inner logic of such views on money led to a

---

of the Birmingham School on one co-operator, William Pare, see R. G. Garnett, 'William Pare, co-operator and social reformer', 13.

[74] R. Owen, *An Explanation of the Cause of Distress*, p. 10 (Owen's emphasis).
[75] W. King, *The Workings of Capital*, Part 2, p. 2.
[76] K. Marx, *Contribution to a Critique of Political Economy*, p. 85: 'goods are to be produced as commodities but not exchanged as commodities'.

repudiation of 'one condition of bourgeois production after another' even though the major concern was '"to reform" the money evolved by commodity exchange'[77] and it was, of course, the aim of most labour exchange theorists ultimately to establish some kind of producers' union, which would go further towards altering the social basis of production than a mere socialising of the means of exchange.[78] In general, therefore, exchanges of the type set up in Birmingham and London were avowedly mere stepping stones on the way to a greater or lesser change in existing social and economic arrangements. However, it cannot be sufficiently stressed how much was expected from these institutions and co-operative trading societies as springboards to the millenium, and these heightened expectations must be considered the logical derivative of a political economy which, at both microeconomic and macroeconomic levels of abstraction, saw the nature and use of money as fundamentally important. It is not surprising that in the hands of these early socialist political economists and to a greater extent in those of their popularisers in the working-class press, the theory of general economic crisis, so fundamental to an effective critique of capitalism, too often degenerated into an obsessive preoccupation with exchange. A potentially revolutionary line of attack often became at best a series of suggestions for currency reform and at worst, as with John Gray, a degenerate and enervating monetary crankiness.[79]

It might seem surprising that such faith was placed in the economic benefits to be derived from a new circulating medium. Yet it should not be forgotten that these writers did tend to see the economic world as a kind of storehouse full to overflowing with material abundance and lacking merely the key to unleash unparalleled prosperity upon a needy populace. The problem for these writers was not that of producing more to satisfy the wants of mankind but rather, 'How ... a nation abounding more than

---

[77] ibid.
[78] 'The founders [of labour exchanges] held that workers should control production as well as marketing; they attacked the profits of the capitalist manufacturer as well as the shopkeeper', W. H. Oliver, 'The labour exchange phase of the co-operative movement', 355.
[79] This is particularly true of Gray's later works, *An Efficient Remedy for the Distress of Nations* (1842) and *Lectures on the Nature and Use of Money* (1848).

any other in the rude materials of wealth, in machinery, dwelling and food, in intelligent and industrious producers should still pine in privation?'[80] or as Owen put it in an 1830 address, 'In the course of our inquiries our attention has been particularly called to the fact, not less true than paradoxical, that the people of this country are experiencing an unprecedented degree of general distress at the moment when the country is abounding in wealth'[81] – abounding, John Gray believed, to the extent that there existed a capacity to furnish a supply of goods and services that would satisfy the needs of the population four times over.[82] Owen even went so far as to suggest that 'Under a well devised arrangement for the working classes they will all procure for themselves, the necessaries and comforts of life, in so short a time, and so easily and pleasantly, that ... occupation will be experienced, to be little more than recreation',[83] while William Heighton stated categorically that the working classes had 'already filled this nation almost to overflowing with every species of wealth'.[84]

At one level this emphasis upon the existence of an actual or potential abundance can be seen as constituting an important component of the critique of existing economic arrangements, for it allowed those writers who developed the idea to counterpose to a reality of generalised distress the possibility of a social and economic order characterised by plenty. Thus the dearth of the status quo could be challenged with the vision of an easily realisable abundance; the desert juxtaposed to the land flowing with milk and honey.[85] Such comparisons called into question the whole rationality and continued viability of competitive capitalism.

Yet as it was developed by early-nineteenth-century socialist writers this element of their critique of capitalism contained a

---

[80] W. Thompson, *Inquiry*, p. xv.
[81] R. Owen, *Address of the Working Classes of Devonshire*.
[82] J. Gray, *A Lecture on Human Happiness*, p. 8.
[83] R. Owen, *Report to the County of Lanark*, p. 26.
[84] W. Heighton, *An Address to the Members of Trade Societies and to the Working Classes generally* (London, 1827), p. 6.
[85] 'Only when the utopian conception of the individual seizes upon *currents already present in society* and gives expression to them ... only then can the existing order be challenged by the striving for another order of existence', K. Mannheim, *Ideology and Utopia* (London, Routledge and Kegan Paul, 1960), p. 187.

number of decided weaknesses. Thus it often served as the basis for the view that general economic distress was simply a problem of distribution and that it was by reference to existing distributive arrangements that its solution should be sought. As Thompson phrased it:

That savage tribes, ignorant of the means of production, disinclined to labor, should be overtaken by want were a matter of no surprise; but where art and nature had run, as it were, a race of emulation in the prodigality of their gifts, to intelligent and industrious millions, that these millions should be disenabled from enjoying these products of their own creation – this is the mystery, this the astounding spectacle. To what but to *a vicious distribution* of wealth can this extraordinary phenomenon be attributed.[86]

Or, as Owen had put it in a letter to some London newspapers in 1817, 'The grand question to be solved is, not how a sufficiency of wealth for all may be produced; but *how the excess of riches, which may be most easily created may be generally distributed... without prematurely disturbing the existing institutions and arrangements of any country*'.[87] Thus by seeing the distribution of a pent-up economic surplus as the solution to the problem of general economic crisis, socialist political economists had a tendency to treat the sphere of distribution as essentially autonomous and so to underplay the determining role (*vis-à-vis* distribution) which the social organisation of production played. Indeed, a particular concern with the factors governing distribution was seen by socialist writers themselves as one of the features which distinguished their political economy from that of the classical economists whose work was viewed as overwhelmingly concerned with production, capital accumulation and economic growth.[88] As Marx put it, 'Nothing is more common than the accusation from "opponents of the political economists" that the political economists regard production too exclusively as an end

---

[86] W. Thompson, *Inquiry*, p. xvi (Thompson's emphasis).
[87] R. Owen, 'A letter published in the London newspapers', 25 July 1817, *Life*, p. 71 (my emphasis). See also, for example, remarks by Robert Owen reported in the *Proceedings of the first general meeting of the British and foreign philanthropic society for the permanent relief of the labouring classes* (London, 1822), p. 29; 'The means to create wealth to an unlimited extent have been discovered but the knowledge how to distribute and enjoy it has been hidden from us.'
[88] See above, pp. 27–30.

The theory of capitalist crisis   183

in itself, and that distribution is equally important. This accusation is itself based on the economic notion that distribution dwells as an autonomous, independent sphere side by side with production',[89] and on the question of general depression, it was just such an understanding and treatment of distribution that characterised socialist political economy. The tendency to general economic depression and breakdown might be eliminated by the more equitable distribution of an existing abundance; a more equitable distribution could be secured by more equal exchanges and more equal exchanges could be secured via labour notes, labour exchanges and co-operative trading societies and between co-operative communities. Once isolated, the problem of distribution could be solved and macroeconomic breakdown prevented without recourse to any immediate attack, theoretical or actual, upon the existing distribution of property and ownership of productive resources. In fact, as the beneficial effects of equal exchanges produced the sought-for distribution of abundance, it was stressed that the very economic antagonisms which might have precipitated such attacks would be dissipated and previously hostile economic interests would be reconciled:

if men were placed in a situation, where, by moderate occupation, without care or agitation of mind, they could procure the necessaries and comforts of life in abundance, they might be trained to dispute as little about the division of them as they now do about the commonly obtainable products of nature.[90]

In such a situation 'the dominion of wealth and the evils arising from the desire to acquire and accumulate riches [would be] ... on the point of terminating'.[91] The distribution of abundance would eliminate class antagonism. Indeed, Owen believed that 'scientific arrangements, founded on foresight' would allow labourers 'to consume a larger portion than heretofore, of that which they produce', and would also permit 'the higher ranks

---

[89] K. Marx, *Preface and Introduction to a Contribution to the Critique of Political Economy* (Peking, Foreign Languages Press, 1976), p. 17. Thus Thompson distinguished 'competitive political economy' from 'That real Social Science, which inquires into the means of distributing wealth ... in such a way as to produce the greatest quantity of happiness to all', *Labor Rewarded*, pp. 40–1.
[90] R. Owen, 'A letter published in the London newspapers', 25 July 1817, *Life*, p. 71.
[91] R. Owen, 'Two memorials', ibid. p. 211.

of society [to enjoy] a much larger surplus than they had ever yet received from the working classes'.[92] Thus abundance was seen as establishing the material basis for a harmony of class interests. Once the problem of distribution had been solved and all material needs satisfied, the possibility of continued conflict would be removed as would the need for further analysis of its origins. In such circumstances it would be easy to ignore wealth and capital accumulated in the past for these would be rendered well-nigh valueless by the sheer volume of consumer and capital goods being produced and distributed.[93] All would be 'capitalists' where capital was plentiful and there would be no need to expropriate the expropriators, however unjustly the latter may have acquired their property.

Such use of the idea of abundance effectively assumed away the possibility that distribution might not prove amenable to significant alteration independently of any alteration in the social mode of production, so obfuscating the fact that distribution was not autonomous and that 'the particular way of participating in production determines the specific form of distribution, the form in which participation in distribution occurs'.[94] Writers such as Owen, Gray and Thompson failed, therefore, to investigate the possibility that the existing mode of production might determine the distribution of output regardless of any attempts to alter it through the rationalisation of exchange relations. For them, an equitable distribution of plenty could be secured independently of any expropriation of capitalist property or the immediate demise of capitalism.

However, there was one further and more fundamental weakness in the early socialist analysis and explanation of economic crisis; a weakness which derived from an understanding of economic breakdown as a function of overvalued commodities and undervalued or exploited labour and which followed from the difficulty which such an analysis has in explaining why a capitalist economy should ever be in anything but a state of general economic depression. For, given the explanation of deficient aggregate demand posited by early socialist writers it

[92] R. Owen, *An Explanation of the Cause of Distress*, pp. 4–5.
[93] On this point see M. Beer, *A History of British Socialism*, p. 224, and G. D. H. Cole, *Socialist Thought, The Forerunners*, p. 94.
[94] K. Marx, *Preface and Introduction*, p. 24.

is difficult to conceive how demand was ever likely to prove sufficient to prevent the occurrence of a general glut of commodities. Thus it can be argued that their analysis explained not how general economic depressions occurred but only why a capitalist economy must be in a permanent and deepening state of economic crisis.

Wage-labour by itself could not generate sufficient demand to take up all commodities offered for sale at prices above their labour values. Thus if wages were exchanged against commodities whose market price exceeded their labour costs by 20% (i.e. if the mark-up of profits, rents, taxes etc. on the labour value of commodities was 20%) then the labouring classes could furnish only five-sixths of the necessary demand and to the extent that profits and rents were increased this deficiency would be exacerbated. Yet what of the additional demand furnished by capitalists? This was something which the early socialist writers do not seem to have confronted directly but it seems likely that they would have discounted the importance of capitalist demand. For example, Owen believed that 'The markets of the world are created *solely* by the remuneration allowed for the industry of the working classes and these markets are more or less extended and profitable, in proportion as these classes are well or ill remunerated.'[95] On the assumption, therefore, that manufacturers, capitalist farmers etc. supplied at prices which included an acceptable level of profits, aggregate demand would be permanently deficient and so the general glutting of markets and a concomitant economic depression would become all-pervasive and permanent features of capitalism. In effect, therefore, the analysis of these writers denied not simply the existence of a prosperous equilibrium towards which the capitalist system tended but also the possibility that it could be in anything other than a state of chronic crisis.

This view of capitalism emerges most clearly in the failure of Owen, Thompson, Gray and lesser writers to explain the periodicity of depressions[96] or even to account for the existence

---

[95] R. Owen, *Report to the County of Lanark*, p. 9 (my emphasis).
[96] Thus it is misleading to suggest that 'Socialism, at its birth, imbibed the dogma that industrialism meant short spells of prosperity, followed by chronic crises, pauperisation of the masses, and the sudden advent of the social revolution', M. Beer, *A History of British Socialism*, p. 182.

of periods when material prosperity was obviously increasing. This is not to suggest that they were oblivious to the distinctively cyclical rhythm which characterised the early-nineteenth-century British economy. Objective economic circumstances did on occasion force a realisation that severe, general economic distress tended to be experienced periodically rather than permanently. For example Thompson, at the outset of *Labor Rewarded*, wrote that, 'As long as the present principle of action remains, crisis will succeed to crisis, at intervals more or less distant'[97] and in the same work he makes mention of the 'temporary effects and alternately flattering and distressing variations',[98] which were produced by fluctuations in the demand for labour. However, for early socialist writers such brief allusion to periodicity is where their analysis of the phenomenon started and finished. For while these writers time and again indicate to their own satisfaction how an economy came to suffer a general depression in economic activity, their works and the writings of their popularisers will be searched in vain for any suggestion as to how and why the economy is likely to recover. In effect, they explain *the* slump, *the* depression, *the* crisis but not the boom. They can explain how the progressive undervaluation or exploitation of labour will lead to a situation of gross underconsumption but, in contrast to Marx, they do not attempt to discover and detail the operative factors likely to lift the economy back to equilibrium. As such, their political economy embodied and purveyed a conception of the functioning of capitalism which deviated as significantly from the economic realities of the 1820s and 1830s as did that of James Mill, Harriet Martineau, Mrs Marcet and the would-be political economists of the Society for the Diffusion of Useful Knowledge.

This is not to suggest that they could or should have formulated a fully fledged theory of economic fluctuations. It would be unfair to have expected them in the 1820s and 1830s to have anticipated the insights and analysis of later trade cycle theorists. Yet what might have been expected was at least the formulation of a theory of capitalist crisis which could accommodate the

---

[97] W. Thompson, *Labor Rewarded*, p. v; Thompson also writes of 'The periodical periods of crises recurring at irregular intervals', ibid.
[98] In any case the word 'crisis' as deployed by Thompson in *Labor Rewarded* has more than purely economic connotations.

The theory of capitalist crisis 187

actuality of periods of relative prosperity; a theory which recognised some of the forces and mechanisms which allowed capitalism to weather the storms of general economic depression and generate periods of economic growth and rising material living standards. Thus while Marx saw economic depression as a means by which capitalism was forcibly returned to some kind of equilibrium,[99] the early socialists saw it, through the medium of their economic theories, as permanent and deepening. For these writers there could only be *one* general economic crisis from which capitalism had insufficient vitality to recover.

This understanding of the nature of general economic depression undoubtedly had a millenarian aspect which was in harmony with important currents of working-class thinking of the period and certainly in accord with the millenial tenor of much Owenite writing.[100] *The* economic crisis would signal the demise of the irrational and redundant principles on the basis of which the nation's affairs, economic and otherwise, had previously been conducted and convince all classes in all nations of the need to create a 'new moral world'. It was essential, therefore, that crisis and breakdown should be interpreted as a once-and-for-all phenomenon, for the millenium loses its cathartic appeal when characterised by cyclical recurrence; the satisfying element of certainty in the expected inevitable transition to a 'new moral world' underpinned by a new economic order is lost if there is no indication as to which downswing in the economic cycle heralds its approach.

Yet despite its theoretical flaws this early socialist theory of general economic depression did progress beyond the simplistic view that crisis was essentially a by-product of political or institutional fiats, and so the ideas of Cobbett and Paine, which had helped to shape the limited popular understanding of the causes of general breakdown, were to a large extent supplanted.[101]

---

[99] 'From time to time the conflict of antagonistic agencies [within capitalism] finds vent in crises. The crises are always but momentary and forcible solutions of the existing contradictions. They are violent eruptions which for a time restore the disturbed equilibrium', K. Marx, *Capital*, Vol. 3, p. 249.

[100] For an assessment of the importance of the millenarian elements in Owen's thought see W. H. Oliver, 'Owen in 1817, the Millenialist Movement', in S. Pollard and J. Salt (eds.), *Robert Owen, Prophet of the Poor*, pp. 165–85; also E. P. Thompson, *Making*, pp. 420–8 and in particular pp. 877–85.

[101] See below, pp. 193–7.

General economic depression ceased to be merely a consequence of high taxation and other exactions of the state and so ceased to be a problem amenable to legislative or political solution. Economic crisis could not, therefore, be eliminated by retrenchment and the requisite remission of taxes. As one defender of Owenism put it:

> as every soldier, sailor and taxgatherer, is as much a consumer as those from whom the taxes are now raised; their being productive or unproductive consumers had little to do with the present situation; and to admit into our reasonings the possibility of the reduction of the National Debt must betray the greatest ignorance of political economy, since no measure could be fraught with more extensive misery to the labouring poor ... the destruction of capital and credit would leave no funds for the employment of labour.[102]

In macroeconomic terms taxes could not simply be seen as so much purchasing power destroyed and thus as a primary cause of deficient aggregate demand. Taxation might be criticised on other grounds but no socialist writer believed that a solution to the problem of generalised distress could be found simply by reducing taxation. Indeed, Owen suggested that government expenditure could prove of positive benefit by providing employment in times of national economic difficulty,[103] while Gray argued that though government expenditure would have no effect on the level of economic activity when the productive powers of a country were fully employed, where this was not the case the rapid increase of the National Debt had in the past helped create a state of affairs where 'prosperity was never so general'. Thus, 'the expenditure of immense sums of borrowed money during the war, created a demand for labour ... [and] called into operation those resources which the country then possessed ... The forced demand for produce, so brought about, made trade brisk [and] ample employment was furnished for existing capital.'[104] While they might prove salutary for other reasons, therefore, reforms reducing unproductive government expenditure were likely to exacerbate rather than solve the problem of economic depression. The elimination of sinecurists

---

[102] Anon., *Letters to Ricardo*, p. 14.
[103] Robert Owen, *A New View of Society*, pp. 170–1.
[104] J. Gray, *Social System*, p. 309.

and placemen was no substitute for resolving the paradox of poverty in the midst of plenty.

Yet despite the more profound understanding of the causes of capitalist crisis evinced by early socialist writers it should be noted, first, that they saw the problem as essentially one of distribution and, because distribution tended to be treated as autonomous, as a problem which might be solved without any direct, fundamental alteration of the existing ownership of the nation's productive means.

Secondly, the understanding of the exploitation or undervaluation of labour upon which the early socialist explanation of depression rested ensured an obsessive concern with the exchange process. This too had the effect of directing attention away from productive relations, with the universality of equal exchanges being seen as a sufficient condition for a restoration of general economic prosperity. Equal labour exchanged for equal labour would guarantee that every commodity produced would find a market and ensure that all available productive resources were fully utilised.[105]

Thirdly, this analysis led to an obsession with the nature and role of money and the desire to introduce a reformed medium of exchange which would cease to facilitate or precipitate the deviation of market prices from natural, labour values, which would function as an immutable standard in terms of which the true value or social utility of commodities could be estimated and which would expand *pari passu* with output. Such a medium of exchange would ensure that aggregate supply and demand remained commensurate and was therefore a fundamental guarantor of future economic stability. In addition, while it might prove the means of effecting a 'revolutionary' transformation of existing economic conditions, it did not require any revolutionary alteration of existing productive relations to prove effective.

Finally, and in contrast to Marx, socialist political economists in the early nineteenth century shackled themselves to a theory

---

[105] cf. Marx's comments on such ideas as expressed by J. F. Bray: 'What has the exchange of equal quantities of labour brought us? Overproduction, depreciation, excess of labour followed by unemployment; in short economic relations such as we see in present-day society'; 'Mr Bray does not see that this equilibrium relation, this *corrective ideal* that he would like to apply to the world, is itself nothing but the reflection of the actual world', *Poverty of Philosophy*, pp. 85, 87 (Marx's emphasis).

of general economic depression which, with every period of economic recovery and sustained economic growth, must have become increasingly tarnished in the eyes of those who used it to make sense of economic events. As they waited for what this analysis must have led them to believe was the inevitable demise of an economic system possessing no capacity for rejuvenation, periodic or otherwise, the upswings in economic activity must have brought with them the same kind of disenchantment with political economy which millenarian sects, disappointed in their hopes of the Second Coming, must occasionally experience with religion.

8

The popular political economy of crisis 1816–34

The radical and co-operative press 1816–24

Writers in the radical and co-operative press of the immediate post-Napoleonic War period did not provide a well-articulated theory of general economic depression. Yet many did highlight the existence of such a phenomenon and stress the truly general nature of the impoverishment which it caused among the labouring classes. Thus they dismissed the classical view that depression must be partial, the consequence of the rundown of a particular industry or trade. As an 'Address and Petition of the Distressed Mechanics of Birmingham' put it:

Upon all former occasions of distress in any Branch of Trade, it was always found that some other channels of industry existed, through which the honest labourer could obtain his bread; but now we find that all other Descriptions of labourers are equally distressed with ourselves. *A general Calamity has fallen upon the whole Nation.* We would indulge the hope that our sufferings are peculiar to ourselves and may have been occasioned by the cessation of War Expenditure, but on whatsoever side we turn our Eyes ... we can perceive nothing but an universal scene of Poverty and Distress.[1]

Nor was the distress occasioned by depression confined to a particular locale:

If the distress indeed, were confined to a certain district, a county, a city or even the metropolis, that district may be left to its fate with whatever cruelty ... But when it spread from one end of the land to the other, when it is equally felt in village and in city, in country and in town, then the danger is indeed imminent [*sic*] to all.[2]

---

[1] *Birmingham Inspector*, 8 (1817), 156 (my emphasis).
[2] *People*, 1 (1817), 19–20, 'Want, Famine, Mortality'.

Or as William Cobbett put it in a 'Letter to the Prince Regent on the Bullion Bill', 'Your Royal Highness has been advised to say that the distress is local ... The cause of the distress is one, it is general; it affects every part of the country and every rank in life and every species of property and of labour'[3] and Cobbett was also quick to attack the 'falsehood, that the distress is temporary; that all things will come round again and that trade and commerce will resume their accustomed channels'.[4]

Economic crisis was, therefore, occupationally and geographically general, it was prolonged and in addition it was characterised by the paradoxical existence of intensified poverty in the midst of an abundance or glut of commodities. Thus popular writers were clear that the 'reality of wealth may exist in a Country, even to superabundance and the body of people be at the same time in the greatest distress, even to misery and starvation'; 'in the midst of apparent wealth and merchandise that baffles description, all are poor and all are complaining'.[5]

In addition to detailing its salient characteristics, popular writers also dismissed conventional explanations of what caused general economic depression. Cobbett, for example, criticised those who explained the existence of general economic distress in traditional terms as the consequence of bad harvests or the failings of agriculture: 'it is manifest that the want of employment which is the great symptom of the present national disease *and which is altogether peculiar to present times*, has not arisen from bad seasons or high prices of food'[6] and in addition he dismissed a range of alternative explanations frequently given for unemployed labour and glutted markets:

All the alleged causes of the misery appear now to be exploded. At first it was a sudden transition from war to peace, that had done this mischief. Then it was a super-abundant produce. Next it was a surplus population: too many mouths and too little food. Next it was the use of machinery and draught horses.[7]

---

[3] *Cobbett's Twopenny Register*, 36, 10 (1820), col. 740.
[4] ibid. 31, 19 (1816), col. 592, 'A Letter to Mr Jabet'.
[5] *People*, 3 (1817), 78, 'A Plan for the Removal and Prevention of Distress, Poor Rates and Mendicity'; *Black Dwarf*, 1, 31 (1817), col. 483, 'Black Dwarf to Yellow Bronze'.
[6] *Cobbett's Twopenny Register*, 33, 6 (1818), col. 170 (my emphasis).
[7] ibid. 36, 11 (1820), cols. 760–1, 'A Letter to Baron Garrow'; see also 32, 18 (1817),

The popular political economy of crisis 1816–34

Yet if conventional explanations were deficient, what was to be put in their place? The radical press, dominated directly or indirectly by the views of Paine and Cobbett, usually provided an explanation of general economic crisis which stressed the disruptive macroeconomic consequences of political decisions affecting such things as the size of the National Debt and the convertibility of the paper currency into gold. The size of the National Debt, for example, was seen as entailing a level of taxation which produced a diminution in the aggregate demand for the products of agriculture and industry. Thus it was believed by most radical writers who touched upon the subject that what was taken and expended for the purpose of debt servicing was subtracted from the purchasing power of the community. The immediate consequence was faltering production and trade and redundancy of labour as manufacturers and others scaled down their productive activity. Cobbett put the argument with characteristic didactic force:

Your distress, that is to say, that which you now more immediately feel, arises from want of employment with wages sufficient for your support. The want of such employment has arisen from want of sufficient demand for the goods you make. The want of a sufficient demand for the goods you make has arisen from the want of means in the nation at large to purchase your goods. The want of the means to purchase your goods has arisen from the weight of the taxes and the bubble of paper money.[8]

And Cobbett went on to pour scorn on that 'race of political economists, bred at Edinburgh and at Oxford who have been putting forth the doctrine ... that taxes do no harm in the end; that if they be taken out of the pocket of one man they are put into the pocket of another'.[9] T. J. Wooler, editor of the *Black Dwarf*, hammered the point home in comparably simplistic terms:

The effect of taxation is always to diminish consumption ... and it is well known that individual as well as national prosperity depends upon the extent of consumption. The more bread is eaten, the more is corn

col. 571, 'Last year the misery was ascribed to the "surplus produce", this year to a "surplus population". Last year food was too plenty: this year food is too scarce.'
[8] ibid. 31, 22 (1816), col. 689, 'A Letter to the Luddites'.
[9] ibid. 32, 19 (1817), col. 598, 'The Grand Exposure'.

demanded and the greater the labour to produce corn. Deprive half a people of the means of earning half the bread they want, the farmer loses the market which their wants create, but which their inability to purchase food destroys ... you rob also the manufacturer and the agriculturist of the market for the produce which these men would otherwise create.[10]

Writers in the radical press also saw taxation as depressing demand through the increase in the price of commodities which it produced: 'Taxation has inflicted as severe a blow upon agriculture as it has done upon manufactures; and by forcing up the price of both agricultural and manufactured produce has lessened the demand for them and consequently the employment for the people.'[11] Thus for most radical writers general economic depression, like labour exploitation, was something which was exogenously precipitated rather than endogenously generated within the economic system. Such a perception of the causes of general distress was also consonant with the view that the major precipitant of economic crisis was the existing monetary system and the manner in which it was insidiously manipulated by the government to the advantage of the rentier class. For, leaving aside the diminished aggregate demand which resulted from labour impoverishment caused by changes in the real value of money,[12] macroeconomic depression was also seen as following automatically from any diminution of the volume of money in circulation and this had been the very policy pursued in the aftermath of the Napoleonic Wars. Cobbett, for example, saw this diminution as resulting primarily from an attempt to facilitate the resumption of cash payments by the Bank of England: 'Here is the cause', he wrote, 'Here is the great cause of the distresses of the country ... and of the starvation in the midst of plenty of the journeyman and the labourer.'[13] To facilitate that convertibility of paper into gold Cobbett believed it had been necessary to reduce the quantity of paper money in circulation: 'in order to pay cash, the quantity of circulating medium must be lessened; ... prices must fall ... a stagnation will take

[10] *Black Dwarf*, 3, 6 (1819), col. 81.
[11] *Medusa*, 20 (1819), 142, 'An Address to the Mechanics and Labourers of the United Kingdom' by 'J.G.'
[12] See above, pp. 115–17.
[13] *Cobbett's Twopenny Register*, 37, 23 (1820), col. 1579, 'A Letter to Earl Grey'.

place ... workmen will want employment'.[14] Thus the government and the Bank of England had impaled themselves upon the horns of a theoretical dilemma. A return to cash payments was necessary to give stability to the monetary system; however, such a policy entailed monetary contraction and this must inevitably precipitate an economic crisis and general depression.[15] For Cobbett this was the unavoidable emetic for the wartime indulgence of an inconvertible paper currency irresponsibly expanded by the ignorant and the self-seeking.

Not all agreed with Cobbett's formulation of the problem. Wooler, for example, put forward the argument that it was the distribution of the circulating medium rather than its quantity which produced general distress. 'Nor do we believe', he wrote, 'that the distress is all owing to a diminished circulation ... it is the more equal distribution of the circulating medium and not any increase which is needed.'[16] However, while diversity of opinion might exist as to the exact causes of general depression and distress, all radical writers who dealt with this question were agreed that the *primus mobile* lay outside the functioning of the economic system. As with labour exploitation this economic evil was seen as the product of the ignorant or malign actions of politicians, sinecurists, placemen and the money jugglers of the Bank. As such the solution lay in institutional and political reform. If general economic depression could be caused by political fiat it could be remedied accordingly.

An alternative explanation of the causes of general economic depression was provided in this period by George Mudie and other writers in the early co-operative paper, the *Economist*. This explanation was essentially, if crudely, Owenite with economic crisis viewed as the necessary consequence of underconsumption,

---

[14] ibid. 36, 10 (1820), col. 738, 'A Letter to the Prince Regent'; for a similar view see *Northern Reformers' Magazine*, 1, 2 (1823), 65–6: 'the present attempt to resume Cash Payments, without adopting concomitant measures of justice and prudence has spread the most indescribable Embarrassment and Distress throughout the Kingdom'.

[15] It would seem, wrong to suggest, therefore, that Cobbett believed that 'a limitation of the monetary supply affects the distribution of income but not its total', F. W. Fetter, *The Development of British Monetary Orthodoxy 1797–1875* (Cambridge, Mass., Harvard University Press, 1965), p. 143.

[16] *Wooler's British Gazette*, 35 (1819), 273, 'The Bursting of the Bank Bubbles, called the Restoration of Cash Payments'.

the primary cause of which was the rapid and uncontrolled application of machinery to industrial and agricultural production and the wholesale displacement and redundancy of labour which that produced: 'a great portion of the available manual labour has been entirely superseded and the value of labour generally has in consequence been severely depressed'.[17] Such unemployment and the resultant loss of purchasing power among the labouring classes meant that the demand for commodities could not possibly keep pace with the ever increasing powers of supply. Disastrous economic consequences must inevitably follow from this manifest imbalance between the power to produce and the ability to consume:

if the extension of machinery obviously depreciates the value of labour, and obviously reduces the bulk of the people to such a situation that they are forced to consume less than they consumed before the extension of machinery then it is obvious that the extension of the machinery, by lessening the home consumption and contracting the home market, is highly injurious.[18]

What prevailed, given existing economic arrangements, was a situation where 'The amazing productive powers which science and mechanism have applied to manufactures are already so stupendous, that an excess of manufactured goods, beyond profitable demand, either exists and *always will exist* or can be always instantaneously produced.'[19]

For writers such as Mudie, therefore, general economic depression was a necessary and permanent feature of competitive, industrial capitalism and the only solution was the more rational utilisation of machinery and technical advances to assist rather than displace labour. This could only be done within the socio-economic framework provided by a co-operative community; only outside the pernicious influence of competitive capitalism could mechanisation proceed without redundant labour, deficient aggregate demand and glutted markets. It was the rational co-operative control of the productive potentialities of machinery which would eliminate the causes of general economic depression and distress.

[17] *Economist*, 5 (1821), 66.
[18] ibid. 5 (1821), 52.
[19] ibid. 3 (1821), 44 (my emphasis); this would suggest that general economic crisis was seen as a permanent state of affairs.

The 'Trades Newspaper' and the co-operative press 1825–30

As with the early radical press, writers in the *Trades Newspaper* saw crisis and depression as a prominent feature of the contemporary economic landscape, though they advanced more varied explanations of its causes. Taxation, money juggles and the prodigality of governments were still seen as important. As one writer put it, 'Taxation' was 'the cause of the present appalling state of the country. It is this which has impoverished our capitalists and abridged the quantity of home consumption.'[20] Here the influence of Cobbett and Paine is obviously still dominant. However, with the monetary explanations of general depression put forward, the attribution of intellectual paternity is more problematic for it becomes increasingly difficult to distinguish which general statements about the disruptive macroeconomic consequences of money juggles were inspired by Cobbett and Paine and which were inspired by Thomas Attwood and the Birmingham School.[21] This is not to suggest that Cobbett and Attwood had similar views on the problems caused by contemporary monetary policy or that they agreed on the means by which these problems could be solved. Cobbett, like most radical writers, attacked the economic instability produced by the expansion of a paper currency not backed by gold and saw economic depression as a necessary deflationary prerequisite for a return to convertibility. Cobbett's solution was not to expand the supply of paper money to counter deflation, as Attwood suggested, but rather to reduce taxation and other financial burdens of the labouring classes in line with the fall in prices, thus maintaining or improving living standards and stabilising or increasing the working-class demand for commodities. Attwood, in contrast, wanted a controlled expansion of paper money in order that the quantity of money in circulation would match the increasing capacity to expand output and so

---

[20] *Trades Newspaper*, 2, 84 (1827), 249.
[21] See A. Briggs, 'The economic background to the Birmingham Political Union 1830–32', *Cambridge Historical Journal*, 9 (1948), 190–216, for a discussion of the economic views of the Birmingham School and their contemporary impact. Attwood's views were expounded in a number of works, e.g. *The Remedy, or Thoughts on the Present Distresses* (London, 1816); *A Letter to Mr Vansittart on the Creation of Money* (Birmingham, 1817); *A Letter to the Earl of Liverpool* (Birmingham, 1819); *The Late Prosperity and the Present Adversity of the Country explained* (London, 1826).

prevent the insufficiency of demand which he saw as resulting from an inadequate supply of money. However, when general statements linking monetary policy with economic depression were made in the *Trades Newspaper* the source of inspiration is not always apparent.[22]

Secondly, there were some writers whose treatment of the deleterious macroeconomic repercussions of heavy taxation shaded into an essentially classical understanding of depression in which taxation and government interference with trade (particularly in corn) were seen as the major causes of general distress. For these writers much was to be expected, therefore, from the repeal of the Corn Laws and similar obstacles to untrammelled free trade. Thus the Corn Laws were seen as ensuring that

> A considerable portion of the high price of bread which is the great regulating standard of the price of all other necessaries, goes at present into the pocket of the landowners... thereby enhancing the price of every article manufactured in the country and causing... *a diminished demand abroad and lowering of wages at home.*[23]

With repeal it was believed that 'trade, manufactures and commerce revive, employment becomes more plentiful, profits and wages advance, incomes enlarge and the good olden times again return'.[24] As one writer phrased it, 'Cheap bread is all that is wanted, and a reduced rate of taxation, to enable our merchants and manufacturers to find a vent for their commodities and our artisans abundance of employment.'[25] Such opinions dominated the *Trades Newspaper* for a period, providing another indication of how the paper did for a time become an important vehicle for the dissemination of popularised classical orthodoxy.[26]

---

[22] One example of a line of argument which was surely inspired by the Birmingham School is 'A Petition of Birmingham Mechanics', *Trades Newspaper*, 2, 96 (1827), 350, which stated that 'the currency of the country is the only means of the distribution of its produce; the demand does not depend on the wants of mankind...; the supply of these wants depends on the productive power of the country and its means of distributing its productions... the productive power cannot be too great as long as the means of distribution are equivalent'.

[23] ibid. 2, 80 (1827), 220, 'On the Corn Laws' (my emphasis). This can be read as a diminished demand abroad and a diminished demand at home.

[24] *Weekly Free Press*, 4, 174 (1828), a letter from 'Cincinnatus' on the repeal of the Corn Laws.

[25] *Trades Free Press*, 3, 118 (1827), 89.

[26] See above, pp. 13–15.

The popular political economy of crisis 1816–34   199

Thirdly, the paper contained elements of that analysis and understanding of general economic depression which was to dominate much of the working-class press in the early 1830s. Thus, for example, one correspondent was adamant in linking what he regarded as a general breakdown of the economic system with the unrelenting and unthinking pursuit of capitalist profit:

A more efficient, a certain cause for it [general distress] is to be found in the over-employment given to the [labourers] at one time by the speculations of the capitalist master manufacturer, which were founded in hopes of advantage and the subsequent want of employment occasioned from them having overstocked the market.[27]

While another saw 'stagnation and ... distress [as] ... the necessary results of the monopolising spirit of the wealthy and influential classes of society'.[28] Yet neither writer developed his insight further. Indeed, contributors to the *Trades Newspaper* tended not to forge any strong theoretical link between labour exploitation and economic crisis but rather stressed the comparatively uncontroversial point that low wages and deficient demand for the products of industry were closely connected:

Is any reaction so stupidly ignorant as not to perceive, that every other class must suffer from ... depriving the working classes of the means of consumption ... and must diminish the prosperity of every trade and occupation whose produce or manufactures are consumed by the working classes.

I think no better means can be pointed out for the employment of the working classes, than by giving them the means to create consumption: consumption will create labour and the country would be ultimately the richer.[29]

Such remarks could, of course, be diversely interpreted according to the theoretical persuasion of the interpreter but it is unlikely, for example, that J. R. McCulloch, a firm believer in the desirability of high wages, would have found in them much with which to disagree.[30]

---

[27] *Trades Newspaper*, 31 (1826), 487, article signed 'A Labourer'.
[28] *Weekly Free Press*, 4, 196 (1829), 4.
[29] *Trades Newspaper*, 16 (1825), 242; ibid. 35 (1826), 566, contribution from John Gast.
[30] 'Indeed McCulloch perhaps more than any other classical economist followed Hume and Smith in stressing the desireability of high wages', D. P. O'Brien, *J. R. McCulloch, a study in classical economics* (London, Allen and Unwin, 1970), p. 365.

Finally, a number of writers in the *Trades Newspaper* explained general economic depression in terms of absolute overproduction[31] and argued that such had been the expansion of the nation's productive capacity that a glut of commodities and a corresponding redundancy of labour were virtually inevitable. One correspondent gave this idea an interesting theological dimension, stating that 'when presumptuous mortals set at defiance the sentence of the Almighty, that by the sweat of his brow man shall eat his bread and attempt by the ingenuity of their minds to reverse this decree, an overproduction can and must be effected',[32] but more often absolute overproduction was explained simply as the consequence of the too rapid mechanisation of productive activity: 'Notwithstanding other co-operative causes of the present distress, blind must be the man who cannot see that machinery is one of the principal evils'; 'The great improvements in machinery is [sic] one of the principal causes why so many thousands are out of employment and can any man of common sense believe that this is the time to promote and encourage it.'[33] Thus for these writers it was the machinery itself or its too rapid application to the productive process which caused general impoverishment and not, as Owenites and cooperators would have argued, the use of machinery in the context of essentially irrational economic arrangements.

If, therefore, the *Trades Newspaper* can be taken as in some sense representative of the state of working-class economic opinion on the question of the causes of economic crisis, popular political economy was in a confused, if fertile, state in the later 1820s. However, consideration must also be given to the co-operative press of the period and here it is possible to perceive the broad outlines of that theory of economic crisis which was to be more fully articulated and more widely disseminated in the working-class press of the early 1830s.

Writers in the co-operative press of the late 1820s saw 'effectual demand' as the crucial determinant of the level of economic

---

[31] See also below, pp. 208–10.
[32] *Weekly Free Press*, 5, 214 (1829), 1, a letter from W. E. Andrews.
[33] *Trades Newspaper*, 46 (1826), 749, article signed 'I.J.'; ibid. 52 (1826), 828, a letter from Thomas Single. However, these opinions were often condemned. For example, taking an absolute overproductionist to task the editor asserted that 'we may fairly ascribe the circumstance of full warehouses to some other cause than overproduction', ibid. 43 (1826), 695.

activity. In the words of one writer, whether an economy prospered or stagnated depended

on the effectual demand; the demand which will at least enable capitalists to obtain what is called the 'natural price' of the produce of labour; that price which will at least enable them to pay the rent of land, the wages of labour and allow them a profit on the stock employed. If this demand ceases; if this natural price cannot be obtained...capital is of course withdrawn, the labourers are... thrown out of employ.[34]

It was upon an adequate effectual demand rather than upon the capital or stock in existence, therefore, that prosperity depended. The problem was that under existing economic arrangements such a demand was not forthcoming both because labour did not receive its full or 'natural' value[35] and because capitalist producers required a profitable demand and did not seek to satisfy the unlimited demand which existed in terms of human wants and needs.[36] Thus implicit and explicit in much co-operative writing was the idea that it was because producers sought a price which yielded profit and rent that markets remained glutted, wants unsatisfied and labour unemployed.

For co-operative writers, general economic depression and distress were essentially a distributive problem, first in the sense of ensuring that labour received its full value and secondly in the sense that goods should be distributed to satisfy needs rather than retained or left to glut markets until a profitable demand was forthcoming. The existence of general distress was certainly not a consequence of dearth or shortage, rather it was 'The present arrangement for distributing the produce of labour [which prevented]...the working classes themselves from participating in the accumulated stores of wealth which glut the

---

[34] *Co-operative Magazine*, 5 (1826), 156, an article signed 'S.F.'; it is interesting to note that this is virtually a paraphrase of a passage from Book 1, chapter 6 of Adam Smith's *Wealth of Nations*.

[35] ibid. 3, 1 (1828), 16, 'The Causes of Poverty': 'when we shall all be usefully employed *and derive the value of our labour*, we shall be able to purchase and consume more commodities' (my emphasis).

[36] The trouble with capitalist manufacturers was that they only gave thought to 'how much...their customers can...pay them for, without the least regard to the satisfaction of our wants', *Magazine of Useful and Co-operative Knowledge*, 2 (1830), 19, 'On the Creation and Distribution of Wealth', reprinted lectures of William Pare.

markets of the world',[37] or, as Robert Dale Owen put it, 'Great Britain has learned to PRODUCE wealth and does produce it most abundantly; but she has not learned to distribute it; and hence her present distress.'[38]

For these writers an actual or potential material abundance existed and scarcity had ceased to be a significant economic problem, an opinion which was expressed with particular force by Robert Owen in an address published in the *Co-operative Magazine* (1827):

> During the French revolutionary war you passed a boundary never before reached in the history of man, you passed the regions of poverty arising from necessity and entered that of *permanent abundance* . . . you have attained the means to ensure the 'Wealth of Nations', the object so long sought for by legislators and political economists.[39]

The nature and causes of the wealth of nations had, therefore, ceased to be *the* important area of economic inquiry. What was now required was a political economy of distribution rather than a political economy of growth; a political economy which would serve to elaborate the principles on the basis of which the existing economic superabundance might best be disbursed. This was the key to the elimination of idle productive capacity, glutted markets and redundant labour.

The difficulty or impossibility of securing an adequate effectual demand, a belief that producers should seek to satisfy the demand represented by the actual wants and needs of the population, the view that this demand should be made effectual through the receipt by labour of its full value and a corresponding emphasis upon the need for a more effective distribution of an existing abundance: these were the distinguishing themes of the co-operative analysis of economic depression. Once again, as with their treatment of labour exploitation, the achievement of these writers was to locate the origins of economic crisis within the economic system and to analyse it as an economic rather than a political phenomenon.

---

[37] *Associate*, 5 (1829), 29; see also, for example, *Weekly Free Press and Co-operative Journal*, 5, 245 (1830), 3, comment made on an article in the *Northern Whig*.
[38] *Co-operative Magazine*, 3, 3 (1828), 61.
[39] ibid. 2, 10 (1827), 436–41, 'An Address to the Agriculturists, Mechanics and Manufacturers of Great Britain'.

The working-class press 1830–4

Given the sources from which they derived their theoretical understanding of labour exploitation, it is not surprising that many writers in the working-class press of the early 1830s developed their analysis and explanation of economic crisis along similar lines to Thompson, Owen and Gray. Certainly the views of Cobbett and other political radicals continued to be disseminated, particularly in papers such as the *Gauntlet*, the *Ballot* and *Cobbett's Twopenny Trash*, but increasingly this *deus ex machina* explanation of general depression was pushed aside to be replaced by one which was more economic than political. Here it will be necessary, first, to outline some of the distinguishing characteristics of this 'new', popular analysis of economic crisis; secondly, to discuss some of the variations on its essential theoretical themes; thirdly, to consider the nature of the solutions to general economic depression which writers derived from their analysis; and finally, to highlight some analytical weaknesses and their possible implications.

Writers in the working-class press of this period moved quickly from the fact that labour was exploited to the conclusion that general economic depression was an inevitable by-product. For, given that labour was exploited and the additional belief that the expenditure of their wages by labour constituted a major market for the commodities of manufacturers, it seemed obvious that a general deficiency of demand must occur. As 'One of the Oppressed' put it in a letter to the *Poor Man's Guardian*, 'you [the labourers] ought to receive as much wages as will enable you to purchase and consume the produce of your own labour yourselves by which means your consumption would keep pace with your industry and your industry with your consumption'.[40]

Specifically, the point was made that it was the addition of profits and other elements to the 'natural' price or value of commodities which prevented this, and the impossibility of a profitable demand for commodities was in fact a common theme in the discussion of the origins of economic crisis. Thus William Carpenter wrote in 1832 that 'The markets are already glutted.

---

[40] *Poor Man's Guardian*, 44 (1832), 358; see also *Herald to the Trades Advocate*, 6 (1830), 89, 'An Address to the Operatives', signed 'D.R.'

There is more now produced than can be PROFITABLY SOLD',[41] while others likewise drew attention to the profit-oriented nature of capitalist production and to the fact that in the absence of profit production would cease with a resultant decline in the general level of economic activity. As one commentator put it, 'The producing classes are set in motion not to supply the natural wants of society, but only as their labour can be rendered profitable to the possessors of money.'[42] Thus it was accepted by many that the need for a profitable demand might prove an obstacle to the expansion of output, while correspondingly output and the employment of adequately remunerated labour might be increased if entrepreneurs would only accept a reduction in the rate of profits, 'capitalists might benefit themselves by removing the restrictions which prevent any use being made of... valuable labour. A small diminution in the rate of profit would immediately set free the creating power of all surplus labourers.'[43]

This idea of profit as a curb upon production and the cause of 'surplus' or redundant labour was also inherent in the view that under existing economic arrangements abundance was the harbinger of crisis. 'Senex' in the *Pioneer* put the matter succinctly when he wrote that 'Plenty [was] perpetually passing the limit of profit, by what the wise men of McCulloch's school call overproduction,' arguing also that the 'influx of plenty' was effectively 'ruinous' to capitalists and their 'profit-mongering system'.[44] For, if profits were to be generated and capitalists thereby encouraged to continue or expand their productive activities and offer employment to labour, supply must remain sufficiently deficient with respect to a given intensity of demand to ensure that the market prices of commodities were pushed above their natural, labour values. As it was, 'The combined forces of ingenuity and industry, of machinery and labour, are creating such plenty, that *profits are nearly impossible*. The capitalist perceives, therefore, an accumulation of goods which he cannot force into the market.'[45] In effect, the abundance produced by

---

[41] *Carpenter's Political Magazine*, February 1832, p. 242 (author's emphasis).
[42] *Voice of the West Riding*, 21 (1833), 167, 'To the Useful Classes', signed 'Z'.
[43] *Poor Man's Guardian*, 167 (1834), 278, an article signed 'Equality'.
[44] *Pioneer*, 38 (1834), 362, 'Letters on Associated Labour'; ibid. 32 (1834), 291.
[45] ibid. 31 (1834), 283, 'Letters on Associated Labour'.

expanding productive powers prevented that shortfall of supply that was necessary to guarantee an acceptable level of capitalist profits. In the absence of such profits production was halted, labour was made redundant and markets remained glutted with 'overpriced' commodities. Thus it seemed that, 'Capital ... suspended as well as expanded production at [its] pleasure',[46] or as another writer phrased it:

> Hitherto production has been carried on at random to serve the purposes of speculators rather than the real wants of society ... but let production be regulated on scientific principles ... called forth by the wants of men and not by the caprices of capitalists, then it will be found that supply will create the demand.[47]

Thus Say's Law would be vindicated, supply would create its own demand, the possibility of future macroeconomic disruption would be eliminated, when production was carried on for the satisfaction of wants rather than for the acquisition of profits. It was the doomed pursuit of profitable demand which condemned the economic system to a state of general depression. The 'Want of employment' which stemmed from 'Want of sale, want of market' could, therefore, be eliminated 'by the voluntary union of the working classes in sufficient number to afford a market to each other by working together for ... the mutual supply of their most *indispensable wants*'.[48]

The components of this understanding of the causes of general economic depression are essentially those which distinguish the work of Owen, Thompson and Gray. On the demand side it is the deficient aggregate demand resulting from the exploitation or undervaluation of labour which is stressed, while on the supply side it was the capitalist's determination to secure a profit, together with the rapid, contemporary expansion of productive capacity, which ensured that markets would be glutted with goods priced above their natural, labour values. Thus popular writers, like their mentors, seem to have recognised both demand and supply side aspects of the problem of macroeconomic

---

[46] *Midland Representative*, 22 (1831), 2, 'Co-operation: A Meeting of the Working Classes and others in Birmingham', reported remarks of 'Bronterre' O'Brien.
[47] *Voice of the West Riding*, 23 (1833), 181.
[48] *Midland Representative*, 22 (1831), 2, 'Co-operation: A Meeting of the Working Classes and others in Birmingham', reported remarks of William Pare (my emphasis).

disequilibrium. Underconsumption and 'overproduction' together ensured glutted markets, underutilised productive capacity and 'surplus labourers'.[49]

Yet if most of those who wrote on the subject of economic depression understood 'overproduction' in terms of an inability of exploited or surplus labourers to consume 'overvalued' commodities, 'overproduction' was also understood in absolute terms by a small number of writers. 'The source of abundance', wrote one, 'is the cause of want ... the workman starves because he produces too much of everything'; or as another put it:

> the immense quantity of goods with which every market is glutted, by the increasing working of our mills ... must on the principle of demand and supply occasion a depreciation of their saleable value, which cannot but constantly increase the hardships and privations of our working population.[50]

This belief that it was absolute overproduction which produced glutted markets and depression frequently went hand in hand with the view that the problem could be solved by the simple expedient of reducing the hours of labour and hence the volume of output coming onto the market.[51] It was assumed, for example, that 'the workman's tasks have been increased until the market has been falling for nearly twenty years'[52] and that this situation had been exacerbated by a tendency for entrepreneurs to extend the hours of labour in a period of falling prices: 'We frequently hear of "dull sales", "no demand", "markets glutted" – and yet in order to quicken the dullness to raise the demand – manufacturers have adopted the very natural remedy of working longer, thus augmenting the evil of which they complain.'[53] Glutted markets and the corresponding general distress of the labouring classes could therefore be alleviated by the pursuit of an opposite course: 'If diminishing the hours [of labour] at first would seem an evil, it would soon work its own cure by

---

[49] *Poor Man's Guardian*, 167 (1834), 278, article signed 'Equality'.
[50] *Lancashire Co-operator*, 1 (1831), 1, 'Introduction'; *Voice of the West Riding*, 6 (1833), 41, 'Working Classes and Political Economists', signed 'Verax'.
[51] See, for example, *Voice of the West Riding*, 7 (1833), 50: 'The Ten Hours Bill combats overproduction which has been one great cause of reduction of wages.'
[52] *Poor Man's Guardian*, 136 (1834), 435, from one of the reported resolutions of a public meeting at Oldham.
[53] *Voice of the West Riding*, 40 (1834), 313.

emptying the markets and increasing their demand, so that wages and profits would be higher than now.'[54]

This absolute overproduction interpretation of the causes of general depression was undoubtedly a minority opinion among writers in the working-class press. It did, however, coalesce with the ideas of those writers who emphasised the adverse economic consequences to be expected from the rapid application of machinery to the production process. These were writers who condemned the application of machinery *per se*, not merely its utilisation in a capitalistic context. The essence of their opinions was neatly encapsulated by a writer in the *Advocate* who stated that 'by the aid of ... machinery he [the manufacturer] may so exceed the power of consumption in hundred and hundred fold degrees, as to render its production useless and it must rot. Population may increase but nature will have its course'[55] – i.e. demand might increase in line with population but still could not conceivably match the increased capacity to produce resulting from mechanisation. Malthus had, therefore, been well and truly stood on his head; man did not press on the means of subsistence, the problem was that he did not press hard enough. The problem of scarcity was replaced by the problem of superabundance.

A similar view was expressed in the *Poor Man's Guardian* in one of a series of articles entitled 'God-made Man v. Gold-made Machine', with the writer arguing that 'as the tendency of machinery is, a priori, to make the supply greater than the demand, it has actually verified this a priori reasoning by glutting the markets'.[56] If a machine could consume like an ordinary labourer, it would 'correct all its mischief as a producer'[57] but as this was impossible, overproduction was a necessary consequence of mechanisation. The opinion of this writer was, therefore, that the use of machinery should be restricted: 'if machinery were moderately restricted, the home consumption would do so much more for the country than all our foreign commerce ever has done or ever can do'.[58] If machinery could be restricted, supply

---

[54] *Voice of the People*, 6 (1831), 47, an article by William Longson; *Poor Man's Advocate*, 6 (1832), 45, article 'On the Cotton Spinners'.
[55] *Advocate*, 2 (1833), 15, an article signed 'G.B.'
[56] *Poor Man's Guardian*, 223 (1835), 668, article by George Burges.
[57] ibid.
[58] ibid. 221 (1835), 653.

would be restricted, prices would rise, wages and profits would increase, more labour would find employment and glutted markets would be emptied. This in essence was the absolute overproductionist's solution to general depression.[59]

The writer of these articles was taken to task for his opinions by O'Brien in the pages of the *Poor Man's Guardian*. O'Brien accused him of 'confounding capital and machines with the system which makes them destructive of the rights of industry'.[60] It is interesting to note, however, that O'Brien believed the writer's 'opinions on machinery, if we mistake not, are those of a very large section of the working classes',[61] though they do not seem to be the opinions of most of those who wrote on the causes and consequences of economic crisis in the working-class press of the early 1830s.

On the question of causes, popular writers tended to remain within the theoretical fold delineated by Thompson, Gray and Owen and likewise accepted the remedies they advocated to restore prosperity. These remedies were, for the most part, concerned with the rationalisation of exchange relations and the overhaul of the exchange medium to allow production and consumption to grow together. Thus labour exchanges were seen as 'all that is necessary to confer upon labour its true value; to give to the producers or holders of wealth the instant power of demanding and obtaining its value in money',[62] and as

---

[59] In this context it is necessary to take issue with M. Berg's view that 'With perhaps greater clarity than any other contemporary issue the machinery question defined the lines of division between these [middle and working] classes', *The Machinery Question*, p. 2; rather it would be more accurate to say that the machinery question revealed profound divisions within the working class itself, with opinions ranging from those who condemned machinery *per se* to those who sought to slow down the introduction of machinery by taxing it, to those who saw machinery as beneficial in the context of different social and economic arrangements. The question which really defined the lines of division between the middle and working classes was the question of exploitation, something clearly recognised by classical popularisers.

[60] *Poor Man's Guardian*, 222 (1835), 655.

[61] ibid. They were certainly the opinions of a number of pamphleteers, for example, Joseph Beddome, *If you ask me, What a Manufacturer by Power Is? I answer a Manufacturer of Poverty* (London, 1834), p. 1, 'My hostility is directed against the mechanical power which is employed to set in motion ... machines, which allows of their being multiplied to any extent, increased to any size, and moved with the utmost rapidity *producing more than man can ... consume*' (my emphasis).

[62] *Birmingham Labour Exchange Gazette*, 3 (1833), 10.

providing 'a new, certain and unlimited Market for the Productions of Industry and Capital'. The establishment of labour exchanges represented the 'creation of a new market for the distribution of wealth which would otherwise neither be distributed nor employed at all'.[63] By valuing labour and commodities correctly, labour exchanges ensured that the sellers of a commodity could be certain of the purchasers or intensity of demand necessary to realise its full value and in such circumstances the absence of an adequate market would no longer represent a barrier to the further development of man's productive power. The existing exploitation or undervaluation of labour ensured that 'the power of consumption is narrowed within an artificial limit, so that by a natural reaction... the power of production, is growing sickly and unhealthy'.[64] However, given different exchange relations, where labour received its true value, the level of demand would prove sufficient to take up all commodities at their natural, labour values. Indeed, so concerned were some writers in the working-class press with establishing the requisite rational and equitable exchange relations that they criticised plans and measures for the alleviation of general economic distress which did not take the need for equitable exchange into account. Thus an attempt made by some Manchester dyers to run their own dyeworks was criticised by one writer on the grounds that

> such an establishment... kept up the old system of competition, by overstocking the market. They went on manufacturing and knew not where they were to find a market. It would be different with a co-operative community, instead of working to overstock the market, they would work for themselves and exchange their productions against each other.[65]

This point was also emphasised by another commentator who wrote of co-operative communities that they were 'dependent upon no other market than that which they themselves created and which their produce and consumption must necessarily

---

[63] *Exchange Bazaars Gazette*, 1 (1832), 1; ibid. 1, 9, a letter from William King.
[64] *Carpenter's Political Magazine*, February 1832, p. 229.
[65] *Voice of the People*, 24 (1831), 189, remark made in a 'Notice' of William Thompson's 'Second Lecture on Co-operation at the Mechanics Institute', 11 June 1831.

maintain *without material fluctuation*',[66] while co-operative trading societies similarly 'increased production and consumption, and thus gave ... employment to a greater number'.[67] It was, therefore, the system of exchange which determined whether new forms of productive enterprise would be able to avoid the evil of glutted markets and general depression.

Simple, co-operative manufacture was also criticised by a writer in the *Lancashire and Yorkshire Co-operator* who argued that productive enterprise which assumed this form would not of itself solve the problem of providing a market for all the commodities produced. Only labour banks could ensure a market co-extensive with production and therefore a demand co-extensive with supply. Labour banks allowed products to create their own markets; co-operative manufacture of itself created 'no new market'.[68] Thus for this writer again it was the form of exchange rather than the mode of production which was fundamental.

As with Gray, Owen, Bray and Thompson, this concern with exchange spilled over into a concern with the medium as well as the mechanism. Thus money, the existing medium of exchange, was seen by many writers in the working-class press as a fundamental cause of general economic crisis. As one commentator put it:

The only just or proper medium of exchange has not yet been introduced into society ... In consequence in the midst of wealth and surrounded by the means of increasing it to an unlimited extent, they [the labouring classes] have for want of this medium suffered the evils and acquired the vices which poverty generates.[69]

Thus leaving aside the reduction in aggregate demand which would result from the exploitative manipulation of the value of money,[70] many writers also regarded the quantity of money in circulation as directly stimulating or depressing the level of economic activity. Indeed, more often than not, the volume of

[66] *Weekly Free Press and Co-operative Journal*, 5, 230 (1830), 2.
[67] *Belfast Co-operative Advocate*, 1 (1830), 8.
[68] *Lancashire and Yorkshire Co-operator*, June 1832, p. 11.
[69] *Midland Representative*, 41 (1832), 3, 'Address to All Classes in the State', the Association for Removing Ignorance and Poverty.
[70] See above, pp. 143–5.

money in circulation was seen as synonymous with the aggregate demand for commodities:

The worlds of producers and capitalists are at a stand in their progress towards independence and happiness, because the old money of the world cannot be brought into circulation as rapidly as the necessaries, comforts and luxuries of life can be made or manufactured... And this is the sole cause of the poverty which exists and all the innumerable evils which it engenders. It is also the cause of so much surplus labour and the necessity in consequence for emigration.

In the present state of things we see the evils which arise from the labouring class, calling on each other for a supply of the necessaries of life, when there is not money enough in circulation, to enable them to effect the transfer... in consequence of this obstacle, no articles or comparatively few are produced.[71]

What was needed, therefore, was a circulating medium which would expand or could be increased in line with production:

The intrinsic value of an article is the labour necessary to produce or obtain it; and in order to have that value correctly represented a circulating medium ought to be employed for the exchange of these productions which will represent accurately the labour required to produce them... and such will be the labour note. This simple expedient will, it is evident, have the immediate effect of securing to every individual the fruits of his own industry, and will create at the same time, a greater demand for labour; for an increased consumption will take place in proportion as the wants of the people can be readily supplied by the aid of their new medium of exchange.[72]

Where commodities were correctly valued and where the medium in which they were valued increased in proportion to the expansion of output, a deficiency of demand could not arise. No overproduction, underconsumption and concomitant economic crisis could occur if 'the circulation of money would be proportioned to the power of production'.[73] For many, the labour note was just the medium of exchange necessary to ensure

---

[71] *Official Gazette of the Trade Union*, 6 (1834), 43, 'Dialogue between a Stranger and a Unionist'; *Crisis*, 2, 18 (1833), 138, reprinted from the 'Report of the Committee of the United Trades Association'.

[72] *Midland Representative*, 41 (1832), 3, 'Address to All Classes in the State', Association for Removing Ignorance and Poverty.

[73] *Pioneer*, 36 (1834), 349, a letter from J. Burr.

that the quantity of money in circulation automatically expanded *pari passu* with output.

It was this rationalisation of exchange relations which provided the key to unlock the existing storehouse of abundance and to do so for the benefit of the labouring classes. For while writers in the working-class press might see existing economic arrangements as a barrier to the further development of productive forces, many nevertheless believed that the productive powers available to mankind were already sufficiently developed to supply all the important wants of society: 'Our productive forces are *far in advance* of the wants of society; there are powers of production now sufficient to secure *any amount of wealth*'; '*Any amount* of real, valuable wealth may now easily be produced in Great Britain and Ireland'; 'twenty of you [labourers] are capable of producing more of the necessaries of life than one hundred of you can rationally consume'; 'England possesses the means and the power of *saturating the whole earth with her* manufactures'.[74]

Consequently, there was a tendency, as with writers in the co-operative press of the later 1820s, to see the problem of general economic depression as one which would be solved merely by an equitable distribution of goods already in existence. As one writer remarked: 'There are some who are aware of the abundance... the excess of all sorts of wealth, which fills the land, [and] cannot close their eyes to the fact that nothing but an improved mode of distributing wealth is required to render all classes happy.'[75] For such writers the problem of production had been solved and only the question of distribution remained. All that was required to eliminate general economic distress was 'an improved mode of distributing wealth' and this would follow automatically from the requisite rationalisation of the exchange process. An overwhelming concern with exchange led many to write, therefore, as if distribution could be altered independently of any fundamental change in productive relations. The problem

---

[74] *Poor Man's Guardian*, 92 (1833), 73; *Crisis*, 1, 13 (1832), 50; *Herald to the Trades Advocate*, 6 (1830), 90, 'Address to the Operatives', by 'D.R.'; *Lancashire Co-operator*, 1 (1831), 'Introduction' (my emphases).

[75] *Birmingham Labour Exchange Gazette*, 1 (1833), 2, 'Address' by the editor; printed also in *Crisis*, 2, 5 (1833), 38; see also, for example, a remark of William Carpenter: 'if we fail to promote distribution the productive power will be rendered proportionally abortive', *Carpenter's Political Magazine*, June 1832, p. 418.

of depression could be solved without the need to impinge upon existing accumulations of capital or to expropriate the expropriators.

The older, radical understanding of crisis and depression was, of course, never entirely displaced by the new, even in the early 1830s when the influence of Thompson, Owen, Gray *et al.* was at its zenith. Taxation, for example, was still considered by some commentators to be the fundamental cause of general economic stagnation and distress. Thus taxation was seen as reducing the funds available for the employment of labour: 'if this unfortunate system [of taxation] had never existed, then all surplus gains would have been lent to commerce, agriculture and manufactures and thus every skill ... would have secured beneficial employment'.[76] Or it was seen as reducing labour's ability to consume, for 'the capital drained off in the name of taxes would be retained by the people and enable them to consume more in proportion ... thereby still further extending the demand for labour'.[77] Similarly the National Debt, 'into which men may be tempted to deposit their money; for the facility of acquiring interest without exertion, drains a certain amount of capital from trade and damps and diminishes the energies of production and the demand for labour. Thus while population multiplies the means for human employment and support are ruinously decreased.'[78] What was required, therefore, was government action to reduce taxation and so restore consumer demand, 'the thing to be aimed at is to give them [labourers] employment; and this employment is to be given them in sufficient quantity only by putting a stop to the transfer of the product of labour to the mouths of those who do not labour ... taking off taxes'.[79]

However, despite this continued emphasis on the primacy of exogenous causes, it was the newer analysis highlighting the endogenous factors making for general economic breakdown which can be said to have predominated in the working-class press of the early 1830s; an analysis which led its proponents

---

[76] *Gauntlet*, 25 (1833), 399, article signed 'T.P.'
[77] *Herald to the Trades Advocate*, 26 (1831), 436.
[78] *Carpenter's Political Letters*, 23 December 1830, p. 3.
[79] *Cobbett's Twopenny Trash*, 1, 6 (1830), col. 130, 'To the Farmers of the County of Kent'.

to attack the irrationality and injustice of existing economic arrangements rather than the malign exercise of political power. This irrationality was epitomised for many by the fact that the labouring classes suffered general economic distress in the midst of an unparalleled material abundance:

> To hunger amidst an abundance of . . . commodities and to be poverty stricken with full pockets are two of the principal arcana which the sagacity of Englishmen has allowed them to reduce to a general practice.

> Our granaries and our warehouses are liberally choked with every description of produce, food included, while the people are starving for want of it.

> There are millions of labourers in this country whose life is but a starvation; who in the midst of abundance and the best of disposition for labour cannot fill their stomachs with the commonest food.

> Yours [the working class] is a state of warfare and your ground of quarrel is the want of the necessaries of life, in the midst of an abundance.[80]

This poverty in the midst of plenty symbolised the bankruptcy of the existing economic system; it demonstrated its essential irrationality and failure; it provided proof positive of the general breakdown of the existing economic order, manifesting at a macroeconomic level the inevitable consequences of the unjust exploitation of labour. In addition, mention of this phenomenon highlighted the possibility of a potential material utopia. It showed that things might indeed be other than they were and that scarcity, impoverishment, vice, misery and a continual pressing against the means of subsistence were not the inevitable lot of the labouring classes. Thus the discussion of general economic depression served the twin critical functions of highlighting, at a macroeconomic level of abstraction, the impending collapse of the existing economic order while holding out the prospect of a prosperous alternative. For these writers the old order had already established the material basis for the new, only inequitable exchange relations barred the way to the promised land.

---

[80] *Carpenter's Political Magazine*, June 1832, 395; *Poor Man's Guardian*, 95 (1833), 98; *Gauntlet*, 1 (1833), 1; ibid. 1, 6; *Poor Man's Guardian*, 16 (1831), 123.

If, therefore, as one writer has suggested,[81] it is at a macroeconomic level of analysis that classical economics can be said to possess a distinctive unity, it is fair to say that by 1834 working-class opinion, in so far as it was expressed through the medium of the working-class press, was directly antagonistic to this unifying feature of classical orthodoxy. In terms of its theoretical coherence this opposition may be dismissed as unimportant. It presented no serious theoretical challenge to any of the forms which Say's Law took in the hands of the classical economists. Malthus, in a theoretical sense, did more damage to the notion that supply created its own demand than Owen, the Smithian socialists and all their popularisers combined. However, the importance of this popular challenge lay not in its theoretical coherence but in the fact that it existed and that it was widely disseminated. It questioned the rationality and stability of early industrial capitalism, it pointed to the need for a new economic order and it suggested some of the means by which this might be established. Together with the theory of labour exploitation, the popularisation of the idea that capitalism had an inherent tendency to economic crisis and breakdown represented a fundamental challenge to the complacency of popularised classical orthodoxy and one which increasingly utilised the language of political economy as depression assumed the form of glut rather than dearth. This was a signal achievement which despite its deficiencies should not be disparaged.

Yet a number of points must be made. First, the understanding of the causes of general economic depression which came to be purveyed most widely in the working-class press of the early 1830s led on to remedies which involved, primarily, the rationalisation of exchange relations, a reform of the mechanisms and a metamorphosis of the medium of exchange. Thus labour banks, labour notes, equitable exchange bazaars and co-operative trading societies were popular panaceas. Some writers, particularly in the co-operative papers, emphasised the need for a more rational, social control of productive forces but even for these writers equitable exchange relations mediated by an invariable standard of value and unit of exchange were considered fundamental.

---

[81] B. A. Corry, 'Keynes and the history of economic thought: some reflections', Queen Mary College, Department of Economics, *Occasional Paper, No. 46* (1977), p. 11.

Secondly, the constant emphasis upon the actual existence of material abundance produced a tendency to treat distribution as an autonomous economic sphere. General economic depression became therefore an essentially distributional problem, the solution to which lay in providing the distributional mechanism to open the floodgates of plenty and empty glutted markets. The problem was that this distributional mechanism, 'the only just or proper medium of exchange', had 'not yet been introduced into society'.[82]

Thirdly, while the periodicity of general depressions was occasionally touched upon, little attempt was made by popular writers to explain why existing economic arrangements might succeed in generating periods of relative prosperity. For writers whose most significant mentors were Thompson, Gray and Owen this might have been expected and in this context it is interesting to note that Cobbett, unconstrained by Owenite or Smithian socialist analysis, did point to the contemporary tendency for the level of economic activity to fluctuate rather than to move inexorably in the direction of slump and inevitable crisis. Thus in one issue of his *Twopenny Register* he remarked:

In the present state of England, there must be *an incessant fluctuation.* Nothing can remain steady for any considerable length of time. The distresses of traders which induced them to glut all the markets abroad as well as at home, produced the ruin of a certain portion of them which resulted in ... some relief of the markets, which had been crammed at the expense of their less opulent brethren.[83]

Thus Cobbett not only noticed the cyclical rhythm of economic life but also provided an interesting if crude explanation of why it occurred, in terms of the periodic diminution of supply to glutted markets which resulted from the bankruptcy of marginal traders.

Yet other examples of this kind of insight are rare. 'One of the Oppressed' in the *Poor Man's Guardian* suggested that the economy might revive periodically through the eventual consumption of those commodities which glutted and depressed markets,[84] while a contributor to the *Magazine of Useful and Co-*

---

[82] *Midland Representative*, 41 (1832), 3, 'Address to All Classes in the State', Association for Removing Ignorance and Poverty.
[83] *Cobbett's Twopenny Register*, 33, 2 (1818), cols. 57–8 (my emphasis).
[84] *Poor Man's Guardian*, 44 (1832), 358.

operative Knowledge also argued that prosperity alternating with lengthening periods of economic stagnation was the characteristic rhythm of economic life:

> And remember that in every period of commercial activity, the means of supply in consequence of the precarious want of employment for capital are increased and accumulated against future demand... So that these periods of activity will gradually become shorter and shorter and the intervals of stagnation will lengthen.[85]

For the most part, however, the understanding of general economic depression disseminated by writers in the working-class press implied that the contemporary economic crisis was a permanent and worsening phenomenon. Even Cobbett and radicals of his ilk, who recognised the existence of booms in economic activity, nevertheless saw them as largely illusory phenomena, the transient products of the irresponsible expansion of paper money which contained the rapidly germinating seeds of future economic catastrophe.

Those who derived inspiration for their economic ideas from Thompson, Owen and Gray or whose economic reasoning was characterised by a similar logic were necessarily driven to the conclusion that general economic depression and impoverishment must be a permanent feature of competitive capitalism. If labour was undervalued or exploited by capitalists and commodities overvalued by the addition of profit to natural value, then there must exist a permanent disparity between the supply price of commodities and the aggregate demand for them, a disparity which must inevitably produce glutted markets: 'The non-employment of capital renders the condition of the great body of the people one of poverty and misery; while the poverty and misery of the great body of the people prevent the productive employment of capital.'[86] This was the vicious circle of economic crisis from which there was no escape except through a transformation of the manner in which exchange was conducted.

The possible repercussions of this analytical deficiency have already been discussed.[87] It is worth reiterating, however, that at a popular level it must have helped to spread a belief in the

---

[85] *Magazine of Useful and Co-operative Knowledge*, 4 (1830), 51, 'On the Creation and Distribution of Wealth', by 'Z'.
[86] *Carpenter's Political Magazine*, February 1832, p. 242.
[87] See above, pp. 188–92.

imminent dissolution of the existing economic order; a conviction which must subsequently have been severely shaken as, with each succeeding bout of prosperity, the capitalist system displayed both its resilience and its continued capacity to flourish.

Conclusion

The years 1816–34 saw the emergence of a popular, working-class political economy viewed by its adherents as distinct from and antagonistic to classical doctrines and looking, for the most part, to anti-capitalist and socialist writers for inspiration. By the early 1830s classical authors and their popularisers were being vigorously rejected by most of those in the working-class press who concerned themselves with economic questions. Yet they did not stop short at mere rejection and, for the most part, eschewed anti-intellectualist attitudes to the discipline of political economy. On the contrary, writers in the working-class press of the 1830s recognised and stressed the importance of a knowledge of political economy, distinguishing the manner in which it could be applied to lay bare the causes of working-class grievances from the manner in which it was abused and reduced to the status of apologetics by classical authors. Classical writers were accused of elaborating theories which bore little relation to the objectively observed economic facts of exploitation, poverty and general depression; of formulating, instead, theories designed to defend the interests of capitalists and landowners; of obfuscating the true causes of general impoverishment and material distress suffered by the labouring classes; of constructing a political economy purged of any ethical dimension; of concerning themselves exclusively with how to maximise the rate of capital accumulation rather than how to optimise the distribution of wealth and, therefore, viewing Man as a means of increasing production rather than regarding his welfare as the sole goal of economic activity.

In thus condemning classical economics, popular writers were effectively defining what they believed should be the nature, function and scope of a working-class political economy. Working-class political economy was to be the polar opposite of 'orthodoxy'; it was to be all that classical political economy was not. Above all it was to be a body of theory which could be utilised to assail the iniquity and inequity of the economic status quo and confound the seemingly quietistic implications of popularised classical orthodoxy. Quite simply, for most writers who discussed the matter in the working-class press, political economy should be directed to the articulation and defence of the interests of the working classes.

This recognition of the positive, critical use to which political economy might be put was undoubtedly, in part at least, a function of the intellectual climate of the period. Political economy was in vogue and in the hands of its 'orthodox' popularisers it represented an ideological onslaught which it would have been difficult for any working-class radical to ignore. It could, of course, have been dismissed with a rhetorical flourish as the philosophy of 'Midas-eared Mammonism', as indeed it was by some of the Romantic writers of the period,[1] but this would have represented the abandonment of high ground to the enemy leaving him able to pour down the unanswerable logic of an unassailable paradigm upon the heads of those who sought to defend the interests of the working classes with rhetoric rather than reason.

Yet did the fact that the classical popularisers had to be answered of itself necessitate a recourse to political economy to provide the substance and medium of an answer, or were there other options open? Two suggest themselves. First, there was the possibility of developing and utilising the *deus ex machina* explanations of poverty and general distress advanced by Cobbett, Carlile, Wooler and other radical writers, and secondly, the possibility of deploying the natural rights analysis to be found in the economic writings of the agrarian radicals. It has been argued, however, that it was not simply the ideological challenge alone which required those who wished to defend the material interests of the labouring classes to have recourse to the analytical tools and theoretical constructs

---

[1] T. Carlyle, *Past and Present* (London, Chapman and Hall, n.d.), p. 124.

of political economy. Rather, the necessity arose because in conjunction with the ideological onslaught of the classical popularisers, the economic developments which characterised early-nineteenth-century industrial capitalism suggested causes of working-class poverty which could not be encompassed in the litany of 'Old Corruption' and which posed theoretical problems of a kind with which the conceptual structure and analytical tools of the agrarian radicals could not cope. To come to terms with the economic realities of nascent industrial capitalism, it was indeed necessary to utilise what classical political economy offered and, in particular, in an increasingly diversified, market-oriented economy, to use it to furnish some kind of theory which would allow anti-capitalists and socialists to think, to reason and to analyse in value rather than in physical terms. This was one of the major achievements of Owen and the Smithian socialists and it was upon this foundation of value theory that their theories of labour exploitation and capitalist crisis were constructed – the twin pillars upon which the whole edifice of popular, working-class political economy came to rest.

Yet among those who defended and articulated working-class interests a definite disenchantment with political economy seems to have set in fairly rapidly after 1834. The symptoms of this disenchantment were many and varied. For example, there was the demise of papers such as the *Pioneer*, the *Crisis* and the *Voice of the West Riding* in 1834 and the *Poor Man's Guardian* in 1835, each of which had devoted significant space to the discussion of economic ideas and issues during its lifetime. In addition, most of the working-class papers which were established in the years 1834–6 proved to be primarily concerned with such matters as universal suffrage and the repeal of the stamp tax on newspapers rather than with specifically economic questions.[2] Thus these papers seem to suggest a move away from popular discussion of and interest in questions of political economy. In this context it is interesting to note the scant attention paid to J. F. Bray's *Labour's Wrongs* by reviewers in working-class papers.[3]

However, what occurred in the years after 1834 was not just a growing disenchantment with economic theorising and economic

[2] See above, p. 5.
[3] It received only lukewarm reviews in the *New Moral World*, the *Chartist* and the *Northern Star*.

discussion but rather the degeneration and disintegration of anti-capitalist and socialist political economy as such. Thomas Hodgskin, for example, increasingly channelled his considerable analytical ability into the defence and advocacy of free trade[4] and eventually became a regular contributor to Charles Wilson's *Economist*.[5] John Gray with the publication of his *Efficient Remedy for the Distress of Nations* (1842) and his *Lectures on the Nature and Use of Money* (1848) took the road of an increasingly extreme monetary crankiness challenging all comers to refute his views for a prize of one hundred guineas. J. F. Bray emigrated to the United States soon after the publication of *Labour's Wrongs* and in any case did not, during the rest of a long life, produce anything comparable to his 1839 work. Robert Owen seems to have displayed negligible interest in socialist political economy after 1834, while the Owenites became increasingly sectarian, evincing a greater relish for fomenting anti-clericalism than for initiating hard thinking on economic questions. Only Thompson's reputation as an economic writer remained unimpaired after 1834, possibly because he died in 1833. By the late 1840s, anti-capitalist and socialist economic theory was in an advanced stage of degeneration and remained so in Britain for the rest of the century.

This study suggests a number of reasons why this should have been the case. Certainly writers such as Hodgskin, Gray, Thompson and Owen had achieved much in the 1820s and 1830s. They had provided the theoretical substance of a distinctive, working-class political economy which was popularly accepted and popularly purveyed. Yet the theoretical foundations upon which this political economy rested had definite weaknesses. Paradoxically, the theories of value, which represented such an important theoretical advance of Smithian socialism over agrarian radicalism and which enabled the Smithian socialists to come to terms with the kinds of question which early industrial capitalism threw up, also proved to be the Achilles heel of early-nineteenth-century anti-capitalist and socialist economic thought. Hodgskin, Thompson, Gray and Bray adopted and deployed a Smithian explanation of the determination of exchange value under capitalism which led to the elaboration of their theories of labour

---

[4] See, for example, his *Lecture on Free Trade in connexion with the Corn Laws*.
[5] E. Halévy, *Thomas Hodgskin*, pp. 184–8.

exploitation along profit-upon-alienation lines. Their additive conception of the determination of exchange value embodied an understanding of exploitation as something which resulted from the constant deviation of market, social or money prices from natural values; rent, profit and other exactions being seen as added to the natural, labour values of commodities, while labour at the same time was bought and sold below its intrinsic worth. Thus the essence of capitalist exploitation lay in the systematic manipulation or distortion of commodity values (labour included); a process of distortion which for formal theorists and their popularisers was both facilitated and masked by the contemporary nature and qualities of money. Analytical attention was focused, therefore, primarily upon exchange relations and their necessary rationalisation, reform or abolition, rather than upon any need for a direct alteration in the existing pattern of property ownership. A fundamental change in the ownership of capital and land could be secured by creating the necessary conditions for equitable exchange rather than by recourse to forcible appropriation and redistribution.

This belief was most obviously reflected in the means by which labour exploitation and general economic depression were to be eliminated. Equitable labour exchanges or bazaars, the establishment of a labour standard or measure of value, the creation of a labour or comparable medium of exchange, the foundation of co-operative trading societies, support – in the case of Hodgskin – for free trade and for the freedom of trade unions to raise the price of labour towards its natural value: these were the inevitable policy corollaries of an additive, profit-upon-alienation theory of labour exploitation.

It is true that this refurbishing of the market and rationalisation of exchange relations was often regarded as merely the first step towards co-operative communities, producer co-operatives and other plans for the eventual, radical alteration of existing social and economic arrangements. Yet two points should be noted here. First, this was a step to which Owen and other socialist writers attached great importance. For them, co-operative trading societies, labour notes, equitable labour exchanges or 'really free trade' were the necessary tickets of admission to a new moral and economic world. With a refurbished market and rationalised exchange relations capital would accumulate in the hands of those who laboured and 'unproductive' capitalists would watch their wealth dwindle as they were forced to consume it to live. Given equal exchanges of labour for labour existing accumulations of capital would diminish and the economic power wielded by the capitalist would atrophy while the ownership of the means of production would be radically altered. Secondly, as is clear from Thompson's *Labor Rewarded*, one of the great economic attractions of co-operative communities was that they represented an institutional embodiment of the abolition of exchanges; they were sanctuaries free from that 'higgling of the market', that manipulation and distortion and of exchange values, which characterised competitive capitalism and permitted exploitation and oppression. A retreat to the sanctuary of autarkic co-operative communities or the refurbishment of the market – these were the panaceas which Smithian socialism implied. In the event neither of these alternatives fulfilled the expectations of their proponents and this must certainly have provoked a profound disillusion with the political economy that had theoretically underpinned them.

In addition, it may be argued that Smithian socialism, due to its theoretical structure, left anti-capitalist and socialist political economy ripe for the degeneration which it underwent in the 1840s and thereafter. It was, for example, a short step from the demand that labour should exchange at its natural value or intrinsic worth, to the opinion that labour should exchange at a 'fair' value or that it should be paid a fair price for its services. Thus while the emphasis upon equitable exchange relations might be seen as pointing in the direction of labour's right to the whole of its product, it is assuredly pointed in the direction of an insipid, non-theoretical labourism which demanded a fair day's pay for a fair day's work. There is, therefore, a sense in which early-nineteenth-century anti-capitalist and socialist political economy contained the seeds of its subsequent degeneration, for an obsession with the phenomena of exchange shades easily and, perhaps, inevitably into a narrow, theoretically crude, pounds-shillings-and-pence concern with the fairness of bargains struck in the labour market. It was just such a collapse of theory which characterised the labourism of the 1850s and 1860s. Also, as the later works of two of the Smithian socialists reveal, where the decay of anti-capitalist and socialist thought did not assume this form, the concern with exchange and exchange relations could as easily lead on to an obsession with the need to free markets in order that the untrammelled operation of natural economic forces determine the value of labour and all commodities (Hodgskin) or to a simplistic concern with the banking system and the minutiae of money (Gray).

This study also suggests the existence of weaknesses and deficiencies at a macroeconomic level of analysis which may account for the collapse of anti-capitalist and socialist theory after 1834. The theories of capitalist crisis advanced by Owen, Gray, Thompson and lesser writers represented a definite analytical achievement providing as they did, at a macroeconomic level of abstraction, some explanation of the *general* nature of the economic distress afflicting the labouring classes, and the dissemination of elements of these theories by popular writers in the late 1820s and early 1830s ensured that the theory of capitalist crisis rapidly became an important component of the contemporary economic *Weltanschauung* of the working classes. These theories represented too an advance, in theoretical terms, on the understanding of general economic depression as a product of exogenous factors which was purveyed by Cobbett and Paine and also a necessary move away from the naturalistic, eighteenth-century perception of crisis as the consequence of scarcity or dearth. Nevertheless, as with exploitation, general economic depression was seen by Thompson, Owen and Gray and their popularisers as, essentially, a product of distorted or inequitable exchange relations. Labour exchanged below and commodities above their natural values and underconsumption, glutted markets, idle capital and redundant labour followed as a necessary consequence. Indeed, this analysis led inexorably to the conclusion that these economic phenomena were and must remain permanent features of capitalism. Thus their theories explained the existence of a slump or steadily deepening depression but could not explain periods of growth or prosperity. The imminence of economic nemesis was, therefore, a logical corollary of the popular political economy of capitalist crisis. Yet it was a nemesis which stubbornly refused to materialise. Capitalism proved to be remarkably and, for these writers, inexplicably resilient and this unfulfilled prediction of general economic breakdown was to hang like an albatross around the neck of anti-capitalist and socialist theory.

Here again we have a powerful reason for disillusionment with political economy as a tool of critical analysis.

However, this is not to suggest that working-class disenchantment with the discipline was exclusively a product of its theoretical deficiencies or lack of predictive power. The fact that from the mid-1830s working-class radicals had numerous outlets for their energies of a practical as opposed to an analytical kind may also be considered significant. For such individuals there were things to do and specific, concrete ends to be achieved — factory reform, the repeal of the stamp tax, the campaign against the 1834 Poor Law Amendment Act and the People's Charter. Yet practical, radical activity should not, in theory at least, have precluded some elaboration or amplification of the theories, ideas and insights bequeathed by Owen and the Smithian socialists, though it might be argued that such activity did require less theoretical justification, in economic terms, than the creation of labour bazaars, co-operative trading societies, co-operative communities or even a Grand National Consolidated Trades Union.

Other factors may also have contributed towards the disenchantment with and degeneration of anti-capitalist and socialist political economy. In particular the economic growth and dynamism of the mid-century period not only negated the apocalyptic macroeconomic implications of early socialist political economy but also helped to create an economic climate likely to dull working-class receptivity to and interest in radical theories, be they economic or political. Thus in circumstances where the material standard of well-being of the bulk of the population was improving, albeit slowly, it might seem reasonable to argue that a political economy based upon theories of labour exploitation and general economic impoverishment would be unlikely to maintain its *popular* momentum. However, while general economic improvement may account in part for the decay of *popular*, anti-capitalist and socialist political economy, the question arises as to whether economic circumstances explain why, at a more formal level, theory degenerated. Did John Gray become a monetary crank, did Hodgskin metamorphose from virulent anti-capitalist to vigorous anti-protectionist, did Robert Owen cease to make any significant contribution to socialist political economy in the 1840s and 1850s because the material well-being of the masses was improving? Such a crude reflectionist view of the link between fact and theory must surely be heavily qualified if not rejected. Increasing material prosperity may go some way to explaining the reduced popular appeal of the economic theories of Owen and the Smithian socialists but it cannot of itself explain why the well-springs of that original economic thinking which characterised their writings in the 1820s and 1830s dried up in the 1840s and 1850s. Perhaps it was a consequence of that erosion of the critical faculties which often accompanies the process of ageing but this fails to explain the non-emergence of a second generation of anti-capitalist and socialist political economists (however small in number) ready to eliminate the theoretical weaknesses and develop the theoretical insights of the first. After all, the economic successes of capitalism have not prevented the emergence of political economies critical of its functioning and predicting its inevitable, eventual demise. Thus the relatively rapid growth experienced by mid-Victorian Britain did not inhibit Marx's elaboration of 'an economic critique of capitalist production'.

The point to make, of course, is that capitalist prosperity will not prevent the formulation of incisive critiques of capitalist production if those critiques can explain capitalism's capacity to deliver the goods. Marx's explanation of the laws of motion of capitalist production could accommodate the phenomenon of prosperity. His critique of capitalism could explain the existence of periods – even prolonged periods – of relative economic growth. Such periods posed, therefore, no major empirical threat to the theoretical core of Marxian political economy. In contrast, Owen and the Smithian socialists were unable to provide an explanation as to why, under existing economic arrangements, periods of relative economic prosperity could and did occur. For these writers such periods of sustained growth were empirical anomalies which could not be accommodated within the theoretical structure which they had elaborated; they represented a fundamental crisis for early anti-capitalist and socialist economic thought which could not be resolved within the prevailing paradigm.

While of itself, therefore, the relative material prosperity of the 1850s and 1860s did not preclude the formulation of an anti-capitalist and/or socialist critique of capitalism, what it may have done was to hinder or obviate the further development of a critical political economy based upon those foundations laid down by Owen, Thompson, Hodgskin, Gray and Bray. It was the reality of mid-Victorian prosperity combined with the specific nature of its internal theoretical structure which may be said to have precipitated the disintegration of anti-capitalist and socialist thought.

A study of the evolution of anti-capitalist and socialist political economy and its popularisation not only highlights, therefore, the positive achievement of its proponents but it also explains, in large measure, the transient nature of that achievement. These writers and their popularisers emphasised the need for a distinctive, working-class approach to the discipline of political economy; they defined the essential characteristics of that approach; they put to critical use some of the tools, concepts and constructs of classical political economy and in so doing they provided, through the formulation of interrelated theories of labour exploitation and capitalist crisis, the theoretical foundations upon which a people's science might rest. Yet the edifice crumbled: anti-capitalist and socialist political economy decayed. The tendency to analytical overconcentration upon exchange and exchange relations finally bore fruit in monetary crankiness, insipid labourism, obeisance to the natural economic laws of the free market or autarkic retreat from the economic world as it existed. Such was the corpse for which J. S. Mill's *Principles* provided a tombstone. For all its rapid and extensive growth, the people's science was a plant doomed to wither before it could establish lasting popular or theoretical roots.

Bibliography

Newspapers[1]

Advocate; or, Artisans' and Labourers' Friend, 1 (16 February 1833) – 10 (20 April 1833), ed. John Ambrose Williams, 'managed by a committee of the Printers' Protection Society ... a miscellany which deplores the effects of machinery'.[2] Price 1d.

Advocate of the Working Classes: and true practical political economist, Winter 1826 – Spring 1827, ed. George Mudie, 'an important source for examining the development of anti-capitalist ideas in the late 1820s'.[3]

Associate, 1 (1 January 1829) – 9 (1 January 1830), then *Associate and Co-operative Mirror*, 10 (1830) – 12 (1830). 'Inspired by the original "Benevolent Fund Association", a co-operative venture set up by some working men in Brighton 1827'.[4] Price 1d.

Ballot, 1 (2 January 1831) – 97 (4 November 1832), ed. Thomas Wakely, a paper of a radical reformist political complexion. Price 7d.

Belfast Co-operative Advocate: the Journal of the Belfast Co-operative Trading Association, 1 (January 1830) – ? Price 1d.

Birmingham Co-operative Herald, 1 (April 1829) – 19 (October 1830), ed. William Pare; a paper outlining the theory of co-operation and the causes of and remedies for working-class distress. Price 1d.

Birmingham Inspector, 1 (4 January 1817) – 16 (23 August 1817), ed. W. Hawkes Smith, 'Organ of radical reform in Birmingham'.[5] Price 4d.

Birmingham Labour Exchange Gazette, 1 (16 January 1833) – 5 (9 February 1833), ed. William Pare. The paper concerned itself primarily with the theory and practice of equitable labour exchanges.

---

[1] The following list includes *some* of the more important newspapers scrutinised in the course of research. For a fuller list of 'labour periodicals' published in the period see R. Harrison, G. Woolven and R. Duncan, *The Warwick Guide to British Labour Periodicals 1790–1970* (hereafter referred to as *Warwick Guide*).
[2] J. H. Wiener, *A Descriptive Find List of Unstamped British Periodicals 1830–36*, p. 2.
[3] G. Claeys, 'George Mudie's *Advocate of the Working Classes 1826–7*', 42.
[4] *Warwick Guide*, p. 19.
[5] ibid. p. 37.

Black Dwarf 1, 1 (29 January 1817) – 12, 21 (December 1824), ed. Thomas Wooler. 'One of the most important, unstamped, ultra-radical periodicals'.[6] Price 4d, 6d.

Carpenter's Monthly Political Magazine, September 1831 – September 1832, ed. William Carpenter. The paper contained articles on political, social and economic questions.

Carpenter's Political Letters and Pamphlets, 1 (9 October 1830) – 34 (14 May 1831), ed. William Carpenter. The paper was largely concerned with radical political reform. Circulation c. 6,000.[7] Price 2d.

Cobbett's Political Register, 1802–36; Cobbett published his *Political Register* throughout this period; however, the cheap, popular, post-Napoleonic War edition of the paper which is referred to as *Cobbett's Twopenny Register* ran from 12 October 1816 to 29 July 1820.

Cobbett's Twopenny Trash, or, Politics for the Poor, 1, 1 (July 1830) – 2, 12 (July 1832), ed. William Cobbett.

Co-operative Magazine and Monthly Herald 1, 1 (January 1826) – 2, 12 (December 1827), then *Co-operative Magazine*, 3, 1 (January 1828) – 3, 10 (October 1829), then *London Co-operative Magazine*, 4, 1 (1 January 1830) – 4, 3 (1 March 1830), then the *British Co-operator*, 1 (April 1830) – 7 (October 1830). 'Organ of the London Co-operative Society'.[8] Price 6d.

The (Brighton) *Co-operator*, 1 (1 May 1828) – 38 (1 August 1830), ed. William King. 'A series of tracts, most of which were written by King'.[9] Price 1d.

The Crisis, or the Change from Error and Misery, to Truth and Happiness, 1, 1 (14 April 1832) – 2, 15 (20 April 1833), then *Crisis and National Co-operative Trades' Union and Equitable Labour Exchange Gazette*, 2, 16 (27 April 1833) – 4, 20 (23 April 1834), ed. Robert Owen, Robert Dale Owen (1832–4) and James E. (Shepherd) Smith; printed for the Association of the Intelligent and well-disposed of the Industrious Classes for removing Ignorance and Poverty by Education and Employment; estimated circulation 5,000.[10] 'Its news accounts and essays disseminate Owenite co-operative principles.'[11] Price 1d, 1½d.

Destructive and Poor Man's Conservative, 1 (2 February 1833) – 45 (7 December 1833), then *People's Conservative and Trade Union Gazette*, 46 (14 December 1833) – 55 (15 February 1834), ed. 'Bronterre' O'Brien. Estimated circulation in September 1833, 8,000; 'A working-class newspaper ... repeatedly attacking the profit system and the "shopocracy"'.[12] Price 2d, 3d.

---

[6] ibid. p. 38.
[7] P. Hollis, Introduction to the *Poor Man's Guardian*, p. xv.
[8] *Warwick Guide*, p. 108.
[9] *Warwick Guide*, p. 112.
[10] *Evening Standard*, 10 September 1833.
[11] J. H. Wiener, *A Descriptive Find List*, p. 12.
[12] *Evening Standard*, 10 September 1833; J. H. Wiener, *A Descriptive Find List*, p. 13.

Economist, a Periodical Paper Explanatory of the New System of Society Projected by Robert Owen Esq., 1 (27 January 1821) – 52 (9 March 1822), ed. George Mudie. A co-operative paper particularly interested in those economic questions which touched on the improvement of the labouring classes. Price 3d.

Gauntlet, a sound Republican Weekly Newspaper, 1 (10 February 1833) – 60 (30 March 1834), ed. Richard Carlile. The paper was mainly a medium for Carlile's republican and anti-clerical sentiments. Estimated circulation in September 1833, 22,000; claimed circulation 23 March 1834, 2,500.[13] Price 3d.

Gazette of the Exchange Bazaars, or Exchange Bazaars Gazette and Practical Guide to the rapid Establishment of Public Prosperity, 1 (22 September 1832) – 9 (24 November 1832) ed. George Mudie. 'The *Gazette* ... is devoted to discussions of the theoretical basis of exchange bazaars, criticisms of their management and plans for their extension.'[14] Price 1d.

Gorgon, 1 (23 May 1818) – 49 (24 April 1819), 'started by John Wade, a woolcomber'.[15] Price 1d, 1½d.

Herald of the Rights of Industry, 1 (8 February 1834) – 16 (24 May 1834). 'Published by the Society for Promoting National Regeneration, a group of factory reformers led by John Doherty'; 'A factory and trades union miscellany that advocates an eight hour working day',[16] ed. John Doherty. Price 1d.

Herald to the Trades Advocate and Co-operative Journal, 1 (25 September 1830) – 20 (5 February 1831); then *Herald to the Trades Advocate*, 21 (12 February 1831) – 36 (28 May 1831). 'Organ of the Trades' Committee of Glasgow ... Probable editors John Tait and Alexander Campbell'; 'a political miscellany ... mainly devoted to encouraging trade union activities'.[17] Price 2d.

Lancashire Co-operator, 1 (11 June 1831) – 6 (20 August 1831), then *Lancashire and Yorkshire Co-operator or Useful Classes Advocate*, 1 (3 September 1831) – 12 (4 February 1832); NS 1 (March 1832) – 12 (October 1832), ed. E. T. Craig, Thomas Hirst. A paper propagating co-operative principles. Price 1d.

London Alfred, or People's Recorder, 1 (25 August 1819) – 12 (17 November 1819), a radical political paper. Price 1½d.

Medusa, or Penny Politician, 1 (20 February 1819) – 2, 1 (28 February 1820), a paper concerned with radical political reform. Price 1d.

Midland Representative and Birmingham Herald, 1 (23 April 1831) – 59 (2 June 1832), ed. 'Bronterre' O'Brien. Concerned for the most part with universal suffrage and annual parliaments. Price 7d.

---

[13] *Evening Standard*, 10 September 1833; J. H. Wiener, *A Descriptive Find List*, p. 18.
[14] G. Claeys, 'George Mudie and the *Gazette of the Exchange Bazaars*', *Bulletin of the Society for the Study of Labour History*, 42 (Spring 1981), 33.
[15] *Warwick Guide*, p. 194.
[16] ibid. p. 208; J. H. Wiener, *A Descriptive Find List*, p. 21.
[17] *Warwick Guide*, p. 208; J. H. Wiener, *A Descriptive Find List*, p. 21.

Mirror of Truth, 1 (10 October 1817) – 2 (7 November 1817), provided an 'Exposition and discussion of Robert Owen's *New View of Society* and schemes for the relief of the poor'.[18] No. 1, p. 14, makes mention of a Board of Editors. Price 1 sh.

Northern Reformers' Monthly Magazine and Political Register, 1 (January 1823) – 4 (April 1823). Concerned with radical political reform. Price 6d.

Penny Papers for the People published by the *Poor Man's Guardian*, 1 (October 1830) – 28 (2 July 1831), ed. Thomas Mayhew. A paper pressing for radical political reform. Price 1d.

People, 1 (19 April 1817) – 15 (26 July 1817), 'Demands universal suffrage, secret ballot, annual parliaments as the key to the problems of the labouring population'.[19]

Pioneer, or Trades' Union Gazette, 1 (7 September 1833) – 44 (5 July 1834). 'One of the best-known trades union and co-operative miscellanies of the decade with an estimated circulation of 20,000',[20] ed. James Morrison. Price 1d, 2d.

Poor Man's Advocate and People's Library, 1 (21 January 1832) – 50 (3 January 1833), then *Poor Man's Advocate and Scourge of Tyranny*, 51 (11 October 1834) – 55 (6 December 1834), ed. John Doherty (1–50) and James Turner (51–5). It was concerned with exposing the abuses of the factory system and advocating legislation to reform them. Price 1d.

Poor Man's Guardian, 1 (7 July 1831) – 238 (26 December 1835), ed. Thomas Mayhew (to December 1831) and 'Bronterre' O'Brien. The paper was concerned with the political and economic grievances of the labouring classes; 'the best-known and most important illegal newspaper of the decade'; estimated peak circulation 15,000[21] but see also the *Evening Standard*, 10 September 1833, which estimated its circulation at 16,000. Price 1d.

Republican, 1, 1 (27 August 1819) – 14, 25 (29 December 1826), ed. Richard Carlile and Julian Augustus St John. The paper was for radical political reform and against organised religion. Price 2d.

Republican, or Voice of the People, 1, 1 (26 March 1831) – 2, 47 (28 July 1832), then *Republican and Radical Reformer* 3, 1 (4 August 1832) – 3, 19 (15 December 1832), then *Republican*, 4, 1 (23 March 1834?) – 4, 6 (27 April 1834), ed. J. H. B. Lorymer. Circulation c. 10,000. The paper was mainly concerned with radical political reform; 'one of the best-known working-class newspapers of the decade'.[22] Price ½d, 1d, 3d, 1d, 1½d.

Trades Newspaper and Mechanics Weekly Journal, 1 (17 July 1825) – 106 (22 July 1827); then *Trades Free Press*, 107 (29 July 1827) – 163 (16 August 1828), then *Weekly Free Press*, 164 (23 August 1828) – 299 (2 April 1831). 'Founded by representatives of the London and Provincial trades',[23] ed. John Robertson, John Anderson and William Carpenter. Price 7d.

---

[18] *Warwick Guide*, p. 320.
[19] ibid. p. 403.
[20] ibid. p. 414.
[21] ibid.; J. H. Wiener, *A Descriptive Find List*, p. 46.
[22] ibid. p. 51; P. Hollis, Introduction to the *Poor Man's Guardian*, p. xvii.

Bibliography 233

Voice of the People, by an Association of Working Men 1, 1 (1 January 1831) – 2, 13 (24 September 1831), ed. John Doherty. 'Organ of the National Association for the Protection of Labour'. Price 7d.

Voice of the West Riding, 1 (1 January 1833) – 53 (7 June 1834), ed. Joshua Hobson and from the end of 1833 John Francis Bray. The paper was a strong advocate of factory legislation, 'a widely circulated working-class newspaper'.[24] Price 1d.

Wooler's British Gazette, 1 (3 January 1819) – 259 (14 December 1823), ed. Thomas Wooler. The paper was mainly concerned with political questions. Price $8\frac{1}{2}$d, 7d.

Working Man's Friend, 1 (22 December 1832) – 33 (August 1833), ed. John Cleave. 'It repeatedly attacks factory abuses, the competition system and the tax on newspapers.'[25] Price 1d.

Books and articles

Altick, R. D. *The English Common Reader, a social history of the mass reading public 1800–1900*, Chicago and London, University of Chicago Press, 1957.

Anon. *Mr Owen's Proposed Arrangements for the Distressed Working Classes shown to be consistent with sound principles of Political Economy: in three letters to David Ricardo Esq., M.P.*, London, Longman, 1819.

Vindication of Mr Owen's Plan for the Relief of the Distressed Working Classes, London, 1820.

A Petition of the Journeymen Broad Silk Weavers of Spitalfields and its vicinity, n.p. 1828.

Words of Wisdom Addressed to the Labouring Classes, Armagh, 1830.

A Plain Statement with respect to Wages, London, 1831.

A Short Address to Workmen on Combinations to raise Wages, London, 1831.

Ashton, T. S. *Economic Fluctuations in England 1700–1800*, Oxford, Clarendon Press, 1958.

Aspinall, A. 'The circulation of newspapers', *Review of English Studies*, 22 (1946), 29–43.

Politics and the Press c. 1780–1850, London, Hone and van Thal, 1949.

Attwood, T. *The Remedy, or Thoughts on the Present Distresses*, London, 1816.

A Letter to Mr Vansittart on the Creation of Money, Birmingham, 1817.

A Letter to the Earl of Liverpool, Birmingham, 1819.

The Late Prosperity and the Present Adversity of the Country explained, London, 1826.

Bain, A. *James Mill, A Biography*, London, Longman, 1882.

Beales, H. L. *The Early English Socialists*, London, Hamilton, 1933.

---

[23] *Warwick Guide*, p. 557.
[24] J. H. Wiener, *A Descriptive Find List*, p. 60.
[25] *Warwick Guide*, p. 615.

Beddome, J. *If you ask me, What a Manufacturer by Power Is? I answer a Manufacturer of Poverty*, London, 1834.
Beer, M. *Pioneers of Land Reform*, London, Bell, 1920.
 A History of British Socialism, 2 vols., London, Allen and Unwin, 1953.
Berg, M. *The Machinery Question and the Making of Political Economy 1815–1848*, Cambridge University Press, 1981.
Blaug, M. *Ricardian Economics, a historical study*, New Haven, Yale University Press, 1958.
 Economic Theory in Retrospect, 3rd edn, Cambridge University Press, 1978.
Bonar, J. *Malthus and his Work*, London, Macmillan, 1885.
Bray, J. F. *Labour's Wrongs and Labour's Remedy or, The Age of Might and the Age of Right*, London School of Economics and Political Science, 1931.
Briggs, A. 'The economic background to the Birmingham Political Union 1830–32', *Cambridge Historical Journal*, 9 (1948), 190–216.
 'The language of class in early nineteenth century England' in A. Briggs and J. Saville (eds.), *Essays in Labour History in Memory of G. D. H. Cole*, London, Macmillan, 1967, pp. 43–73.
Brougham, H. *Practical Observations on the Education of the People, addressed to the Working Classes and their Employers*, London, 1825.
Butt, J. 'Robert Owen in his own time 1771–1858' in *Robert Owen and his Relevance to our Times*, Co-operative College Papers, No. 14, Loughborough 1971, pp. 15–22.
Carlyle, T. *Past and Present*, London, Chapman and Hall, n.d.
Carpenter, W. *The Proceedings of the Third Co-operative Conference*, London, 1832.
Carr, H. J. 'John Francis Bray', *Economica*, 7 (1940), 397–415.
 'The social and political thought of John Francis Bray', unpublished PhD thesis, University of London, 1942.
Chabert, A. 'Aux sources du socialisme anglais: un pré-marxiste méconnu: Charles Hall', *Revue d'Histoire Economique et Sociale*, 29 (1951), 369–83.
Chalmers, T. 'On Mechanics Schools and on political economy as a branch of popular education', *Glasgow Mechanics Magazine*, 5 (3 June 1826), 217–21.
Church, R. A. and Chapman, S. D. 'Gravener Henson and the making of the English working class' in E. L. Jones and G. E. Mingay (eds.), *Land, Labour and Population in the Industrial Revolution*, London, Edward Arnold, 1967, pp. 236–61.
Claeys, G. 'George Mudie and the *Gazette of the Exchange Bazaars*', *Bulletin of the Society for the Study of Labour History*, 42 (Spring 1981), 33.
 'Four letters between Thomas Spence and Charles Hall', *Notes and Queries*, NS, 28, 4 (August 1981), 317–21.
 'Benjamin Scott Jones alias "Philadelphus": an early Owenite socialist', *Bulletin of the Society for the Study of Labour History*, 43 (Autumn 1981), 14–15.
 'George Mudie's *Advocate of the Working Classes* 1826–7', *Bulletin of the Society for the Study of Labour History*, 44 (Spring 1982), 42–3.
Clapham, J. H. 'The Spitalfields Acts 1773–1824', *Economic Journal*, 20 (1916), 459–71.

Coats, A. W. 'The classical economists and the labourer' in A. W. Coats (ed.), *The Classical Economists and Economic Policy*, London, Methuen, 1971, pp. 144-79.
Cobbett, W. *Paper Against Gold*, London, 1815.
Cole, G. D. H. *A History of Socialist Thought*, 5 vols., Vol. 1, *Socialist Thought: The Forerunners 1789-1850*, London, Macmillan, 1977.
Cole, M. 'Owen's mind and methods' in S. Pollard and J. Salt (eds.), *Robert Owen, Prophet of the Poor*, London, Macmillan, 1971, pp. 188-213.
Corry, B. A. 'Keynes and the history of economic thought: some reflections', Queen Mary College, Department of Economics, *Occasional Paper No. 46*, 1977.
Deane, P. *The First Industrial Revolution*, 2nd edn, Cambridge University Press, 1979.
Deane, P. and Cole, W. A. *British Economic Growth 1688-1959, Trends and Structure*, University of Cambridge, Department of Applied Economics, Monographs, 8, 1962.
Derry, J. W. *The Radical Tradition, Tom Paine to Lloyd George*, London, Macmillan, 1967.
Desai, M. *Marxian Economic Theory*, London, Gray Mills, 1974.
Dinwiddy, J. R. 'Charles Hall, early English socialist', *International Review of Social History*, 21 (1976), 256-76.
Dobb, M. *Theories of Value and Distribution since Adam Smith*, Cambridge University Press, 1979.
Douglas, P. H. 'Smith's theory of value and distribution' in J. M. Clark (ed.), *Adam Smith 1776-1926: Lectures to commemorate the sesquicentennial of the publication of the 'Wealth of Nations'*, New York, Kelley, 1966, pp. 77-115.
Driver, C. 'Thomas Hodgskin and the individualists' in F. J. C. Hearnshaw (ed.), *The Social and Political Ideas of Some Representative Thinkers of the Age of Reaction and Reconstruction*, London, Harrap, 1932, pp. 191-219.
Eatwell, J. 'The interpretation of Ricardo's *Essay on Profits*', *Economica*, 42 (1975), 182-7.
Empson, W. 'Mrs Marcet – Miss Martineau', *Edinburgh Review*, 57 (April 1833), 1-39.
Engels, F. W. *The Condition of the Working Class in England*, London, Panther, 1974.
Preface to the first English edition of *Capital*, Moscow, Progress Publishers, 1974, pp. 13-17.
Socialism, Utopian and Scientific, London, Allen, 1911.
Feinstein, C. H. 'Capital accumulation in the industrial revolution' in R. Floud and D. N. McCloskey (eds.), *The Economic History of Britain since 1700*, 2 vols., Cambridge University Press, 1981, Vol. 1, pp. 128-42.
Fetter, F. W. 'Economic articles in the *Edinburgh Review*, 1802-47', *Journal of Political Economy*, 61 (1953), 232-59.
'Economic articles in the *Quarterly Review*', *Journal of Political Economy*, 66 (1958), 47-64, 154-70.
'Economic articles in *Blackwood's Magazine*', *Scottish Journal of Political Economy*, 7 (1960), 85-107, 213-31.

'Economic articles in the *Westminster Review, 1824–51*', *Journal of Political Economy*, 70 (1962), 576–96.
The Development of British Monetary Orthodoxy 1797–1875, Cambridge, Mass., Harvard University Press, 1965.
Flood, J. W. 'The Benthamites and their use of the press', unpublished PhD thesis, University of London, 1974.
Foxwell, H. S. Introduction to the English translation of A. Menger, *The Right to the Whole Produce of Labour*, London, Macmillan, 1899.
Garnett, R. G. *Co-operative and Owenite Socialist Communities in Britain and America 1825–45*, Manchester University Press, 1972.
'William Pare, co-operator and social reformer', *Co-operative College Paper*, No. 16, Loughborough, 1973.
Gayer, A. D., Rostow, W. W. and Schwartz, A. J. *The Growth and Fluctuation of the British Economy*, 2 vols., Oxford, Clarendon Press, 1953.
Ghosh, R. N. 'Malthus on emigration and colonization', *Economica*, 30 (1963), 45–61.
Gide, C. and Rist, C. *A History of Economic Doctrines*, 2nd edn, London, Harrap, 1948.
Goldstrom, J. M. 'Richard Whately and political economy in schoolbooks 1833–80', *Irish Historical Studies*, 15 (1966–7), 131–46.
Gordon, S. 'The *London Economist* and the high tide of laissez-faire', *Journal of Political Economy*, 63 (1955), 461–88.
Graham, W. *Socialism, New and Old*, London, Kegan Paul, 1890.
Gray, A. *The Socialist Tradition, Moses to Lenin*, London, Longman, 1967.
Gray, J. *A Lecture on Human Happiness*, London School of Economics and Political Science, 1931.
The Social System, A Treatise on the Principle of Exchange, Edinburgh, 1831.
An Efficient Remedy for the Distress of Nations, Edinburgh, 1842.
Lectures on the Nature and Use of Money, Edinburgh, 1848.
Gray, S. alias Purves, G. *All Classes Productive of National Wealth; or, the Theories of M. Quesnai, Dr Adam Smith and Mr Gray Concerning Various Classes of Men, as to the Production of Wealth to the Community Analysed and Examined*, London, 1817.
Gray, S. 'Remarks on the production of wealth', *Pamphleteer*, No. 17 (1820).
Hale, W. *An Appeal to the Public in Defence of the Spitalfields Act*, London, E. Justins, 1822.
Halévy, E. *Thomas Hodgskin*, translated with an introduction by A. J. Taylor, London, Benn, 1956.
Hall, C. *The Effects of Civilisation*, London, 1805.
Observations on the principal Conclusion in Mr Malthus's Essay on Population, London, 1805.
Hall, R. *An Appeal to the Public on the subject of the Framework Knitters Fund*, 2nd edn, Leicester, T. Combe, 1820.
Hardach, G., Karras, D. and Fine, B. *A Short History of Socialist Economic Thought*, London, Edward Arnold, 1978.
Harrison, J. F. C. *Learning and Living 1790–1960: A Study in the History of the Adult Education Movement*, London, Routledge and Kegan Paul, 1961.

Bibliography 237

Owen and the Owenites in Britain and America, the quest for the new moral world, London, Routledge and Kegan Paul, 1969.

Harrison, R., Woolven, G. and Duncan, R. *The Warwick Guide to British Labour Periodicals 1790–1970: A Check List*, Hassocks, Harvester Press, 1977.

Harrison, S. *Poor Men's Guardians, a record of the struggles for a democratic newspaper press 1763–1973*, London, Lawrence and Wishart, 1974.

Heighton, W. *An Address to the Members of Trade Societies and to the Working Classes generally*, London, 1827.

Henson, G. *The Civil, Political and Mechanical History of the Framework Knitters in Europe and America*, Nottingham, 1831.

Hodgskin, T. *Labour Defended against the Claims of Capital*, 2nd edn, London, Steil, 1831.

Popular Political Economy, Four Lectures delivered at the London Mechanics Institute, London, 1827.

The Natural and Artificial Rights of Property Contrasted, London, Steil, 1832.

A Lecture on Free Trade, in connexion with the Corn Laws, London, 1843.

Letters, 1826–7, in the *College Correspondence Collection of University College London*.

Hollander, S. G. 'The development of Ricardo's position on machinery', *History of Political Economy*, 3 (1971), 105–35.

'Ricardo's analysis of the profit rate 1813–15', *Economica*, 40 (1973), 260–82.

'Ricardo and the corn profit model, reply to Eatwell', *Economica*, 42 (1975), 188–202.

The Economics of David Ricardo, London, Heinemann, 1979.

'The post-Ricardian dissension: a case study in economics and ideology', *Oxford Economic Papers*, 32 (1980), 370–410.

Hollis, P. Introduction to reprint of the *Poor Man's Guardian*, 4 vols., London, Merlin, 1969.

The Pauper Press: a study in working-class radicalism of the 1830s, Oxford University Press, 1970.

Class and Conflict in Nineteenth Century England 1815–50, London, Routledge and Kegan Paul, 1973.

Holyoake, G. J. *A History of Co-operation*, London, Unwin, 1906.

Hovell, M. *The Chartist Movement*, Manchester University Press, 1925.

Hunt, E. K. 'Value theory in writings of the classical economists', *History of Political Economy*, 9 (1977), 322–45.

'Utilitarianism and the labour theory of value', *History of Political Economy*, 11 (1979), 544–71.

'The relation of the Ricardian socialists to Ricardo and Marx', *Science and Society*, 44 (1980), 177–98.

Hyndman, H. M. *The Historical Basis of Socialism in England*, London, Kegan Paul, 1892.

Jackson, W. *An Address to the Framework Knitters*, Leicester, J. Fowler, 1833.

Jeffrey, F. 'Political economy', *Edinburgh Review*, 43 (November 1825), 1–23.

Johnson, R. 'Really useful knowledge, radical education and working-class culture 1790–1848' in J. Clarke, Chas. Critcher and R. Johnson (eds.),

Working-Class Culture, Studies in History and Theory, London, Hutchinson, 1979, pp. 75–102.

Jones, E. L. 'Agriculture 1700–80' in R. Floud and D. N. McCloskey (eds.), *The Economic History of Britain since 1700*, 2 vols., Cambridge University Press, 1981, Vol. 1, pp. 66–86.

Jones, G. Stedman. 'Class struggle and the industrial revolution', *New Left Review*, No. 90 (March/April 1975), 35–69.

Kamata, T. 'The life and thought of Thomas Hodgskin up to the first parliamentary reform (1832)', paper presented to the *Ninth conference of the History of Economics Society*, 25 May 1982.

Kaufmann, M. *Utopias; or schemes of social improvement: from Sir Thomas More to Karl Marx*, London, 1879.

Kay, J. P. *The Moral and Physical Condition of the Working Classes employed in the Cotton Manufactures in Manchester*, Manchester, 1832.

Kelly, T. *George Birkbeck: Pioneer of Adult Education*, Liverpool University Press, 1957.

A History of Adult Education in Great Britain, Liverpool University Press, 1970.

Kemp-Ashraf, P. M. 'An introduction to the selected writings of Thomas Spence' in Anselm Schlösser (ed.), *Essays in Honour of Willie Gallacher*, Berlin, Humboldt University, 1966, pp. 271–91.

Keynes, J. M. 'The end of laissez-faire' in *Essays in Persuasion*, ed. D. E. Moggridge, *The Collected Works of John Maynard Keynes*, London, Macmillan, 1972, Vol. 9, pp. 272–94.

Kimball, J. *The Economic Doctrines of John Gray 1799–1883*, Washington, Catholic University of America Press, 1946.

King, J. E. 'Perish commerce! Free trade and underconsumption in early British radical economics', *Australian Economic Papers*, 20 (1981), 235–57.

'Utopian or scientific? A reconsideration of the Ricardian socialists', *History of Political Economy*, 15 (1983), 345–73.

King, W. *To the Useful Working Population*, London, 1831.

The Workings of Capital, at present represented by money, London, 1831.

Kirkup, T. *A History of Socialism*, London, Black, 1892.

Knight, C. *The Results of Machinery*, London, 1831.

The Rights of Industry, London, 1831.

Passages in a Working Life during half a century, 3 vols., London, 1864–5.

Capital and Labour including the Results of Machinery, London, 1873.

Larcher, A. *The Good and Bad Effects of High and Low Wages; or, a Defence of the Spitalfields Acts*, London, 1823.

Link, R. G. *English Theories of Economic Fluctuations 1815–48*, New York, Columbia University Press, 1959.

Longfield, M. *Lectures on Political Economy*, Dublin, Milliken, 1834.

Lovett, W. *The Life and Struggles of William Lovett in Pursuit of Bread, Knowledge and Freedom*, London, Bell, 1920.

Lowenthal, E. *The Ricardian Socialists*, New York, Longman, Green & Co., 1911.

McCormac, H. *An Appeal in Behalf of the Poor*, Belfast, 1831.
McCulloch, J. R. 'The opinions of Messrs Say, Sismondi and Malthus on the effects of machinery and accumulation', *Edinburgh Review*, 35 (March 1821), 102–23.
'Political Economy', Supplement to the *Encyclopaedia Britannica*, 6th edn, Edinburgh, 1824.
The Principles of Political Economy, Edinburgh, 1825.
Syllabus of a Course of Lectures on Political Economy, London, 1825.
'The rise, progress, present state and prospects of British cotton manufacturers', *Edinburgh Review*, 46 (June 1827), 1–39.
Malthus, T. R. *Principles of Political Economy*, London, 1820.
Mannheim, K. *Ideology and Utopia*, London, Routledge and Kegan Paul, 1960.
Marcet, J. *Conversations on Political Economy*, London, Longman, 1816.
John Hopkins's Notions of Political Economy, London, 1833.
de Marchi, N. B. 'The success of Mill's *Principles*', *History of Political Economy*, 6 (1974), 119–57.
Marsh, J. H. 'Economics education in schools in the nineteenth century: social control', *Journal of the Economics Association*, 3 (1977), 116–18.
Martineau, H. *Illustrations of Political Economy*, No. 25, *The Moral of Many Fables*, London, Knight, 1834.
Marx, K. *The Poverty of Philosophy*, London, Lawrence and Wishart, 1954.
Preface and Introduction to a Contribution to the Critique of Political Economy, Peking, Foreign Languages Press, 1976.
Contribution to a Critique of Political Economy, London, Lawrence and Wishart, 1971.
Capital, 3 vols., Moscow, Progress Publishers, 1974.
Theories of Surplus Value, 3 vols., Moscow, Progress Publishers, 1969–72.
Mathias, P. *The First Industrial Nation: An Economic History of Britain, 1700–1914* London, Methuen, 1969.
Meek, R. L. 'The decline of Ricardian economics in England', *Economica*, 9 (1950), 43–62
Studies in the Labour Theory of Value, London, Lawrence and Wishart, 1973.
Merle, G. 'Weekly Newspapers', *Westminster Review*, 10 (April 1829), 466–80.
Mill, J. 'Thomas Smith on money and exchange', *Edinburgh Review*, 13 (October 1808), 35–68.
The Elements of Political Economy, 3rd edn, London, 1826, in D. N. Winch (ed.), *Selected Economic Writings of James Mill*, Edinburgh, Oliver and Boyd, 1966.
Mill, J. S. *Essays on Some Unsettled Questions of Political Economy*, London School of Economics and Political Science, 1948.
Mineka, F. E. (ed.). *Collected Works of John Stuart Mill*, Vol. 12, *The Earlier Letters of J. S. Mill*, Toronto University Press, 1963.
Mitchell, B. R. and Deane, P. *An Abstract of British Historical Statistics*, University of Cambridge, Department of Applied Economics, Monographs, 17, 1971.

Morgan, J. M. *Remarks on the Practicability of Mr Owen's Plan to Improve the Condition of the Lower Classes*, London, Samuel Leigh, 1819.
The Revolt of the Bees, London, 1826.
Musson, A. E. and Kirby, R. G. *'The Voice of People', John Doherty, 1798–1854, trade unionist, radical and factory reformer*, Manchester University Press, 1975.
Myrdal, G. *The Political Element in the Development of Economic Theory*, London, Routledge and Kegan Paul, 1953.
O'Brien, D. P. *J. R. McCulloch, a study in classical economics*, London, Allen and Unwin, 1970.
O'Brien, P. K. and Engerman, S. L. 'Changes in income and its distribution during the industrial revolution', in R. Floud and D. N. McCloskey (eds.), *The Economic History of Britain since 1700*, 2 vols., Cambridge University Press, 1981, Vol. 1, pp. 164–81.
Ogilvie, W. *An Essay on the Right of Property in Land* (1781) in M. Beer, *Pioneers of Land Reform*.
Oliver, W. H. 'The labour exchange phase of the co-operative movement', *Oxford Economic Papers*, 10 (1958), 355–67.
'Owen in 1817, the Millenialist Movement', in S. Pollard and J. Salt (eds.), *Robert Owen, Prophet of the Poor*, London, Macmillan, 1971, pp. 165–85.
Owen, R. *A New View of Society, Essays on the Formation of Human Character*, Harmondsworth, Pelican, 1970.
Observations on the Effect of the Manufacturing System, London, 1815.
'Letter published in the London newspapers', 25 July 1817, in *The Life of Robert Owen written by Himself*, Vol. 1A.
'Report to the Committee for the Relief of the Manufacturing Poor', 1817, in *The Life of Robert Owen written by Himself*, Vol. 1A.
'Two memorials on behalf of the working classes', 1818, in *The Life of Robert Owen written by Himself*, Vol. 1A.
'An address to the working classes', April 1819, in *The Life of Robert Owen written by Himself*, Vol. 1A, Appendix P, p. 230.
An Address to the Master Manufacturers of Great Britain, Bolton, 1819.
Development of the Plan for the Relief of the Poor, London, 1820.
Report to the County of Lanark of a Plan for Relieving Public Distress, Glasgow University Press, 1821.
An Explanation of the Cause of Distress which pervades the civilized parts of the World, London, 1823.
The Address of the Working Classes of Devonshire, Exeter, 1830.
An Address to All Classes in the State, London, 1832.
The Revolution in the Mind and Practice of the Human Race, London, 1849.
The Life of Robert Owen written by Himself, 2 vols., London, E. Wilson, 1857–8.
Owen Correspondence, Co-operative College, Manchester.
Paine, T. *The Decline of the English System of Finance*, London, 1796.
Agrarian Justice (1797) in M. Beer, *Pioneers of Land Reform*.
Pankhurst, R. K. P. *William Thompson, Britain's Pioneer Socialist, Feminist and Co-operator*, London, Watts, 1954.

Parsinnen, T. 'The revolutionary party in London 1816–20', *Bulletin of the Institute of Historical Research*, 45 (1972), 266–82.
Perkin, H. *The Origins of Modern English Society, 1780–1880*, London, Routledge and Kegan Paul, 1981.
Place, F. *Illustrations and Proofs of the Principle of Population*, London, 1822.
Place Collection, BM Add. MSS. 27, 791.
Plummer, A. 'The place of Bronterre O'Brien in the working-class movement', *Economic History Review*, 2 (1929–30), 61–80.
 Bronterre, A Political Biography of Bronterre O'Brien, London, Allen and Unwin, 1971.
Pollard, S. 'Robert Owen as an economist' in *Robert Owen and his Relevance to Our Times*, Co-operative College Paper No. 14, Loughborough, 1971, pp. 23–36.
Potter (Webb), B. *The Co-operative Movement in Great Britain*, London, Sonnenschein, 1891.
Proceedings of the first general meeting of the British and foreign philanthropic society for the relief of the labouring classes, London, 1822.
Prothero, I. *Artisans and Politics in early Nineteenth Century London, John Gast and his Times*, Folkestone, William Dawson, 1979.
Pryme, G. *A Syllabus of a Course of Lectures on the Principles of Political Economy*, Cambridge, 1816.
 An Introductory Lecture and Syllabus to a course delivered in the University of Cambridge on the Principles of Political Economy, Cambridge, 1823.
Radical, Roger (pseud.), *Why are we poor? An Address to the Industrious and Labouring Classes of the Community*, London, 1820.
Ravenstone, P. (pseud.), *Thoughts on the Funding System and its Effects*, London, 1824.
Ricardo, D. *On the Principles of Political Economy and Taxation*, ed. P. Sraffa, *The Works and Correspondence of David Ricardo*, Cambridge University Press, 1981, Vol. 1.
Robinson, J. *An Essay on Marxian Economics*, London, Macmillan, 1949.
Rodbertus, K. *Overproduction and Crises*, English translation, London, Sonnenschein, 1898.
Roll, E. *A History of Economic Thought*, Homewood, Irwin, 1974.
Rose, J. H. 'The unstamped press', *English Historical Review*, 12 (1897), 711–26.
Routh, G. *The Origin of Economic Ideas*, London, Macmillan, 1977.
Ryan, C. C. 'The fiends of commerce: Romantic and Marxian criticisms of classical political economy', *History of Political Economy*, 13 (1981), 80–94.
Samuelson, P. A. 'Economists and the history of ideas', *American Economic Review*, 52 (1962), 1–18.
Saville, J. 'J. E. Smith and the Owenite movement, 1833–4', in S. Pollard and J. Salt (eds.), *Robert Owen, Prophet of the Poor, Essays in Honour of the Hundredth Anniversary of his Birth*, London, Macmillan, 1971, pp. 115–44.
Schumpter, J. S. *Economic Doctrine and Method*, London, Allen and Unwin, 1954.

Schwartz, P. *The New Political Economy of J. S. Mill*, London, Weidenfeld and Nicolson, 1968.
Scrope, G. P. 'The rights of industry – the banking system', *Quarterly Review*, 47 (July 1832), 407–57.
Senior, N. W. 'Political Economy', *Westminster Review*, 8 (July 1827), 177–89.
Three Lectures on the Rate of Wages, 2nd edn, London, Murray, 1831.
Sever, J. 'James Morrison of the *Pioneer*', unpublished monograph, 1963.
Smith, A. *An Inquiry into the Nature and Causes of the Wealth of Nations*, ed. R. H. Campbell, A. S. Skinner and W. B. Todd, 2 vols., Oxford, Clarendon Press, 1976.
Sowell, T. *Say's Law: an historical analysis*, Princeton University Press, 1972.
Spence, T. *Lecture on Land Reform to the Newcastle Philosophical Society* (1775) in M. Beer, *Pioneers of Land Reform*.
The History of Crusonia or, Robinson Crusoe's Island (1782) in Anselm Schlösser (ed.), *Essays in Honour of Willie Gallacher*, Berlin, Humboldt University, 1966, pp. 297–307.
The Real Rights of Man, London, 1793.
The Rights of Infants, London, 1795?
The End of Oppression being a Dialogue between an Old Mechanic and a Young One concerning the Establishment of the Rights of Man, 2nd edn, London, 1796.
The Meridian Sun of Liberty or The Whole Rights of Man displayed, London, 1796.
The Restorer of Society to its Natural State, London, 1801.
Sraffa, P. Introduction to D. Ricardo, *The Works and Correspondence of David Ricardo*, Vol. 1, *On the Principles of Political Economy and Taxation*, Cambridge University Press, 1981.
Stephen, L. *The English Utilitarians*, 2 vols., London, Duckworth, 1900.
A History of English Thought in the Eighteenth Century, 3rd edn, 2 vols., London, Smith, Elder and Co., 1902.
Stigler, G. J. 'Ricardo and the 93% labour theory of value' in *Essays in the History of Economics*, University of Chicago Press, 1965, pp. 326–42.
Thomas, W. E. S. 'Francis Place and working-class history', *Historical Journal*, 5 (1962), 61–70.
Thompson, E. P. 'The moral economy of English crowd in the eighteenth century', *Past and Present*, No. 50 (1971), 76–136.
The Making of the English Working Class, Harmondsworth, Pelican, 1975.
Thompson, N. W. 'Ricardian socialists/Smithian socialists: what's in a name?', *Faculty of Economics and Politics Research Paper*, University of Cambridge, 1976.
Thompson, W. *An Inquiry into the Principles of the Distribution of Wealth most conducive to Human Happiness*, London, Longman, 1824.
Labor Rewarded: The Claims of Labor and Capital Conciliated, By One of the Idle Classes, London, Hunt and Clarke, 1827.
Practical Directions for the Speedy and Economical Establishment of Communities, London, 1830.

Torrens, R. 'Mr Owen's plans for relieving the national distress', *Edinburgh Review*, 32 (October 1819), 453–77.
Tribe, K. *Land, Labour and Economic Discourse*, London, Routledge and Kegan Paul, 1978.
Tufnell, E. C. *The Character, Object and Effects of Trades' Unions*, London, Ridgway, 1834.
von Tunzelmann, G. N. 'Technical progress during the industrial revolution' in R. Floud and D. N. McCloskey (eds.), *The Economic History of Britain since 1700*, 2 vols., Cambridge University Press 1981, Vol. 1, pp. 143–63.
Tyrell, A. 'Political economy, Whiggism and the education of working-class adults in Scotland 1817–40', *Scottish Historical Review*, 48 (1969) 151–65.
Ure, A. *The Philosophy of Manufactures; or, an exposition of the scientific, moral and commercial economy of the factory system of Great Britain*, 3rd edn, London, Bohn, 1861.
Vaughan, M. and Archer, M. S. *Social Conflict and Educational Change in England and France 1789–1848*, Cambridge University Press, 1971.
Wallas, G. *The Life of Francis Place*, 2nd edn, London, Allen and Unwin, 1918.
Warden, B. *The Rewards of Industry*, Bovington, 1832?
Webb, R. K. *The British Working Class Reader, 1790–1848, literacy and social tension*, London, Allen and Unwin, 1955.
  'The Victorian reading public', *Universities Quarterly*, 12 (1957–8), 24–44.
Whately, R. *A Letter to his Parishioners on the Disturbances which have lately occurred*, London, 1830.
  Introductory Lectures on Political Economy, London, 1831.
  Village Conversations in Hard Times, London, 1831.
  Easy Lessons on Money Matters, Commerce, Trade, Wages etc. etc. for the Use of Young People as well as Adults of all Classes, Dublin, 1835.
Wiener, J. H. *The War of the Unstamped, the Movement to Repeal the British Newspaper Tax 1830–36*, Ithaca, Cornell University Press, 1969.
  A Descriptive Find List of Unstamped British Periodicals 1830–36, London, The Bibliographical Society, 1970.
Yeo, E. M. J. 'Social science and social change 1830–80', unpublished PhD thesis, University of Sussex, 1972.

Index

Abundance
  and critique of capitalism, 180–1, 183–4
  and economic crisis, *see* Economic crisis
  and existing distribution of property, 184
  and Gray, *see* Gray, J.
  and Owen, *see* Owen, R.
  and poverty in the midst of, 55, 115, 169, 181, 192, 202, 210–11, 214
Advocate, 207n
Advocate of the Working Classes, 15n
Agrarian radicals
  inapplicability of analysis, 40, 43–8, 52–3, 221
  and natural rights, 40–2, 47–51, 220
  and physical nature of analysis, 42
Altick, R. D., 60n
Antagonism of interests, 67–8, 69, 80, 95, 103, 109, 124, 140, 151–3, 184
Anti-capitalist political economy, *see* Ricardian socialists
Archer, M. S., 62n
Ashton, T. S., 54n
Aspinall, A., 4n, 6n
Associate, 15n, 202n
Associate and Co-operative Mirror, 15n, 132n, 133n, 134n
Attwood, T., 178, 197–8

Bain, A., 154n
Ballot, 144, 203
Bank Restriction Act, 114, 116
Barton, J., 16n
Beddome, J., 208n

Beer, M., 2, 20, 65n, 84n
Belfast Co-operative Advocate, 134n, 135n, 143n, 145n, 210n
Berg, M., 61n, 64n, 203n
Birkbeck, G. 14n, 60
Birmingham Co-operative Herald, 15n, 131n, 135n
Birmingham Inspector, 114n, 191n
Birmingham Labour Exchange Gazette, 19, 141n, 212n
Birmingham School, 178, 197, 198n
Black Dwarf, 8, 9, 24, 112n, 113n, 117n, 192n, 193–4
Black, J., 57
Blaug, M., 63n, 65n, 85, 162n
Bonar, J., 84n
Bray, J. F., 4, 64n, 82–3, 85, 221, 222
  on capitalists, 109
  on economic antagonism, 109
  on exchange, 94, 95–6, 98
  on exploitation, 94, 95–6, 98, 109
  on money, 97–8, 177
  on value, 91
Briggs, A., 197n
British Co-operator, 15n, 132n
Brougham, H., 29, 59

Capital
  displacing labour, 159
  growing importance of, 52, 54
  as a means of exploitation, 123, 134, 143, 149
  as money, 147–8
  ownership of, *see* Production, means of

245

Capitalism
  and abundance, 182, 184
  and economic crisis, 163, 168, 185, 187, 196, 199, 204
  and exchange, 76, 93, 97, 105, 145
  and impoverishment of labour, 35–6, 74, 148
  and prosperity, 227
Capitalists
  and economic crisis, 169–70, 173, 204–5
  as exploiters, 108–9, 125, 127, 130, 139–40
  power of, 70, 128, 134, 138, 145
Carlile, R., 8, 9, 10, 116, 148, 220
Carlyle, T., 220n
Carpenter, W., 13, 32n, 204, 212n
Carpenter's Political Letters and Pamphlets, 17, 24n, 149n, 213n
Carpenter's Political Magazine, 136n, 204n, 212n, 214n, 217n
Carr, H. J., 82n, 84
Chabert, A., 65n
Chalmers, T., 59n
Chapman, S. D., 37n, 38n, 39n
Church, R. A., 37n, 38n, 39n
Clapham, J. H., 38n
Clarke, J., 6n
Classical populisers
  antipathy to anti-capitalist and socialist political economy, 153–7
  apologia for capitalism, 61–3
  attack on by working-class press, 23–5, 29, 34
  perception of role, 56–7, 58
  and Mechanics Institutes, *see* Mechanics Institutes
  and Place, *see* Place, F.
Coats, A. W., 162n
Cobbett, W
  on economic crisis, 192–3, 194–5, 197–8, 203, 216–17, 225
  on exploitation, 113–15, 148–9, 220
  on labour and value, 112–13, 116
  on money, 114–15, 116, 197–8
  on the National Debt, *see* National Debt
  on political economy, 8–9, 10
  on taxation, 116
Cobbett's Twopenny Register, see Cobbett, W.
Cobbett's Twopenny Trash, 148, 203, 213n

Cole, G. D. H., 2, 65n, 85
Cole, W. A., 45n
Colquhoun, P., 93
Competition, 36–9, 67, 75, 76, 79, 95, 97, 99–100, 101, 106, 118, 122, 123, 128, 132, 140, 209
Co-operative communities, 100–2, 123, 146, 165–6, 167, 168–9, 179, 210, 223
Co-operative Magazine, 15n, 16n, 22, 131n, 132n, 134n, 135n, 201n
Co-operative Magazine and Monthly Herald, 15n
Co-operative press
  circulation, 6, 229–3
  and economic crisis, 191, 201–3
  on exchange, 132–5
  on exploitation, 121–4, 132–6
  on political economy, 10–12, 15–16, 22, 27
  on value, 131–2
Co-operative trading societies, 132–6, 146, 180, 210, 215, 223
Co-operator, 15n, 131n, 132n, 133n, 134n
Corn Laws, 14, 127, 129, 198
Corry, B. A., 215n
Crisis, 5, 18, 19n, 136n, 139n, 140n, 141n, 142n, 143n, 149n, 211n, 212n
Critcher, C., 6n

Deane, P., 35–6, 45n, 53–4, 55n
Demand
  deficiency of *see* Economic crisis
  as need, 166–7, 169, 201, 205, 211
Derry, J. W., 9n
Desai, M., 105n
Destructive, 5, 17, 19, 24n, 149n
Dinwiddy, J. R., 20n, 72n
Distribution
  autonomous treatment of, 182–3, 212–13, 217
  and economic crisis, 182, 189, 202
Douglas, P. H., 86
Driver, C., 84n

Eatwell, J., 44n
Economic crisis, 1, 2
  and abundance, 180–2, 216
  and Attwood, 202, 204–5, 212, 214
  and Birmingham School, *see* Birmingham School
  changing nature of, 53–6
  and classical economists, 158–62

Index 247

and Cobbett, *see* Cobbett, W.
and co-operative communities, 165–6, 167, 168–9, 195–7
and the co-operative press, *see* Co-operative press
and deficiency of demand, 169, 171, 172–4, 201, 204–5, 206, 209, 212, 213
and distribution, *see* Distribution
and exploitation, 172–3, 177, 199, 209
general nature of, 54–5
and government expenditure, 188–9
and Gray, *see* Gray, J.
and Hodgskin, *see* Hodgskin, T.
and labour exchanges, 168
and machinery, 196, 200, 207–8
and Marx, *see* Marx, K.
and money, 160–1, 168, 174–6, 189, 193, 194–6, 197–8, 210–12
and overproduction, *see* Overproduction
and Owen, *see* Owen, R.
periodicity of, 53–4, 185–7, 190, 216–17
permanency of, 185, 187, 190, 217–18, 225
and the radical press, *see* Radical press
and Ricardo, *see* Ricardo
and taxation, *see* Taxation
and Thompson, *see* Thompson, W.
and the *Trades Newspaper*, 197–201
and the working-class press, *see* Working-class press
Economist, 10, 27, 121n, 122–3, 196–7
Ellis, W., 60
Empson, W., 1, 154
Encyclopaedia Britannica, 57–8
Engels, F. W., 53, 80, 105
Engerman, S. L., 54n
Exchange
  abolition of, 102, 103, 224
  equitable and inequitable, 89, 92–3, 95–6, 101, 102–3, 122, 132–3, 138–42, 146, 164, 177, 189, 209, 223–5
  medium of, 94, 134, 141
  rationalisation of, 94–5, 102–3, 111, 133, 141, 144, 165, 178, 184, 209
  relations of, 92, 96–7, 104, 132–3, 135, 139, 144–6, 209, 223–5
Exploitation
  and capitalists, *see* Capitalists

and Cobbett, *see* Cobbett, W.
and the co-operative press, *see* Co-operative press
and economic crisis, *see* Economic crisis
endogenous perception of, 110, 120, 123
and exchange (*see* Exchange, equitable and inequitable)
exogenous perception of, 110, 114, 116–17, 121
and Gray (*see* Gray, J.)
and Hall (*see* Hall, C.)
and Hodgskin, *see* Hodgskin, T
and inadequacy of physical theory of, 43–7, 53
and Marx, *see* Marx, K.
and Owen, *see* Owen, R.
and profit-upon-alienation, 96, 140, 144, 223
and the radical press, *see* Radical press
and taxation, *see* Taxation
and Thompson, *see* Thompson, W.
and the *Trades Newspaper*, *see* Trades Newspaper
and the working-class press, *see* Working-class press
Exploiters, 67, 69, 72, 107, 108–10, 117, 120, 125, 129–30, 139–40, 145, 149–50

Feinstein, C. H., 46n
Fetter, F. W., 57n, 195n
Foxwell, H. S., 83–4
Framework knitters, 36–9
Fry, C., 134

Garner, E., 134
Garnett, R. G., 167n
Gast, J., 127, 129, 199n
Gauntlet, 203, 213n, 215n
Gayer, A. D., 53
Ghosh, R. N., 26n
Gide, C., 80n
Godwin, W., 62
Goldstrom, J. M., 155n
Gorgon, 9–11, 24, 118–21
Graham, W., 83
Gray, A., 2, 65n, 84
Gray, J.
  on abundance, 181

on economic crisis, 163–5, 169n, 174–5, 177–8, 225
on exchange, 93–4, 97, 179–80
on exploitation, 93–4, 109
and Marx, *see* Marx, K.
on the means of production, 96
on money, 97, 174–5, 177–8, 180, 222, 226
and Owen, 107
and Ricardo, 84
on value, 91, 93
and the working-class press, 15
Gray, S., 58–9

Hale, W., 38–9
Hall, C., 2, 15n, 65, 85
and antagonism of interests, 69
causes of dearth, 68–9
and exploitation, 66–7, 69–71
on manufactures and trade, 67–8
physical mode of analysis, 68–71, 73
rights to land, 66
value theory, 71–3
Hall, R., 37–8
Harrison, J. F. C., 59, 60n, 81n
Harrison, R., 3
Harrison, S., 3n, 4n
Heighton, W., 181
Henson, G., 38n, 39
Herald to the Rights of Industry, 139n
Herald to the Trades Advocate, 149n, 204n, 212n, 213n
Hodgskin, T., 1, 11–12, 17, 27, 52, 60, 155n, 226
on economic antagonism, 109
on economic crisis, 169–72
on exchange, 99
on exploitation, 92, 93, 108
on free markets, 98, 222, 223
and Marx, *see* Marx, K.
and O'Brien, *see* O'Brien, J. B.
and Owen, 107–8
on political economy, 12, 20–2
and Ricardo, 84–5, 93–4
and Smith, 93–8
on trade unions, 223
and the *Trades Newspaper*, *see* *Trades Newspaper*
on value, 90–1, 92, 93–4
Hollander, S. G., 44n, 86
Hollis, P., 4n, 138n, 148n, 173n
Holyoake, G. J., 16, 83

Hovell, M., 20, 84
Hunt, E. K., 106n
Hyndman, H. M., 83

Jackson, W., 38
Jeffrey, F., 59n
Johnson, R., 6n
Jones, E. L., 45n
Jones, G. S., 52n

Kamata, T., 155n
Kaufmann, M., 83
Kay, J. P., 152n
Kelly, T., 60n
Kemp-Ashraf, P. M., 49n
Keynes, J. M., 63n
Kimball, J., 86
King, J. E., 106n, 171n
King, Dr. W., 131n
King, W., 23, 133, 142, 176n, 179
Kirkup, T., 83
Knight, C., 153, 154, 155

Labour
banks, 141, 146, 176–7, 210, 215
and classical popularisers, 62–3
exchanges, 141, 146, 168, 176–7, 178–80, 209, 215, 223
exploitation of, *see* Exploitation
and a fair wage, 39, 120, 128, 224
impoverishment of, 50, 52, 54–5, 61–2, 66–7, 73–4, 76–7, 79, 102, 117, 123, 132, 148, 150, 163, 191
legislative protection of, 36–7, 39, 126, 128–9
notes, 135, 143, 176–7, 211–12, 215, 223
right to the whole product of, 33, 95, 101, 134–5, 141, 153, 224
source of value, 76, 90–1, 103, 111–14, 121, 124–5, 131, 136, 142, 147
and unemployment, 53–4, 127, 159–60, 164, 173–5, 193–6, 199–202, 211
value of, 74–5, 80, 89, 113, 116–17, 118–20, 122, 124–5, 131, 136, 142, 147
vulnerability of, 38, 40–2, 54, 66–7, 74, 76–7, 81, 122–3, 127
Labouring class, *see* Labour
Lancashire and Yorkshire Co-operator, 17, 139n, 144, 210

Lancashire Co-operator, 17, 206, 212n
Larcher, A., 37
London Alfred, 115
London Co-operative Magazine, 15n
Longfield, M., 156
Lovett, W., 16
Lowenthal, E., 85–6

Machinery, 96, 130, 159, 196–7, 200, 207–8
McCormac, H., 169
McCulloch, J. R., 1, 3, 14, 15, 25, 30, 59, 159n, 160n, 200n
Magazine of Useful and Co-operative Knowledge, 201n, 217
Malthus, T. R., 8, 15, 20, 26n, 215
Mannheim, K., 182n
Marcet, J., 1, 56–7, 154, 162n
de Marchi, N. B., 34n
Market
  freeing of, 98–9
  hostility to, 101, 126–29
  imperfections of, 105-6, 111, 119–20, 126, 129
Marsh, J., 57n
Marshall, J., 59
Martineau, H., 1, 23, 25, 59–60, 154, 161n
Marx, K., 156–7, 183, 227
  on economic crisis, 168
  on economic cycles, 53, 187, 227
  on exploitation, 105, 106–7
  on Gray, 179–80
  on Hodgskin, 98–9
  on value, 104–5
Mathias, P., 55n
Mechanics Institutes, 60, 171
Mechanics Magazine, 14n, 170
Medusa, 4n, 112n, 113, 116, 117n, 194n
Meek, R. L., 90n
Merle, G., 6n
Middlemen, 139–40
Midland Representative, 136n, 146n, 155n, 205n, 211n, 216n
Mill, J., 15, 30–1, 56, 153–4, 159–60
Mill, J. S., 160–1, 168, 228
Mirror of Truth, 10
Money
  and Cobbett, *see* Cobbett, W.
  and the co-operative press, *see* Co-operative press, on exchange, *and* on exploitation
  and economic crisis, *see* Economic crisis
  and Gray, *see* Gray, J.
  and Owen, *see* Owen, R.
  and the working-class press, *see* Working-class press
Monopolists, 98, 99n, 115, 120, 130, 143, 145, 149, 199
Moral economy, 27–8, 29, 100, 107
Morgan, J. M., 10, 15n, 17n
Mudie, G., 10, 135n, 146–7, 150–1, 195–7
Myrdal, G., 86n

National Debt, 62, 149, 188, 193, 213
Natural value, *see* Value
Nichol, J., 161
Northern Reformers' Monthly Magazine, 112n, 195n

O'Brien, D. P., 200n
O'Brien, J. B. ('Bronterre'), 6, 17–18
  on capital, 143
  on economic crisis, 205, 208
  on exchange, 141
  on Hodgskin, 17
  on political economy, 23, 29, 33
  on taxation, 149–50
O'Brien, P. K., 54n
Ogilvie, W.
  on industrial labour, 42
  on natural rights to land, 41–2, 49–50
  physical mode of analysis, 43, 50
  on rent, 42
Oliver, W. H., 179n, 180n, 187n
Overproduction, 165, 168, 172–4, 200, 204–5, 206–8, 212
Owen, R., 1, 10, 13, 16, 17, 152, 222, 226
  on abundance, 181, 183–4, 202
  and the classical economists, 73–4
  and competition, *see* Competition
  and distribution, 182
  and early co-operative press, 123–4
  on economic crisis, 163–6, 167n, 169–70, 173n, 174, 175–7, 178, 188, 225
  and exploitation, 77–81
  on harmony of interests, 78, 80
  on mechanisation, 74–5
  millenarian implications of political economy, 179, 189, 190

on money, 175–6, 178–9
and the Ricardian socialists, 76–8, 107–10
on value, 75–6, 166, 175–7, 179
on villages of mutual co-operation, 78–9, 179
on working-class poverty, 73–81
Owen, R. D., 202

Paine, T., 9n, 18, 47, 50–1, 193, 225
Pankhurst, R. K. P., 28n
Pare, W., 139, 205n
Parsinnen, T. M., 148n
Penny Magazine, 25
Penny Papers for the People, 136n
People, 115–16, 191n, 192n
Perkin, H., 60n, 150
Pioneer, 6
  on economic crisis, 204n, 212n
  on exploitation, 138n, 142n, 143n, 151n, 152n
  on political economy, 23, 24n
Place, F., 20, 60–1, 62n
  as a classical populariser, 58n, 118, 120–21, 130n, 154, 155
  and the *Trades Newspaper*, 13–15, 24, 61, 126, 130n
Plummer, A., 17n
Political and Moral Magazine, 155
Political economy
  anti-capitalist, *see* Ricardian socialists
  and classical popularisers, 56–7, 58, 153–7
  and the co-operative press, *see* Co-operative press
  and framework knitters and silk weavers, 36–9
  and Hodgskin, *see* Hodgskin, T.
  and living standards, 35
  and Mechanics Institutes, *see* Mechanics Institutes
  and the radical press, *see* Radical press
  and Thompson, *see* Thompson, W.
  and the *Trades Newspaper*, *see* Trades Newspaper
  working-class need for, 35–64
  and the working-class press, *see* Working-class press
Pollard, S., 23n
Poor Man's Advocate, 137, 152n

Poor Man's Guardian, 5, 6, 15
  on antagonism of interests, 151, 152
  on economic crisis, 204n, 206, 207–8, 212n, 214n, 216–17
  on exploitation, 136n, 137, 138n, 139n, 141, 143n, 149–50
  on exploiters, 140n, 150
  on means of production, 145n, 146
Potter, B., 83
Production, means of, 47, 48, 52–3, 66–7, 68, 72, 88, 89–90, 96, 102, 106–7, 111, 128–9, 134–6, 145–7, 183
Profit
  inverse relation to wages, 109, 119
  as a limit to output, 169–71, 201–2
  Owen on, 77–8, 123
  upon cost price, 76n, 122, 132, 169, 173n, 174
Property, 51, 66, 108,113
Prothero, I., 14n
Pryme, G., 56

Radical press, 3, 4n
  circulation, 6, 229–33
  and economic crisis, 191–5
  and exploitation, 111, 114–21
  and political economy, 8–11
  and value, 111
Ravenstone, P., 63n
Rent, 63, 108, 123
Republican, 4n, 8, 9, 10, 113, 115, 116n, 117n
Republican (*Voice of the People*), 149n
Ricardian socialists
  and capitalists, 108–10
  degeneration of theoretical reasoning, 222–3, 224–6
  and economic crisis, 163–90
  and exchange, 93, 96, 111–12, 223, 228
  and exploitation, 2, 92, 102–3, 221, 223
  exploitation theories and labourism, 224
  and historians of economic thought, 83
  and influence on the working-class press, *see* Working-class press
  and means of production, 96, 223
  mode of discourse, 63–4

Index

as precursors, of Marx, 106
and Owen, *see* Owen, R.
and Ricardo, 84–6, 90, 103–4
and Smith, 85, 89–90, 91, 104
as Smithian socialists, 93, 105–6
and value theory, 90, 221, 223–4
Ricardo, D., 1, 8, 13n, 15, 20, 30, 103–4, 118–19, 159–60, 168n
Rist, C., 80n
Robertson, J., 14n
Robinson, J., 163n
Rodbertus, K., 163n
Roll, E., 84
Rose, J. H., 20
Rostow, W. W., 53
Routh, G., 155n, 156n
Ryan, C. C., 19n

Salt, J., 23n
Samuelson, P. A., 63
Saturday Magazine, 156n
Saville, J., 23n
Say, J-B., 57, 161
Say's Law, 158, 160, 161, 215
Schumpeter, J. A., 28n
Schwartz, A. J., 53
Schwartz, P., 86
Scrope, G. P., 79n, 155
Senior, N., 1, 58, 59, 62n
Sever, J., 23n
Silk weavers, 14n, 36–9, 126
Smith, A., 8, 10n, 11, 14, 118
and the Ricardian socialists, *see* Ricardian socialists
and value theory, 87–9
Smith, J. E. ('Shepherd'), 6, 23n
Smithian socialists, *see* Ricardian socialists
Socialist political economy, *see* Ricardian socialists *and* Owen, R.
Society for the Diffusion of Useful Knowledge, 23, 25, 34, 155
Sowell, T., 158n
Spence, T., 148
and natural rights to land, 40–1, 47–8
physical mode of analysis, 43
on rent, 41
Sraffa, P., 44n
Stamp duty, 4n
Stephen, L., 62n, 84n
Stigler, G. J., 89n

Taxation
and economic crisis, 187–8, 193–4, 197, 199, 213
and exploitation, 116–17, 148–9
Thomas, W. E. S., 61n
Thompson, E. P., 15n, 20, 43n, 44n, 187n
Thompson, W., 1, 11–13, 16, 17, 222
on abundance, 181
on antagonism of interests, 109
on capitalists, 108–9
on competition, 99–101
on co-operative communities, 100–2, 165–6, 167, 224
on distribution, 182
on economic crisis, 163–69, 173–4, 225
on exchange, 92, 101–2, 175
on exploitation, 92, 101–2, 106, 108–9, 110
on the means of production, 96, 134
on moral economy, 27–8, 100
and Owen, 107
on periodicity of crisis, 186
on political economy, 20–2, 27–9, 32n
and Ricardo, 84
on value, 91, 92, 165–6
Thomson, W., 19
Torrens, R., 1, 57
Trades Free Press, 126n, 199n
Trades Newspaper
and classical influence, 60–1, 126, 198–9
and the Corn Laws, 127
and economic crisis, *see* Economic crisis
and exploitation, 125–31
and Hodgskin, 12–15, 124, 125, 129
and Place, *see* Place, F.
and political economy, 12–16, 24, 30–1
and Robertson, *see* Robertson, J.
and value theory, 124–5
Tribe, K., 28n
Tufnell, E. C., 162n
von. Tunzelmann, G. N., 36n
Tyrell, A., 60n

Underconsumption, *see* Economic crisis, and deficiency of demand

Unstamped press, 4–5, 16
Ure, A., 153

Value
  and Bray, *see* Bray, J. F.
  and the co-operative press, *see* Co-operative Press
  and Gray, *see* Gray, J.
  and Hodgskin, *see* Hodgskin, T.
  importance of theory, 46, 48, 52–3
  labour theory, of, 76, 89–92, 103–4, 112–13, 119, 130
  natural, 75, 76–7, 90, 92, 93–4, 104–5, 122, 139, 141, 144–5, 172, 177, 179, 189, 201, 206
  and Owen, *see* Owen, R.
  and the radical press, *see* Radical press
  and the Ricardian socialists, *see* Ricardian socialists
  and Ricardo, *see* Ricardo, D.
  and Smith, *see* Smith, A.
  surplus, 87, 105, 107
  in use, 144, 165, 167, 168
  and the working-class press, *see* Working-class press
Vaughan, M., 62n
Voice of the People, 146n, 152n, 207n, 210n
Voice of the West Riding, 5, 18n, 24n, 139n, 204n, 205n, 206n, 207n

Wade, J., 9–10, 118–20
Wages, *see* Labour, value of
Wallas, G., 58n, 60n, 149n
Warden, B., 176
Webb, R. K., 6n
Weekly Free Press, 13n, 130n, 198n, 199n, 200n
Weekly Free Press and Co-operative Journal, 133n, 134n, 202n, 210n
Whately, R., 155–6
Wiener, J. H., 16n, 18n, 19
Wooler, T. J., 8, 9, 193–5, 195, 220
Wooler's British Gazette, 195n
Working-class press (early 1830s)
  and antagonism of interests, 140, 151–3
  and capital, 146–7
  and circulation, 6, 229–33
  and economic crisis, 199, 201, 203–18
  and exchange, 95, 138–46, 150–1
  and exploitation, 95, 137–46, 148–51
  and exploiters, 139–40
  and Gray, *see* Gray, J.
  and the means of production, 145–48
  and money, 141–4, 147–8, 210–12
  and political economy, 2, 5, 16–20, 22–5, 29–34, 219–20
  Ricardian socialist influence on, 2, 17–18, 34, 139, 144, 150–1, 206, 215
  and taxation, 213
  and value, 136–39, 141–4

Yeo, E. M. J., 179n

Zero sum game, 69, 151